T0301716

# BEYOND BARTER
Lectures in Monetary Economics
After 'Rethinking'

# BEYOND BARTER
## Lectures in Monetary Economics
## After 'Rethinking'

## John Smithin
### York University, Canada

**World Scientific**

EW JERSEY · LONDON · SINGAPORE · BEIJING · SHANGHAI · HONG KONG · TAIPEI · CHENNAI · TOKYO

*Published by*

World Scientific Publishing Co. Pte. Ltd.

5 Toh Tuck Link, Singapore 596224

*USA office:* 27 Warren Street, Suite 401-402, Hackensack, NJ 07601

*UK office:* 57 Shelton Street, Covent Garden, London WC2H 9HE

Library of Congress Cataloging-in-Publication Data
Names: Smithin, John N., author.
Title: Beyond barter : lectures in monetary economics after 'rethinking' /
    John Smithin, York University, Canada.
Description: New Jersey : World Scientific, [2022]
Identifiers: LCCN 2021047939 | ISBN 9789811244421 (hardcover) |
    ISBN 9789811245381 (ebook) | ISBN 9789811245398 (ebook other)
Subjects: LCSH: Macroeconomics. | Interest rates | Barter.
Classification: LCC HB172.5 .S638 2022 | DDC 339.5--dc23
LC record available at https://lccn.loc.gov/2021047939

**British Library Cataloguing-in-Publication Data**
A catalogue record for this book is available from the British Library.

For any available supplementary material, please visit
https://www.worldscientific.com/worldscibooks/10.1142/12488#t=suppl

Desk Editors: Nimal Koliyat/Thaheera Althaf

Typeset by Stallion Press
Email: enquiries@stallionpress.com

Printed in Singapore

# Preface

These *Lectures* explain the approach to monetary macroeconomics set out in my *Rethinking the Theory of Money, Credit, and Macroeconomics*[1] in a clear, concise, and up-to-date manner.

The mainstream approach to macroeconomic theory and policy has failed because it is based on the wrong premises. It does not address the real complexities of the social ontology of the macroeconomy and tries to explain all economic activity on the model of barter exchange, treating money as nothing more than a 'medium of exchange'. According to the conventional theory, money may help to facilitate trades that would take place anyhow, but its existence does not change anything fundamental in economic life. This is an ontology based on false conjectures about money's historical evolution, and the entire approach is misguided. What is truly important about money is that it is a 'means of payment', specifically a means of payment of debt. As the work of the Cambridge University sociologist Geoffrey Ingham has made clear, money is a social relation involving debt and credit.[2] While it is true that in a monetary economy many debts are indeed incurred in the process of making trades and fulfilling the associated contracts, the focus on debt marks a fundamental change of emphasis. The analyst is forced to recognize the importance of bank

---

[1] John Smithin, *Rethinking the Theory of Money, Credit, and Macroeconomics: A New Statement for the 21st Century* (Lanham, MD: Lexington Books, 2018).
[2] Geoffrey Ingham, 'Money is a social relation' (*Review of Social Economy* 54, 1996); *The Nature of Money* (Cambridge: Polity Press, 2004).

credit creation and endogenous money for the generation of profit and, in turn, for the scale and structure of economic activity.

Confusion arising from basic misunderstandings about the nature of money was revealed in dramatic fashion in recent policy debates in the USA about modern monetary theory (MMT). MMT was championed by some radical politicians, and just as strongly resisted by those of a different political persuasion. As Graham Hubbs has argued, however, what the debates have really shown is that all along the protagonists have essentially been arguing about the ontology of money, without perhaps being fully aware of it.[3]

The core argument of MMT rests on the logically unassailable proposition that the central government of an economy with its own sovereign currency and a floating exchange rate (to which I would also add a 'fixed but adjustable' exchange rate) faces no binding financial constraints. Under these circumstances, fears about 'unsustainable' budget deficits are nonsense. None of this, however, applies to jurisdictions that have an irrevocably fixed exchange rate or to those embedded in a currency union. Nor does it apply to the individual Provinces or States in a federal system. And by no means does this purely financial insight settle any of the debates about macroeconomic policy alternatives, which must still be debated on the merits of the policies themselves. Critically, the core proposition does not settle debates about the correct level of interest rates, or about whether to define interest rates in 'real' or 'nominal' terms. *Beyond Barter* provides an in-depth analysis of all these issues.

As I wrote in *Rethinking* in 2018, I saw that volume as the culmination of a long series of works beginning with my doctoral dissertation on *The Incidence and Economic Effects of the Financing of Unemployment Insurance*; through *Macroeconomics After Thatcher and Reagan*; two editions of *Controversies in Monetary Economics*; *Macroeconomic Policy and the Future of Capitalism*; *Money, Enterprise and Income Distribution*; and *Essays in the Fundamental Theory of Monetary Economics and Macroeconomics*.[4] In the dissertation I had already included such key

---

[3] Graham Hubbs, 'Philosophical explanations of the nature of money' (paper presented to the *Aurora Philosophy Institute*, Aurora ON, November 2020).

[4] John Smithin, *The Incidence and Economic Effects of the Financing of Unemployment Insurance* (PhD thesis in Economics, McMaster University, 1982); *Macroeconomics after Thatcher and Reagan: The Conservative Policy Revolution in Retrospect* (Aldershot: Edward Elgar, 1990); *Controversies in Monetary Economics: Ideas, Issues and Policy*

concepts as bank-credit creation and endogenous money. Later, there were further developments such as the eventual complete abandonment of problematic mainstream concepts such as the supposed 'natural rates' of interest, unemployment, and growth. Also, there was the introduction of one version or another of my fundamental idea of a 'real interest rule'. I then developed the notion of a 'wage curve', or 'wage function', specifying a positive relationship between the *level* of the average or aggregate real wage rate and the *rate* of economic growth. This is what has sometimes been called a 'mixed' equation in that it makes the level of a distributional variable depend on the growth rate of another variable.[5] Such formulations have been known to cause difficulties for econometricians, and therefore this type of specification has usually been avoided in the construction of economic theory. Unfortunately for the theorists, however, and as with the ontology of money, this relation is actually fundamental to real world political economy. It cannot be avoided. *Lecture 8* that follows will explain some of the technical issues that are involved in more detail.

In the sequence from *Money, Enterprise, and Income Distribution* (MEI) through *Essays* to *Rethinking,* there was another very important progression. By the time of *Essays* and *Rethinking* the demand-side relationship between inflation and economic growth, which in MEI I had called the 'demand for inflation' (*DI*) schedule, was upward-sloping rather than downward-sloping, in what I now take to be a thoroughly Keynesian manner. In *Beyond Barter,* this relationship is far more appropriately called the 'effective demand' (ED) schedule. The significance of this, I think, is that Keynes's original schedule of 'effective demand' and the 'aggregate supply function' in the *General Theory* were both upward-sloping, albeit with different variables on the horizontal and vertical axes.[6]

(Cheltenham: Edward Elgar, 1994); *Macroeconomic Policy and the Future of Capitalism: The Revenge of the Rentiers and the Threat to Prosperity* (London: Routledge, 1996); *Controversies in Monetary Economics: Revised Edition* (Cheltenham: Edward Elgar, 2003); *Money, Enterprise and Income Distribution: Towards a Macroeconomic Theory of Capitalism* (London and New York: Routledge, 2009); *Essays in the Fundamental Theory of Monetary Economics and Macroeconomics* (Singapore: World Scientific Publishing, 2013).
[5] Clive Grainger, *Empirical Modelling in Economics: Specification and Evaluation* (Cambridge: Cambridge University Press, 1999).
[6] John Maynard Keynes, *The General Theory of Employment, Interest, and Money* (London: Macmillan, 1936).

*Beyond Barter* is a necessary (and was probably an inevitable) further step beyond *Rethinking*. I have tried to refine the various ideas, concepts, and arguments employed, explain them more clearly, and put them in the correct order for the most effective exposition. Once having finished a book such as *Rethinking*, the writer can always think of all sorts of ways in which the argument could be improved, made clearer, how the order of topics might be re-arranged, and so on. And also, needless to say, no matter how hard one tries or how many times the copy is proof-read, there are going to be typos, mathematical and algebraic slip-ups, algebraic signs reversed, transcription errors, *etc.* Seldom (in fact, I would claim never) do these seriously affect the intellectual argument, but they are nonetheless extremely irritating whenever they are discovered, or have been pointed out to me, *ex-post.* Therefore (although I make no guarantees about this!) reworking the material in *Lecture* format does give a real opportunity to try to re-state the argument in a final, and hopefully definitive, form.

In the past, I have often quoted Keynes's remarks to George Bernard Shaw during the writing of his own *General Theory.* Keynes wrote to Shaw as follows[7];

> To understand my own state of mind ... you have to know that I believe myself to be writing a book on economic theory which will largely revolutionise — not I suppose at once but in the course of the next ten years — the way the world thinks about economic problems. When my new theory has been duly assimilated and mixed with politics and feelings and passions, I can't predict what the final upshot will be in its effects on actions and affairs. But there will be a great change and, in particular, the Ricardian foundations of Marxism will be knocked away ... I can't expect you, or anyone else, to believe this at the present stage. But for myself I don't merely hope what I say — in my own mind I am quite sure.

I suppose it is debatable whether or not Keynes himself ultimately achieved this goal. Many of the problems that have arisen along the way will be discussed in the *Lectures* that follow. Nonetheless, I would claim

---

[7]John Maynard Keynes, *Collected Writings XXVIII*, edited by Donald Moggridge (London: Macmillan, 1982).

that the ideas presented in *this* book are in themselves quite capable of bringing about such a change, provided they are taken seriously.

I have been lecturing on this sort of material to different audiences, and at different levels of academic preparation, for around 30 years now (rather longer than Keynes's expectation of the 10 years that he thought it would take to effect a change). And, as the intellectual arguments have been developing, so too has the content of the *Lectures*. I think that they have also now coalesced into something like a final form. Between 1992 and 2016, for example, I taught both a third-year undergraduate course in *Monetary Economics: Financial Markets and Institutions* and a graduate course in *Advanced Monetary Economics* in the Department of Economics and the Faculty of Graduate Studies at York University, Toronto. At one time, I also regularly taught a second-year MBA elective at the Schulich School of Business which dealt with much the same sorts of monetary and financial issues. During the years that I was teaching the latter course, some of the students were kind enough to pay me the compliment of following through the entire sequence of all three courses in their undergraduate and graduate work. (I *do* flatter myself that they all learned something new each time.)

In 2014, assisted by Frederick Zhou, I delivered a mini-course on *Monetary Macroeconomics* as part of the INET[8] Young Scholars Initiative (YSI) at the Fields Institute for Mathematical Research at the University of Toronto. This was an invited program for second-year PhD students from all over the world, and the resulting *Lectures* are available on the Internet. Five years later, in 2019, I taught an online course on *Monetary Economics*, in the *Canada Summer Overseas* program, out of Wuhan, China and Toronto ON, this time at the senior undergraduate level. This was a program for students resident in China, who were able to gain credit in Canadian universities. Finally, in Fall 2021 I taught a course at Glendon College, Toronto (the bi-lingual liberal arts College of York University) on *Monetary Theory and Policy: Canadian Context*, based precisely on this most recent set of *Lectures* published here.

I therefore think that the material will be accessible to students with all levels of preparation, always allowing for the appropriate differences in emphasis in each case. That has certainly been my experience. For example, graduate students would be required to write a full-scale research paper on the topic, employing the full range of philosophical

---

[8] INET is the acronym for the *Institute for New Economic Thinking*.

arguments, mathematical analysis, and research methodologies that are involved. On the other hand, for undergraduates it was important to grasp some of the novel ideas in social ontology and political economy that they were being introduced to for the first time. As I have just said, all of the different groups, I think, do learn something new. After all, this is an entirely novel approach to political economy. Moreover, it is one that I think is essential for very many people, not just academics and students, to be able to grasp if we are ever to make any progress in the future. I would therefore be quite comfortable, and indeed enthusiastic, to discuss this material with any audience regardless of their background level of preparation; academics, students, policymakers, practitioners, and the interested general public.

Several of the students who took the course *Advanced Monetary Economics* in graduate school went on to complete PhD theses in monetary economics and related fields. I would like to mention specifically the work of John Paschakis who wrote about *Real Interest Rate Control,* Eric Kam whose subject was *Monetary Non-Superneutrality,* D'Ansi Mendoza who was interested in *Money, Credit, and Philosophy,* Aqeela Tabassum (supervised by Professor Brenda Spotton Visano) who wrote on *The Impact of Financial Innovation on Monetary Policy,* and Reid Collis who examined in detail *The Soundness of the Alternative Monetary Model.*[9] Each of these theses has contributed a vital piece to the intellectual puzzle that I hope will finally be solved in this book.

In *Rethinking,* I mentioned the fact that in all my previous works I have acknowledged the contributions of the many people who have helped me to come to understand monetary macroeconomics over the years — and that I would like those acknowledgements to stand. (This includes all of the contemporary scholars whose names have been mentioned above.)

---

[9] John Paschakis, *Real Interest Rate Control and the Choice of an Exchange Rate System* (PhD thesis in Economics, York University, 1993); Eric Kam, *Three Essays on Endogenous Time Preference and Monetary Non-Superneutrality* (PhD thesis in Economics, York University, 2000); D'Ansi Mendoza, *Three Essays on Money, Credit and Philosophy: A Realist Approach per totam viam to Monetary Science* (PhD thesis in Economics, York University, 2012); Aqeela Tabassum, *Three Essays on the Impact of Financial Evolution on Monetary Policy* (PhD thesis in Economics, York University, 2013); Reed Collis, *Three Essays on Monetary Macroeconomics: An Empirical Examination of the Soundness of the Alternative Monetary Model and Monetary Policy in Canada* (PhD thesis in Economics, York University, 2018).

Those who have specifically helped with the current book know very well who they are, and how grateful I am to them all. Their assistance has been very deeply appreciated and is further acknowledged at all the relevant points in the footnotes and references to follow. I would just like to make two further general acknowledgements. The first is to my editor Lum Pui Yee, with whom I have successfully worked on several previous projects for more years, probably, than either she or I would like to remember. And also, to Alla Marchenko, my fellow Executive Co-Director, and President and Chair of the *Aurora Philosophy Institute* (API). The influence of the 'Philosophy of Money' on these *Lectures* should be plain for all to see. My collaboration with Alla has (so far) been much shorter than that with Pui Yee. Nonetheless, the activities of the API have been a decisive influence on my current intellectual interests, their development, and on the direction they will likely take in future.

# About the Author

**John Smithin** is Executive Co-Director and Fellow of the Aurora Philosophy Institute, and Professor Emeritus of Economics and Senior Scholar at York University, Toronto, Canada. He previously held teaching appointments at the University of Calgary and Lanchester Polytechnic at Coventry (now Coventry University) in England. In the academic year 1995–1996, he was elected Bye Fellow at Robinson College, Cambridge. He holds a PhD and an MA from McMaster University and a BA (Honours) from the City of London Polytechnic (now London Metropolitan University). His research interests are in the fields of macroeconomic policy, monetary theory, and the philosophy of money and finance. He is the author and/or editor of *Debates in Monetary Macroeconomics* (2022), *Rethinking the Theory of Money, Credit, and Macroeconomics* (2018), *Essays in the Fundamental Theory of Monetary Economics and Macroeconomics* (2013), *Money, Enterprise, and Income Distribution* (2009), *Controversies in Monetary Economics* (2003, 1994), *What is Money?* (2000), *Macroeconomic Policy and the Future of Capitalism* (1996), *Macroeconomics after Thatcher and Reagan* (1990), and *Keynes and Public Policy After Fifty Years* (1988).

# Contents

# Lecture 1

# An Introduction to Money

## 1.1 Introduction

On many occasions, including most recently in my book *Rethinking the Theory of Money, Credit, and Macroeconomics*,[1] I have insisted that;

> Common-sense tells us that capitalism [so-called] is all about money. We continually speak and write about making money, spending money, saving money, and so forth.

Similarly, Geoffrey Ingham in *The Nature of Money*[2] writes as follows;

> ... [money] ... arguably the most important institution in capitalist society ... has received far less attention ... [from social science and business disciplines, including economics] ... than it deserves ...

The existence of electronic money in the twenty-first century makes no difference to the truth of these statements. This has only been a change of form not of substance. But we do need to be clear that the innovations in information technology in themselves, such things as crypto-currencies, computerized payments systems, smart cards, and so forth (whatever the latest innovation happens to be) are not 'money' and will never replace 'money'.

---

[1] Smithin, *Rethinking.*

[2] Ingham, *Nature of Money.*

To understand why this is so we will need to understand exactly what money is, and what is its nature. This is what a philosopher would call the *ontology* of money. Usually in economics emphasis is placed (quite wrongly, I think) on the supposed role of money as *medium of exchange*, which is an ontology derived from conjectures about how money did arise historically. But, in fact, these conjectures about history, to the effect that money evolves from a pre-existing system of markets conducted by barter, have never been anything more than that (conjectures), and the entire approach has turned out to be misguided.[3] In reality, there are many and various different ways of physically making trades, including straightforward barter itself. We literally need to move *Beyond Barter*. What seems to be truly important about money, as that institution functions in actual economies, is that it is a *means of payment*, specifically a means of payment of debt. This is not the same thing as a medium of exchange, although in a genuinely monetary economy it is certainly true that many of the debts will indeed have been incurred in the process of making trades and fulfilling the associated contracts. Above all, money is a social relationship involving debt and credit.[4]

In a credit or claim theory of money, money is not thought of primarily as a physical object, nor as somehow representative of any pre-existing value, but as entries in a ledger, in a system of accounts, or a balance sheet. The purpose of the entries is to record the various social relations of indebtedness. Debts are incurred and paid off by balance sheet and accounting operations.[5] It then becomes a key issue for the analyst to decide exactly what it is, in a given system, that 'counts as'[6] making payments (discharging debt) in the particular circumstances. This has nothing to do with the technology whereby payments are effected.

Up to the present day mainstream economics, an academic discipline that is also frequently called 'neoclassical' economics, has usually tried to argue that money is not all that important. There are several slogans and catch-phrases expressing this view, such as 'money is neutral', 'money is a veil', 'money does not matter', and so forth. Money only seems to be

---

[3] David Graeber, 'The myth of barter', Ch.2 of *Debt: The First 5000 Years* (Brooklyn, NY: Melville House Publishing, 2011).

[4] Ingham, 'Money is a social relation'.

[5] Alain Parguez and Mario Seccareccia, 'The credit theory of money: The monetary circuit approach', in John Smithin (ed.), *What is Money?* (London: Routledge, 2000).

[6] John Searle, *The Construction of Social Reality* (New York: The Free Press, 1995).

noticed when a crisis occurs, as in the twentieth century with the 'Wall Street Crash' of 1929 and the subsequent 'Great Depression' of 1929–1933, and in the twenty-first century with the 'Global Financial Crisis' (GFC) followed by the 'Great Recession'. When this sort of thing happens, it always causes great surprise and confusion, and even a questioning of the underlying intellectual framework for a while. But rarely does it lead to any lasting change in the way professional economists go about their business.

## 1.2 A Barter Economy or a Real Exchange Economy *versus* a Monetary Economy

The basic premise, then, of mainstream or neoclassical economics is that beneath the veil of money economics should deal primarily with the real exchange of goods and services, and the determination of the *relative* prices of goods and services (how many apples can be exchanged for how many oranges), rather than *money* prices expressed in terms of dollars, euros, rupees, rmb, yen, *etc.* Again the underlying economic model is essentially that of barter.

In the closely related concept of the *real exchange economy*,[7] it might be allowed that a sort of 'money' is in use, but as medium of exchange only. This would have to be either a commodity money, a token money, or a *fiat* money. For obvious reasons modern economists no longer think of money as being literally a physical commodity, but they do very definitely believe that an economy with (say) token money or *fiat* paper money should behave exactly 'as if' it were a commodity money regime. Money of this type is assumed to be *neutral* in its effects on economic outcomes, and to have no impact on relative prices. Implicitly, all the trades are made on the basis of spot exchange, and therefore do not give rise to the creation and discharge of debt. It is precisely this sort of hypothetical or theoretical system that is mainly studied in university and college courses on economics. In principle, a real exchange economy does not really differ from barter, and (therefore) also bears little or no relation to what actually goes on in the real world. Most real-world economic

---

[7] John Maynard Keynes, 'The distinction between a co-operative economy and an entrepreneur economy', 1933 (as reprinted in *Collected Writings* XXI, Donald Moggridge, ed., London: Macmillan, 1979).

issues do involve money in the full sense of the term, as a social relation. This is true of all such events as booms and depressions, financial crises, inflation and deflation, changes in interest rates and exchange rates, changes in the balance of payments, and so on. The conclusion to be drawn from this is that a truly monetary economy is an altogether different thing than either a barter economy or a real exchange economy. These *Lectures* therefore necessarily approach the issues in a different manner than do most university courses in economics, which do not accept the distinction.

## 1.3  Real Analysis *versus* Monetary Analysis

In his posthumously published *History of Economic Analysis,* the Austrian-American economist Joseph Schumpeter made a similarly important distinction, also highly relevant to our discussion here, between *real analysis* and *monetary analysis* in economics.[8]

Real analysis is conducted solely in terms of inputs and outputs of physical quantities of goods and services (or volume indices of these quantities), and the attitudes of human beings toward them. It takes for granted that all economic knowledge can be acquired simply by studying the relationships between these commodities. As already sufficiently stressed, the basic model is barter. In monetary analysis, however, money and monetary variables are 'introduced on the very ground floor of the analytical structure'.[9] Monetary analysis abandons the idea that all essential features of economic life can be represented as barter. To quote Geoffrey Ingham again, monetary analysis takes into account a separate and 'relatively autonomous'[10] monetary sphere over and above the purely material aspects of exchange and production. The leading exponent of monetary analysis, according to Schumpeter, was John Maynard Keynes, author of *The General Theory of Employment Interest and Money.*[11]

---

[8] Joseph Schumpeter, *History of Economic Analysis,* 1954 (as reprinted by Routledge, London: 1994).

[9] Schumpeter, *History.*

[10] Ingham, *Nature of Money.*

[11] Keynes, *General Theory.*

## 1.4 The Monetary Economy, the Monetary Circuit, and the Monetary Theory of Production

Of all people, and even though he explicitly assumed the existence of a commodity money, Karl Marx, author of *Das Kapital*, made an important early contribution to the (much later) eventual development of monetary analysis, *via* his notion of the monetary circuit.[12] Keynes, writing in 1933 as he was preparing his own major work for publication, had this to say about Marx[13];

> The distinction between a co-operative economy and an entrepreneur economy bears some relation to a pregnant observation by Marx — though the subsequent use to which he put it was highly illogical. He pointed out that the nature of production in the actual world is not, as economists seem often to suppose, a case of $C \rightarrow M \rightarrow C'$ ... of exchanging a commodity (or effort) to obtain another commodity (or effort). That may be the standpoint of the private consumer. But it is not the attitude of business, which is a case of $M \rightarrow C \rightarrow M'$ ... parting with money for a commodity (or effort) in order to obtain more money.

Keynes is by no means endorsing Marx or Marxism. He rightly says that the use to which Marx himself put this otherwise useful idea is 'illogical'. Elsewhere, in correspondence with George Bernard Shaw for example, Keynes was quite clear in stating that the impact of his own work would be to 'knock away the Ricardian foundations of Marxism'.[14]

Nonetheless, the idea of the circuit, $M \rightarrow C \rightarrow M'$, which we will later expand to $M \rightarrow C \rightarrow C' \rightarrow M'$, is a crucially important insight. Even if Marx himself did not really contribute to monetary analysis *per se,* the concept of the monetary circuit is indispensable to it. In effect, the difference $C'$ minus $C$ represents what a modern economist would call the real value-added in the economy, and $M'$ minus $M$ is the total or aggregate money profit. There are several important questions that can be asked about the relationships between these magnitudes, but most notably how is it even possible for $M'$ to be greater than $M$, and hence for monetary profits to exist? This obviously cannot happen if the money supply is fixed, but this is so often precisely the

---

[12] Keynes, 'The distinction …'.

[13] Karl Marx, *Das Kapital,* vol. 2, 1885 (as reprinted by Penguin Books: London, 1976).

[14] Keynes, *Collected Writings* XXVIII.

assumption made in economics textbooks. As we will see in later *Lectures*, the answer to this puzzle can only be credit creation (and thereby money creation) by the banking system. Marx did not answer, or even ask, this important question, but it follows directly from the $M \rightarrow C \rightarrow M'$ set-up.

Keynes, on the other hand, did (try to) follow up his thoughts about the monetary circuit with what he called a 'monetary theory of production' in the *General Theory*. But when he came to write that work, he misguid-edly decided to 'let technical monetary detail fall into the background' in his exposition.[15] This was a mistake. Much of that detail, such as an expla-nation of the circuit itself, and stress on the endogeneity of money and the importance of credit creation, would have been absolutely necessary to fully explain the argument, and head off numerous misunderstandings by both critics and would-be interpreters in the years afterwards.

## 1.5   Methodological Problems in Monetary Macroeconomics

The ontological and epistemological problems faced by many contempo-rary scholars in all such disciplines as monetary economics, macroeco-nomics, and finance, seem to arise from the fact that they reflexively apply only real analysis to all economic problems (including those of money, credit, and finance themselves).

Keynes's work is now either forgotten, misunderstood, or misinter-preted. It is usually mentioned only dismissively, if at all. To call someone a 'Keynesian' is frequently meant merely as a criticism or to imply, despite Keynes's clear statements about Marx and Ricardo, that the author is a sup-porter of left-wing political positions. It seems to me, however, that these attitudes are ultimately based on nothing more than a basic lack of knowl-edge of, and/or interest in, the actual issues and arguments. In the present course of *Lectures*, it will be necessary to take exactly the opposite approach. We must revert to the appropriate level of monetary analysis in the tradition started by Keynes but here brought up to date for the twenty-first century.

The textbook discussions often start with the notion of identifying the functions of money. The 'functions' are often given as a triad, namely (1) a unit of account, (2) a medium of exchange, and (3) a store of value. The idea is that money can be defined as the asset which best performs the three functions in any given state of society. Keynes, using a slightly

---

[15] Keynes, *General Theory*.

different terminology, had actually argued that the unit of account function was fundamentally important,[16] but this view is not shared by modern
textbook writers. They don't seem to think it important at all. This is a
serious mistake. If there were no unit of account, it would be impossible
to conduct business on a rational basis by quoting prices, keeping
accounts, and obtaining the necessary finance. On the other hand, we have
already seen that the notion of a medium of exchange *is* regarded as
important, because of the analogy to barter. Another mistake. Finally, in
standard theories of the demand for money and portfolio choice the idea
of money as a store of value continues to be emphasized. Also an error.
Experience over long periods shows that money is certainly not the only
store of value, and not necessarily the best, often far from it.

Interestingly enough, the late Sir John Hicks, in his posthumously
published *A Market Theory of Money*,[17] broke entirely with the usual
three-fold classification. Translated into the terminology we have been
using here, Hicks's argument was that the two main functions of money
were (1) a *unit of account*, and (2) a *means of payment*. Ultimately, in
practice, money will be that asset in which the two functions are combined.[18] The store of value aspect is downplayed.

How does the notion of a means of payment differ from that of the
medium of exchange? Hicks's answer is that in reality the typical transaction is not a straightforward 'spot' exchange of goods for money or *vice
versa*. Particularly for the more important large value transactions, some
sort of agreement, an explicit or implicit contract, is required for trade to
take place. The timing of delivery and payment is highly variable. Debts
are continually being created and extinguished, but it is not possible to be
dogmatic about exactly when. In some cases the buyer must pay 'cash in
advance', before delivery of the item. In others, payment is made later 'in
arrears'. Spot payment is only a special case. In all three cases it is
implicit that money, the thing offered in payment, is in a different category
altogether from the goods and services being offered for sale. Otherwise,
when trading apples for oranges why not consider either one of them
'money'? The concept of a means of payment also extends quite naturally
to cover the case of purely financial transactions.

---

[16] John Maynard Keynes, *A Treatise on Money*, vol. 1, *The Pure Theory of Money* (London: Macmillan, 1930).
[17] John Hicks, *A Market Theory of Money* (Oxford: Oxford University Press, 1989).
[18] John Smithin, *Controversies in Monetary Economics: Ideas, Issues, and Policy* (Aldershot: Edward Elgar, 1994).

The store of value aspect does not need to be stressed. Historically, money has always continued to perform the unit of account and means of payment functions long after inflation rates have reached very high, and even hyper-inflationary, levels. This makes a mockery of the idea of storing value. To make such a case is not to deny that money might be more useful in capitalism if its real value could be kept more stable. Indeed, in *Lecture 7* to follow a method will be suggested by which this goal might be achieved. But it is not a primary. It is not part of the ontology of money.

The next question to ask is how all this works out in an actual economy. The school of modern monetary theory (MMT), recently prominent in the public policy debate in the USA, explains this by their mantra that 'taxes drive money'.[19] Consider the following two quotations, the first by Geoffrey Ingham once again,[20] the second by Hicks himself[21];

> All money is debt in so far as issuers promise to accept their own money for *any* debt payment by any bearer of the money.[22]

> Money is what is paid for a discharge of debt when that debt [itself] has been expressed in terms of money.

The state has the power to tax, and if it is prepared to accept its own liabilities in payment of those taxes, it will establish its liabilities as a sovereign money. The liabilities of other institutions, such as commercial banks may also count as money due to (a) an explicit or implicit commitment to convertibility, and (b) the fact that those liabilities are also accepted in payment of taxes.

## 1.6 The Monetary Base, the Money Supply, and Bank Reserves: Definitions

To further explain the ideas set out above in terms of the notation used in textbooks we will next use the basic definitions of various 'monetary aggregates', as set out in *Table 1.1*.

---

[19] L. Randall Wray, *Modern Money Theory: A Primer on Macroeconomics for Sovereign Monetary Systems* (New York: Palgrave Macmillan, 2012).

[20] Ingham, *Nature of Money*.

[21] Hicks, *Market Theory of Money*.

[22] As we will see in what follows, the converse is not true. It is not the case that 'all debt is money'.

*Table 1.1*: Definitions

| |
|---|
| $H$ = the monetary base |
| $M$ = the money supply |
| $CU$ = currency in the hands of the non-bank public |
| $D$ = redeemable deposits held by the non-bank public in the commercial banks |
| R = bank reserves |

In *Table 1.1,* the symbol $H$ stands for the *monetary base*, which lettering (the $H$) is a throwback to the heyday of 'monetarism', in the third quarter of the twentieth century, when the base was called *high-powered money* in the context of money multiplier analysis.[23] The notion of the money multiplier was never a particularly useful idea, but was somehow just plausible enough to mislead several generations of economists. There is indeed an algebraic relationship between $H$ and the overall money supply $M$ which takes the form $M = [(1 + CU/D)/(R/D + CU/D)]H$, but this is of no causal significance because all of these magnitudes and ratios are endogenous variables. The days are long gone since the authorities would attempt to influence monetary conditions *via* futile interventions such as a legally binding reserve/deposit ratio ($R/D$). Nevertheless, even today it is handy to retain a different symbol, $H$, for the base than for the overall money supply, $M$.

The monetary base in a modern economy consists mainly of items on the liabilities side of the balance sheet of the state central bank. In symbols;

$$H = CU + R. \qquad (1.1)$$

The base is therefore equal to 'cash in the hands of the non-bank public', $CU$, plus 'bank reserves', $R$. Bank reserves, in turn, are the deposits that the commercial banks themselves hold with the central bank[24] plus 'vault and till cash', that is, currency held by the banks to be paid out to their customers on demand. To put it another way, the monetary base thus comprises the

---

[23] Charles Goodhart, 'Monetary base', in John Eatwell *et al.* (eds.), *The New Palgrave: Money* (London: Macmillan, 1989).

[24] In the USA, for example, these sums of money are called 'federal funds', which explains the situation quite well.

liabilities of the central bank to their commercial bank customers plus the total cash outstanding in the economy.

A generic definition of the overall money supply will comprise the same currency in the hands of the non-bank public already counted in the base, and (much more important quantitatively) some subset of the total amount of bank deposits held by the public.

$$M = CU + D. \tag{1.2}$$

As already mentioned, it is certainly possible to imagine an entirely 'cash-less' economy in the future. There would only be electronic money. In that case $CU = 0$, and;

$$H = R, \tag{1.3}$$

$$M = D. \tag{1.4}$$

But we should be quite clear that the cash-less economy would not be 'money-less', far from it. There would still be a monetary economy in place and, from the ontological point of view, money will continue to be what it always has been, a social relation between people. The only difference is that in a cash-less economy that relation is expressed exclusively by electronic means.

## 1.7  Illustrative Numerical Examples of the Monetary Aggregates

We next provide some hypothetical numbers to illustrate the numerical relationships. Suppose that at a given point in time we have $CU = \$19.7$ billion, $D = \$244.4$ billion, and $R = \$6.4$ billion. (These figures are very loosely based on the orders of magnitude typically reported in Canada some years ago, at a time when central banks, including the Bank of Canada, routinely reported several *different* alternative sets of statistics for the monetary aggregates. These were given labels like M0, M1, M2, M2+, M2++, M3, and so on. The figure for '$D$' is based on the M2 aggregate). *Table 1.2* then calculates totals for the hypothetical monetary aggregates and banking ratios.

This all seems very neat, but in practice it is virtually impossible to arrive at an accurate figure for the nominal (dollar) supply of money.

*Table 1.2*: Monetary Aggregates

| | | | |
|---|---|---|---|
| $H$ | $= CU + R = 19.7 + 6.4$ | $= \$26.1$ billion, | monetary base |
| $M$ | $= CU + D = 19.7 + 244.4 = \$264.1$ billion, | | money supply |
| $CU/D$ | $= 19.7/244.4$ | $= 0.08,$ | cash/deposit ratio |
| $R/D$ | $= 6.4/244.4$ | $= 0.03.$ | reserve/deposit ratio |

Indeed, this is quite obvious just from the existence of all the competing definitions. There would have to be separate tables for all of the 'Mn'. Which deposits, in which financial institutions, should be included and how is it possible to count them? There is no definitive answer. It may well be possible in principle to define the money supply as something like the total of all redeemable deposits in all deposit-taking institutions. However, all the official statistics tend either to omit items which should be included, or to include items which should be omitted, such as irre-deemable deposits (notice or term deposits), foreign currency deposits, or short-term money market instruments. And financial innovation takes place all the time.

The concept of the money supply is nonetheless an extremely impor-tant one and it certainly does seem to exert a definite influence in the economy, which shows up *via* such things as changes in nominal interest rates and inflation rates. In monetary analysis, therefore, given the endo-geneity of the money supply, we must find some way around the problem of counting it. For example, by treating the nominal policy rate of the central bank itself as the monetary policy instrument.

## 1.8  Real Money Balances

The actual purchasing power of the aggregate money supply (as opposed to its nominal quantity) is given by the expression $M/P$, where $P$ is the *aggregate price level* as calculated by an appropriate statistical price index. For example, if the price index in the current year comes out to 118.2, the total of *real money balances* in the above example will be given by;

$$M/P = 244.4/1.182 = 206.8 \text{ billion constant dollars.} \qquad (1.5)$$

This concept of *constant dollars* is an attempt to re-express all the nominal quantities in the income statements and balance sheets each year in terms of the prices that prevailed in the *base year*. The base year is the year from which the price index is calculated. The index for the base year is always set at $P = 100$ and when we have (*e.g.*) $P = 118.2$, as in our example, it should be taken to mean that prices in the current year are on average 18% higher than in the base year. Deflating the dollar numbers by 1.182 then allows for an inflation-adjusted comparison of the current year numbers with the base year.

Once again it seems obvious that the total amount of real purchasing power in existence must be an important determinant of economic outcomes. But, as we have just explained how difficult it is to count even the nominal supply of money, the same must be true for any attempt to estimate the total of real money holdings. For the purposes of monetary theory, therefore, there will have to be another work-around to avoid the problem. For example, in this case we might think about the consequences of changes in the real rate of interest caused by monetary policy, rather than just the nominal rate.

# 1.9  The Aggregate Price Level and the Rate of Inflation

To define the rate of inflation (*i.e.*, the rate of change of the aggregate price level), let the symbol $P$ continue to stand for the price level itself, and chose lower case $p$ to stand for the inflation rate. Thus;

$$p = (P - P_{-1})/P_{-1}   (\times 100). \tag{1.5}$$

Once the statisticians have worked out the price index, they (or we) can then calculate the inflation rate as in *Table 1.3*. The base year for the index has been chosen as year 4.

*Table 1.3:* The Price Level and the Rate of Inflation

| Year | P (price level) | p (inflation rate) |
|------|-----------------|--------------------|
| 1    | 99.1            | -----              |
| 2    | 101.4           | 2.3%               |
| 3    | 98.7            | $(-)$ 2.7%         |
| 4    | 100.0           | 1.3%               |
| 5    | 103.5           | 3.5%               |

The indices for other years then show whether prices were on average higher or lower than in the base year. When prices are higher between one period and the next, there has been *inflation*. On one occasion, however, the aggregate price level actually fell. This happened between years 2 and 3. Rather than inflation there was therefore a period of *deflation* (falling prices) at the time.

## 1.10  Nominal and Real Interest Rates

Turning now to a discussion of concepts involving the rate of interest, let the symbol $i$ stand for the nominal market rate of interest on loans of money, and $p$ once again for the currently observed rate of inflation. Therefore, $p_{+1}$ is the expected rate of inflation between the current period and the next. Then let $r^e$ stand for the *expected* real rate of interest, and $r$ for the inflation-adjusted or *ex-post* real rate of interest. Therefore, we have;

$$r^e = i - p_{+1}, \qquad\qquad (1.6)$$

$$r = i - p. \qquad\qquad (1.7)$$

In economic theory, the concept of the real rate most frequently employed is that of the expected real rate of interest, $r^e$. However, in the real world, the future inflation rate is not known with certainty. In practical policy analysis, therefore, the inflation-adjusted real rate, $r$, using currently observed inflation, is often used to get some sort of 'guesstimate' of the expected real rate. Formally, the currently observed inflation rate is taken as a 'proxy for' the expected inflation rate.[25]

There is a major problem, however, with usual treatment of the rate of interest in mainstream macroeconomics which arises because of the bias toward real analysis. For at least two hundred and seventy years,[26] and contrary to the common-sense view of the matter, the orthodox approach to interest rate determination has been that the rate of interest is *not* primarily a monetary or financial phenomenon. It is thought to be determined rather

---

[25] John Taylor, 'Discretion versus policy rules in practice' (*Carnegie-Rochester Conference Series on Public Policy*, 39, 1993).

[26] David Hume, *Essays Moral, Political, and Literary*, 1752 (as reprinted by Liberty Classics: Indianapolis, 1987).

by the putatively real forces of 'productivity and thrift'.[27] Over a century ago, Knut Wicksell,[28] for example, wrote in this vein about the supposed existence of a 'natural rate' of interest, and provided a definition;

> This natural rate is roughly the same thing as the real interest of actual business. A more accurate, though rather abstract, criterion is obtained by thinking of it as the rate which would be determined by supply and demand if *real* capital were lent in kind without the intervention of money. (emphasis added)

Most economists down to the present day have shared Wicksell's opinion. However, it should have immediately been clear from his wording that the idea of a natural rate of interest, influential though it has been throughout the history of economics, is untenable. Wicksell invokes an entirely hypothetical world with no money but which nonetheless has a fully-fledged market economy, presumably conducted by barter. As already explained, in spite of its lasting popularity with those seeking a purely materialist or reductionist account of social phenomena, this notion is a fiction. To put the point in as straightforward a manner as possible, how can there be 'actual business' without a money of account and credit creation? There cannot be.

In the *General Theory*, on the other hand, Keynes had a much more plausible definition of the rate of interest, that conforms to commonsense, and is entirely appropriate to a monetary analysis;

> [It is] ... (n)othing more than the inverse proportion between a sum of money and what can be obtained for parting with control over that money for a stated period of time.

Moreover, also in the *General Theory,* Keynes explicitly repudiated the notion of the natural rate. Writing about his own past views from the earlier *Treatise on Money*, he frankly admits that;

> (I)t was a mistake to speak of the natural rate or to suggest ... [it] ... would yield a unique value for the rate of interest irrespective of the level of employment ... I am no longer of the opinion that the concept

---

[27] Thomas Humphrey, 'Can the central bank peg real interest rates?' Ch. 4 of *Money, Banking and Inflation: Essays in the History of Monetary Thought* (Aldershot: Edward Elgar, 1993).
[28] Knut Wicksell, *Interest and Prices: A Study of the Causes Regulating the Value of Money*, 1898 (as reprinted by Augustus M. Kelley, New York: 1965).

of the natural rate of interest has anything useful or significant to contribute to our analysis.

In reality, there is no such thing as a natural rate of interest. Nonetheless, the concept of the real rate of interest, as just discussed, still remains important. Notions of the natural rate of interest and the real rate of interest are by no means synonymous. The real rate is what it is. It is simply the nominal rate less some measure of inflation or expected inflation. But, contrary to the assumptions of very many economists, it can take on any value. It is not tied down by reference to any non-monetary natural rate.

## 1.11  The Policy Rate of Interest

Another important interest rate concept is that of the *policy rate* of interest. The policy rate is the interest rate on loans of base money between the commercial banks, typically in the overnight market. It is called the policy rate because it is effectively dictated by the central bank as a matter of policy. They can do this because the central bank is the monopoly supplier of base money. In the USA, the policy rate is called the *federal funds rate* and in Canada it literally used to be called the *overnight rate*. At various other times and places it has gone by other names, or aliases, such as the *overnight call rate* in Japan or the *main refinancing rate* in the Euro-zone. In the literature on the history of economic thought, reference was also made to such expressions as *bank rate* or *discount rate*.

If $i_0$ is the nominal policy rate, and $p$ is the currently observed rate of inflation, another important variable, the inflation-adjusted real policy rate, or $r_0$, is given by

$$r_0 = i_0 - p. \tag{1.8}$$

From the point of view taken in these *Lectures*, the value of the inflation-adjusted real policy rate, $r_0$, is, in fact, the most important indicator of the stance of monetary policy. Even if central bankers do not admit it, the real policy rate defined in this way is an *exogenous* policy variable. The implication is that central banks should start to pay explicit attention to this variable, something they have usually failed to do in the past.

## 1.12  The Transmissions Mechanism of Monetary Policy

Empirically, the transmissions mechanism of monetary policy in most jurisdictions can be represented as something like[29];

$$i = m_0 + m_1 i_0, \quad m_0 > 0, \ 0 < m_1 < 1 \tag{1.9}$$

Here, the term $m_0$ is the mark-up between deposit rates and lending rates in the commercial banks. This is how the commercial banks themselves 'make money', so clearly it must be reflected in the general level of interest rates. The term $m_1$, meanwhile is the *pass-through coefficient*, that is, the amount by which commercial banks raise the interest rate that they charge to their own customers whenever there is an increase in the policy rate. Empirically, it is usually less than one. If $m_1$ is around 0.8, for example, and the central bank increases the policy rate ($i_0$) by a full percentage point, the commercial banks will respond by increasing their own lending rate ($i$) by 8/10 of a percentage point. In this way, they pass on some of the increase to their customers. If the prime lending rate was previously 3%, for example, it will now be increased to 3.8%. Thus, the commercial banks decide by how much to raise the rate for their customers based on their own subjective perceptions of what is needed to continue to make a profit.

Equation (1.9) is also important in explaining the relationship in monetary economics between the real rate of interest and the inflation rate. To see this, subtract the currently observed inflation rate $p$ from both sides. As $r = i - p$ and $r_0 = i_0 - p$, this gives;

$$r = m_0 + m_1 r_0 - (1 - m_1)p. \tag{1.10}$$

In principle, there is a negative relation between the inflation rate and the real interest rate. This is the so-called *forced saving effect* as was frequently discussed in the history of economic thought. In the twentieth century, the idea was rediscovered and labeled the *Mundell–Tobin* effect,

[29] Eric Kam and John Smithin, 'A simple theory of banking and the relationship between the commercial banks and the central bank' (*Journal of Post Keynesian Economics* 34, 2012).

after two Nobel Prize-winning economists.[30] The idea of 'forced saving' is that an increase in inflation reduces the real income of the so-called 'rentiers' (the recipients of interest income) in favour of other groups who are more likely to spend money on investment goods. (The term forced *saving* is therefore not really a particularly good description of the actual process. It arises because of the confused notions prevalent in the era of classical economics about the relationship between saving and investment.)

This notion of forced saving has always been highly controversial for two main reasons. Firstly, it definitely goes against the idea that the real rate of interest depends solely on productivity and thrift, not on monetary factors. Equation (1.10), however, seems to establish its relevance in a way that leaves little room for disagreement. Secondly, an ethical argument has sometimes been made about the (im)morality of income redistribution away from the rentiers. But, in fact, there is a strong argument that a 'fair' rate of interest, in real terms, is itself zero.[31] Therefore, as long as the real rate of interest is positive, there is always scope to reduce it further. Equation (1.10) also reinforces the idea that there is a positive relation between the real policy rate and the inflation-adjusted real market rate.

## 1.13 A Numerical Example of the Real Policy Rate

As already mentioned, the inflation-adjusted, or *ex-post*, real policy rate is given by the formula;

$$r_0 = i_0 - p \qquad (1.11)$$

Therefore, if $i_0 = 0.01$ (1%) and $p = 0.013$ (1.3%), we will have;

$$r_0 = 0.01 - 0.013 = -0.003. \quad (-0.3\%) \qquad (1.12)$$

---

[30] Robert Mundell, 'Inflation and real interest' (*Journal of Political Economy* 71, 1963); James Tobin, 'Money and economic growth' (*Econometrica* 33, 1965).

[31] John Smithin, 'Interest rates, income distribution, and the monetary policy transmissions mechanism under endogenous money: what have we learned thirty years on from *Horizontalists and Verticalists?*' (*European Journal of Economics and Economic Policies: Intervention* 17, 2020).

These were the actual numbers reported one day on the Bank of Canada website a few years ago. The central bank was obviously disregarding (as always) my advice that the real policy rate should be 'low but still positive', or zero. The real policy rate is negative, not by much, but still negative. The important point, however, is that in a quite definite sense the central bank had chosen this result. They chose the nominal policy rate and knew *p* beforehand. (That number was already recorded on the website.)

## 1.14   Nominal and Real Gross Domestic Product (GDP)

Traditionally, in macroeconomics the symbol *Y* stands for *real gross domestic product* (real GDP). Therefore, $P \times Y$ (or *PY*) is nominal GDP (the dollar value of GDP). Trivially, therefore;

$$Y = PY/P. \tag{1.13}$$

Next, use the symbol *$C* to denote the dollar value of total *consumption* spending, and *$I* for the total dollar value of '*investment*' spending (although, because of the insuperable problems existing in capital theory, it would probably be better to call this expenditure simply *firm* or *business* spending). Also, let *$G* stand for the total dollar value of *government expenditure* on goods and services and $\$(X - IM)$ for the total dollar value of *net exports*. The 'expenditure breakdown' of nominal GDP is thus;

$$PY = \$C + \$I + \$G + \$(X - IM). \tag{1.14}$$

For theoretical consistency, the various nominal quantities in equation (1.14) should be taken as referring to actual *flows of funds* (that is, transactions in which money has actually changed hands within the period), as opposed to the imputed values provided by the statisticians. The latter are not 'stock-flow consistent'.[32] Only if the sums of money recorded in an income statement are actually receivables will it be possible to make the correct entries in the corresponding balance sheet. But this is not the case in the calculations of the national income and product accounts. This

---

[32] Wynne Godley and Marc Lavoie, *Monetary Economics: An Integrated Approach to Credit, Money, Income, Production and Wealth* (London: Palgrave Macmillan, 2007).

*lacuna* may not present a major problem in the working out of pure economic theory, but it does mean that the various statistical measures used in empirical work can only ever be approximate.

In principle, nominal GDP should be the sum of the $$C + $$I + $$G + $$EX$ spent on goods and services produced domestically. However, in practice the statistics for $$C + $$I + $$G$ will also include spending on foreign made goods. There is no way to sort out the separate figures. This is why it is necessary to subtract the total amount of spending on exports ($$IM$) to arrive at an accurate estimate. Dividing through by $P$;

$$Y = C + I + G + (EX - IM). \tag{1.15}$$

This is the expenditure breakdown of real GDP (real value-added) in a modern economy, where $C$ = real consumption, $I$ and $G$ are real firm and government spending, and $EX - IM$ = real net exports.

## 1.15 Real GDP and the Rate of Economic Growth

Although many textbooks still present discussions of macroeconomic theory in what I call 'static' terms (that is, in graphs or diagrams with the price level, $P$, on one axis and the level of real GDP, $Y$, on the other), in real-world economic debate the emphasis is always on the rate of inflation and the rate of economic growth. In our notation, the rate of economic growth, lower case $y$, is given by;

$$y = (Y - Y_{-1})/Y_{-1} (\times 100) \tag{1.16}$$

Therefore, given some numbers for nominal GDP, and using the same aggregate price index as in *Table 1.3*, we can calculate the level of real GDP and its growth rate as in *Table 1.4*.[33]

According to the numbers worked out in *Table 1.4*, the level of real GDP in constant dollars actually fell between years 1 and 2. The growth rate was negative. This would be called a *recession*. On the contrary, it would be fair to call the period of high growth between years 3 and 4 a *boom*. When there is a boom, economic conditions are good for most people, and the opposite is true in a recession. For example, during a boom the unemployment rate falls, and after-tax real wages rise.

---

[33] For example, $1{,}598/0.991 = 1{,}613$.

*Table 1.4:* Real GDP and the Rate of Economic Growth

| Year | Nominal GDP (*PY*) | *P* | Real GDP (*Y*) (constant dollars) | Growth (*y*) |
|------|------|------|------|------|
| 1 | $1,598 *trillion* | 99.1 | 1,613 *trillion* | ----- |
| 2 | $1,612 *trillion* | 101.4 | 1,590 *trillion* | −1.4% |
| 3 | $1,588 *trillion* | 98.7 | 1,609 *trillion* | 1.2% |
| 4 | $1,681 *trillion* | 100.0 | 1,681 *trillion* | 4.5% |
| 5 | $1,783 *trillion* | 103.5 | 1,723 *trillion* | 2.5% |

The relationship between the growth rate and the unemployment rate may be illustrated with a relationship called *Okun's Law*, based on research in the mid-twentieth century by the late American economist Arthur Okun.[34] Okun's empirical findings were that to bring the unemployment rate down by one percentage point the growth rate might have to increase by as much as 2.5 or 3.0 percentage points. A somewhat simplified version of this relationship might therefore be;

$$u = u_0 - u_1 y. \tag{1.17}$$

In more recent work on Canada, Reed Collis reports that the Okun coefficient there is around $u_1 = 0.29$.[35] Therefore, if the intercept term, $u_0$, were as high as (say) 0.05, the growth rate would have to be around 4% *per annum* to get the unemployment rate down below 4%. If there was a recession of the same magnitude, the unemployment rate would increase to over 6%.

Similarly, the relationship between after-tax real wages and growth may be described, again in simplified form, by the expression in equation (1.18), which I have previously called either a 'wage curve' or 'wage function'[36];

---

[34]Arthur Okun, 'Potential GNP: Its measurement and significance' (*Proceedings of the American Statistical Association* 7, 1962).

[35]Reed Collis, *Three Essays on Monetary Macroeconomics: An Empirical Examination of the Soundness of the Alternative Monetary Model and Monetary Policy in Canada* (PhD thesis in Economics, York University, Toronto, 2018).

[36]John Smithin, *Money, Enterprise, and Income Distribution: Towards a Macroeconomic Theory of Capitalism* (London: Routledge, 2009).

$$w - t = h_0 + h_1 y \qquad (1.18)$$

Here, $w - t$ is the natural logarithm of the average after-tax real wage rate *per* employed person, $h_0$ is a variable indexing the socio-political power of labour, and $h_1$ is the sensitivity of the after-tax real wage rate to an increase in growth. (The distinction between nominal and real wage rates is further discussed in what follows.) The obvious reason why growth tends to increase after-tax real wages is that it improves the bargaining position of labour. Suppose then that the value of $h_1$ is 0.2, that the growth rate is 2.5%, the average tax rate is 0.38, and the gross average real wage is $10,000 constant dollars *per annum*. The after-tax real wage rate is therefore $6,200 constant dollars *per annum*, and $w - t = 8.7$ (as *ln* 6,200 = 8.7). This may be broken down as follows;

$$w - t = \mathbf{8.2} + 0.2(2.5) = \mathbf{8.2} + 0.5 = 8.7 \qquad (1.19)$$

Using these numbers we can work out that the intercept term $h_0$ must be 8.2, as shown in bold type. If the growth rate then increases to 4%, the natural logarithm of the after-tax real wage rate will increase to 9.0, implying an actual increase in average after-tax real wages *per* annum of $1,903 constant dollars (that is from $6,200 to $8,103).[37]

$$w - t = 8.2 + 0.2(4.0) = 8.2 + 0.8 = 9.0 \qquad (1.20)$$

These figures are only meant to be illustrative. There will be other factors involved in a real world version of equation (1.18), such as the real exchange rate. Nonetheless, the principle is clear.

In spite of these relationships, however, the objective of achieving a high rate of economic growth (and therefore real wage growth and improved economic security for the middle and working classes) is not always popular with the different political factions, neither on the 'right' nor the 'left'. From expressions like (1.10) and (1.18), the explanation for concerns about inflation and growth from the traditional political right seems quite clear. They are proxies for positions taken in the debate about income distribution. At the same time, the political left of the present day is also notably unenthusiastic about economic growth.

For example, the concerns often expressed in the media, and elsewhere, about the supposed effects of economic growth on the physical

---

[37] *ln* 8,103 = 9.0.

environment, are attributable mainly to those on the left side of politics. They have become part of the general debate about comparative systems. The underlying argument is that the industrial production associated with consumer capitalism inevitably leads to deleterious effects on the physical environment. In recent times, this has been described by such well-known phrases, or slogans, as 'global warming' or 'climate change'. Therefore, or so the argument goes, on these grounds alone some other form of economic organization, that supposedly uses up less resources, would be desirable. But the implications for income distribution are likely to be just the same. This seems incongruous, because traditionally or historically the left-wing political parties were supposed to be the champions of the working class.

The simplest explanation is that the constituencies of the political parties have changed. Although identifying with the political left, most of those who canvass slower or zero economic growth, less consumerism, and so forth, will tend to be those who already feel economically secure. At the global level, for example, they will likely be people living in the richer countries rather than in the developing economies. Within the more prosperous economies, the advocates of slower growth are often those engaged in occupations in which they personally are unlikely to suffer from unemployment or income instability, such as academia, the government bureaucracy, the public sector generally, the media, *etc.* Finally, the persons funding the various political campaigns are also (almost by definition) the 'super-rich', those among the famed '1%' at the top of the income distribution.[38] These trends seem to be part and parcel of the seismic shifts in political alignments taking place at the present time, pitting the social and educational 'elites' against the general population.

As far as the strictly environmental issues are concerned, in my own view is that what is occurring here is simply the confusion (or identification) of physical, biological, and engineering concepts with questions of social process and organization. There are, however, at least three main reasons why it is important to keep these issues distinct. The first is that although there are some historical examples of societies that have

---

[38] I am writing these words during the difficult year, 2020, characterized by historically unprecedented economic 'shutdowns' imposed in response to the COVID-19 pandemic. These events seem to have fully borne out the consequences for income distribution and unemployment suggested here with the main burden falling on private sector employment and small business, and little or none on the politicians, bureaucrats, epidemiologists, media, *etc.* advising on, canvassing, and administering the response.

collapsed as a result of environmental degradation,[39] these have all (obviously) been on local scale. And, even more importantly, all past examples of environmental collapse have happened in the context of non-capitalistic economies. They all occurred in either 'customary' or 'command' economies as these terms will be defined in the next chapter.

A second consideration is that predictions of eventual widespread economic breakdown due to the depletion of natural resources have been commonplace for over two hundred and fifty years now, ever since the earliest days of capitalism. Frequently, as is the case today, they have been a dominating force in the popular culture but have somehow always failed to materialize. It was Malthus's original *Essay on the Principle of Population*,[40] after all, predicting mass starvation as population growth outstripped agricultural productivity, that gave rise to the notion of economics as the 'dismal science'.[41] Another example, in the nineteenth century, was Jevons's book *The Coal Question,* which predicted the exhaustion of the coal mines in Britain, the leading industrial power of the day, and the collapse of the mid-Victorian industrial system.[42] In reality, it was over a hundred years later (in the 1980s) when the remaining mines were abandoned, the fuel no longer being required. Into the twentieth century, now about half a century ago, there were the dire warnings of the *Club of Rome* about the global *Limits to Growth,* which should have been reached well before now.[43] In another prominent example, in 2006 the former US Vice President Al Gore released a documentary film about what, at the time, was called 'global warming' with the title *An Inconvenient Truth* (sic). This famously gave only a ten-year window, now long past, for changes to be made if climate catastrophe is to be avoided. Clearly, 'de-bunking' arguments of this type will

---

[39] Jared Diamond, *Collapse: How Societies Choose to Fail or Succeed* (New York: Viking, 2005).

[40] Thomas Robert Malthus, *An Essay on the Principle of Population, or A View of its Past and Present Effects on Human Happiness*, 1798 (as reprinted by Ward, Lock and Co., London: 1890).

[41] The world population at that time, 1798, was around 800 million. It is around 7.8 *billion* today in 2020.

[42] William Stanley Jevons, *The Coal Question: An Inquiry Concerning the Progress of the Nation and the Possible Exhaustion of our Coal Mines* (London: Macmillan, 1865).

[43] D.H Meadows, D.J. Meadow, J. Randers and W.W. Behrens III, *The Limits to Growth* (New York: University Press, 1972).

never be 100% convincing to those who continue to believe (or remain persuaded by) the latest arguments, but they do justify a certain sense of *déjà vu*.

A third point to be made is more subtle, but is nonetheless potentially decisive. This is that, under capitalism, notions of value and profit, and the very definitions of a good or a service, are sufficiently flexible and/or subjective that they cannot be uniquely identified with any particular pattern of resource use. If 'green' or environmentally friendly production methods are genuinely regarded as 'goods' by the public at large, and therefore perceived as being more privately profitable to those organizing production than the alternatives, then that is what society will get and *vice versa*. Either way, there can be 'rapid economic growth', and increases in income and wealth as measured in subjective value-added terms. Public policy on these questions then boils down to a question of providing the appropriate sets of incentives. None of the foregoing observations will settle the essentially political disputes about the status of any specific set of predictions, but they do serve to sharply separate ecological issues from those of comparative economic systems.

## 1.16  Nominal and Real Wages

Symmetrically with such concepts as the nominal and real money supply, it is also important to distinguish between nominal and real wage rates. The nominal wage rate, $W$, is the wage rate in money terms and the real wage rate, $W/P$, is the nominal wage rate divided by the price index, $P$. This gives the actual purchasing power of the wages. These concepts are applicable at both the microeconomic level (to one's own individual situation when asking for a raise) and at the macroeconomic level.

To help to understand how the concept of real wages might be applicable in macroeconomics, suppose that, in the national income and product accounts of a given economy for a certain year, real GDP is calculated as 100,000 million constant dollars. Also, that the number of persons counted as being employed ($N$) is 10 million. Further, that the labour share in the distribution of income is 55%. Thus;

$$Y = 100{,}000 \text{ million constant dollars.} \tag{1.21}$$

$$N = 10 \text{ million persons.} \tag{1.22}$$

Therefore, average labour productivity, $A$, and the gross real wage rate *per* employed person, $W/P$, are;

$$A = Y/N = 10,000 \text{ constant dollars } per \ annum \qquad (1.23)$$

$$W/P = \text{average real wage} = 5,500 \text{ constant dollars } per \ annum \ (1.24)$$

The remainder of the real income available *per* employed person, in this case 4,500 constant dollars annually, is distributed between the other two income shares, interest and profit.

## 1.17  The International Economy and Exchange Rates

One way of thinking about the international economy is as a set of competing currency networks, each with its own central bank. Exchange rates between the different currencies can be either *floating* (flexible), or *fixed*. To illustrate, let the symbol $E$ stand for the *nominal spot exchange rate,* defined as the foreign currency price of one unit of domestic currency. For example, suppose that $C0.75 = $US1.00. In that case (if Canada is the domestic economy), $E = 0.75$. The authorities may either try to fix the exchange rate at its present level or, as is currently the case in Canada, may allow it to float (find its own level in international currency markets). In any event, what really matters for *international competitiveness* is not the nominal exchange rate (in spite of all the attention lavished on it by government, business, and the media) but actually the *real exchange rate, Q.* If as before $P$ stands for the domestic price level, then $Q$ is given by;

$$Q = EP/Pf. \qquad (1.25)$$

If Canadian 'widgets' cost $C25.00 *per* unit, the domestic price level for this single item is $P = 25$. If US widgets cost $US21.00, the foreign price level is $Pf = 21$. With $E = 0.75$;

$$Q = (0.75 \times 25)/21 = 0.89 \qquad (1.26)$$

Therefore, Canadian goods (the widgets) are actually *less* expensive than the equivalent US goods, appearances to the contrary. (So-called purchasing power parity, or PPP, where the prices are equal in real terms, would be $Q = 1$.) In the present case, Canadian goods are actually cheaper, or more 'competitive', than are US goods, and Canadian widgets will outsell US widgets. This would be good for the Canadian *balance of payments* (BOP). Using the above definition of the nominal exchange rate, we can say that a *depreciation* (fall) in the real exchange rate would be good for exports, whereas an *appreciation* (a rise) in the real exchange rate would have the opposite effect.

These circumstances lead to a highly confused situation in international political economy, in which attempts to stabilize the economy by fixing the *nominal* exchange rate end up by *destabilizing* it. Even if the authorities like to think that they can keep the nominal exchange rate at (say) $E = 0.75$ for ever, under endogenous money it is impossible to do the same for either $P$ or $Pf$. (In any event, the foreign price level is entirely beyond domestic control.) Therefore, even if $E$ is fixed, the ratio $P/Pf$ is bound to change eventually, in one direction or another. Once a given trend is established, up or down, the real exchange rate will continuously be changing. Historically, including in very recent times, many societies have suffered from, or been held hostage to, this error. A basic lack of understanding on the part of the supposed 'experts'.

## 1.18  Conclusion: The Key Questions in Monetary Macroeconomics?

One thing that has been emphasized in this first *Lecture* is that in a monetary economy it is necessary continuously to be aware of the difference between nominal, or money, values and real values. Therefore, perhaps the two most important questions in monetary theory are about how the real interest rate, $r$, and the real exchange rate, $Q$, are determined.

According to a real analysis, the real rate of interest is determined not by monetary or financial factors but by the rate of time preference, the marginal product of capital, or some such. And the real exchange rate is determined by the barter terms of trade. The implication of both assumptions is that neither fiscal, monetary, nor financial policies are ever going to 'matter'. All that is supposed to be going on, even in a highly complex international economy, is essentially barter. This is the underlying premise of both the macroeconomic theory, and the trade theory, currently taught in universities. In monetary analysis, however (in spite of the labels), the 'real' interest rate and the 'real' exchange rate are indeed determined by monetary and financial factors. The real economy itself must adjust accordingly. In this case, the pursuit of the correct economic policy certainly does matter, very much indeed, for good or ill. In the terminology of the late Professor Meyer Burstein,[44] should there be a 'real theory of the *real* rate of interest', or a 'monetary theory of the *real* rate of interest'? Also, should there be a 'real theory of the *real* exchange rate', or a 'monetary theory of the *real* exchange rate'? Burstein, I think, understood the issue very well in terms more or less identical to those discussed here. His view, however, was that a real analysis is the most appropriate. On the contrary, a genuinely monetary analysis suggests that the second answer to each question is correct. This is the premise of the present set of *Lectures*.

---

[44] Meyer Burstein, *Classical Macroeconomics for the Next Century*, mimeo, York University, Toronto, 1995.

# Lecture 2

# Money, Capitalism, and Enterprise

## 2.1  Introduction

I began the first *Lecture* in this series with some quotes from my own *Rethinking* and Geoffrey Ingham's *The Nature of Money*, and I will do the same sort of thing here. We start with a 'quote within a quote' from the first chapter of my earlier *Money, Enterprise, and Income Distribution*[1];

> According to [the late] Margaret Thatcher '... 'capitalism' ... is one of the few words which the right have appropriated from the left rather than *vice versa*'. The former British Prime Minister is ... using these terms in their standard meanings in late 20th/early 21st century politics, and the inference is that conservatives have adopted the expression capitalism as a term of approbation for the ... system they favour, as opposed to the negative spin ... by generations of Marxists and socialists. The positive associations ... Thatcher wants to suggest are ... summed up [in] the title of Milton Friedman's ... [book], *Capitalism and Freedom* ...

I went on to argue, however, that what is striking about recent intellectual history is that many of those professionally charged with the investigation of economic questions, namely the academic economics establishment, seem much less enthusiastic about the study of capitalism, conceived of as an ongoing socio-economic system, than do some of the politicians. For example, in contributions toward the end of the twentieth century, Robert

---

[1] Smithin, *Money*.

Heilbroner and William Milberg complained about the lack of a 'vision' of the capitalist economic process on the part of the academic economists of the day.[2] And up to the time of writing, nothing much has changed. Nobody would suggest that the contents of 'top-tier' economics journals today differ markedly from those of a couple of decades back. Heilbroner and Milberg suggest that the malaise dates back to at least the late 1960s/early 1970s.

Similarly, Paul Davidson asserts that after about 1970 articles expressing dissenting views (which must have had *some* sort of vision, positive or negative) have been excluded from the most prestigious academic journals.[3] Granted its existence, the problem is a long-standing and continuing one.

The term vision derives from Schumpeter, and refers to the 'pre-analytical cognitive act' that is nonetheless an indispensable precursor to analysis.[4] In Heilbroner's view, although a 'vision' necessarily has an ideological character, it is free of the pejorative connotations usually associated with ideology. However, the argument does not work with the idea of 'capitalism', as that term is politically loaded and misleading. The very concept of capital has always been vague and ambiguous. Is it supposed to be a sum of money, a collection of machines, or a set of personal and social characteristics (*cf.* 'human capital' or 'social capital')? It is rare that writers on economic issues feel any need to clarify these points. Nonetheless, they write extensively about things like the 'capital stock', the 'accumulation of 'capital', the 'marginal product of capital', and so on, without ever properly defining them. Keynes used to tell his students that the only way out of these difficulties is to be clear precisely 'what one feels one means by capitalism' in each specific context.[5] I have argued that it might be better to do away with the ambiguous notion of capital (and hence of 'capitalism') altogether. The best alternative descriptor of the system would be Max Weber's 'method of enterprise', defined as, 'the provision of human needs by ... enterprise, which is to say by private business seeking profit'.[6]

[2] Robert Heilbroner, 'Analysis and vision in the history of modern economic thought' (*Journal of Economic Literature* 28, 1990); Robert Heilbroner and William Milberg, *The Crisis of Vision in Modern Economic Thought* (New York: Cambridge University Press, 1995).

[3] Paul Davidson, 'Setting the record straight on a *History of Post Keynesian Economics*' (*Journal of Post Keynesian Economics* 26, 2003/04).

[4] Heilbroner, 'Analysis ...'.

[5] A.F.W. Plumptre, 'Maynard Keynes as a teacher', in Milo Keynes, ed., *Essays on John Maynard Keynes* (Cambridge: Cambridge University Press, 1975).

[6] Randall Collins, *Weberian Sociological Theory* (Cambridge: Cambridge University Press, 1986).

## 2.2  The 'Scope and Method' of Economics?

One reason why adherents of the academic mainstream feel no need of a vision is that (judging by their own methodological writings) they are not really all that much interested in their ostensible subject matter. They are seemingly not concerned with the behaviour of 'the economy', in the way in which business economists, stock market investors, or even social activists would be. Nor do they wish their activities to be seen as part of the broader project of social science, if this means investigating the social structures that condition economic activity. To many practitioners the *only* point of the discipline of economics is the construction of a pure theory of rational choice, regardless of institutional context.

This stance is consistent with the narrow definition of economics set down by Robbins in the 1930s, restricting the subject to a study of 'human behaviour as a relationship between given ends and scarce means which have alternative uses',[7] but not with the broader definitions favoured (rightly so, in my opinion) by scholars from other disciplines such as economic sociologists.[8] The latter are typically much closer in spirit to Adam Smith's original *Inquiry into the Nature and Causes of the Wealth of Nations*.[9] Moreover, ever since the publication of Samuelson's *Foundations* in the next decade, the further requirement that the rational choice theory be capable of some form of complicated mathematical expression has grown ever stronger.[10] The preferred vehicle for the mathematics is subject to various fads and fashions, be it optimal control, linear algebra, game theory, or the ubiquitous 'dynamic stochastic general equilibrium' (DSGE) model, but the focus of academic research comes to be only on the development of the various techniques. Actual economic events are interesting only to the extent they can be explained by one or another of the mathematical choice theories. Otherwise they can be put to one side as a 'puzzle'. Economics is defined solely by the methods it uses, rather than its subject matter. Such writers have no use for a vision of any

[7] Lionel Robbins, *The Nature and Significance of Economic Science* (London: Macmillan, 1932).

[8] Carlo Triglia, *Economic Sociology: State, Market and Society in Modern Capitalism* (Oxford: Basil Blackwell Publishers, 2002).

[9] Adam Smith, *An Inquiry into the Nature and Causes of the Wealth of Nations*, 1776 (as reprinted by Liberty Fund: Indianapolis IN, 1981).

[10] Paul Samuelson, *Foundations of Economic Analysis*, 1947 (second enlarged edition, Cambridge, MA: Harvard University Press, 1983).

particular social system, whether it be called capitalism, the method of enterprise, or anything else.

## 2.3  Systems of Material Reproduction

In a contribution to a volume that I edited twenty years ago, Heinsohn and Steiger quote a rhetorical question from Harold Demsetz '... what has mainstream economics being doing for 200 years if ... not ... studying capitalism?'[11] The time frame for the implied negative response is an exaggeration, but the answer is that for much of that time, at least since the marginalist revolution of the 1870s, the mainstream has not studied the system in its entirety at all but focused exclusively on the rational choice theory just outlined, and how such choices are reflected in the price mechanism.

On the other hand, in a literature (broadly speaking) in the tradition of Karl Polyani,[12] it is argued that, in spite of diversity in detail, at the most fundamental level there have been just three 'distinctive systems of material reproduction' that have existed in history. In a standard terminology, these are (I) the customary or tribal society, (II) the command or feudal society, (III) the property-based society. In the customary society, production and distribution are organized by time-honoured procedures, differing in specific content in each case, but based essentially on the principle of *reciprocity*. The individuals who make up the society, however, are not free in the sense that there is any independent system of law to which they could appeal to enforce the rules. In the command society (such as systems of slavery, or feudalism, or the totalitarian systems of the 20th century), the reigning principle is *coercive redistribution*. In these cases, production and distribution are organized by a ruling class, or cadre, who extract levies from a subordinate class of serfs. The latter are also not free, and likewise have no independent system of justice to which to appeal. In a property-based society, however, production is said to be organized by *market exchange* and a system of contracts between free

---

[11] Gunnar Heinsohn and Otto Steiger, 'The property theory of interest and money', in John Smithin, ed., *What is Money?* (London: Routledge, 2000).
[12] Karl Polyani, *The Great Transformation*, 1944 (as reprinted by Beacon Press, Boston, MA: 1985).

individuals, who can appeal to independent courts of law for enforcement.

Each system involves the activity of *provisioning*, meaning the production of the means of subsistence and the distribution of the resulting goods and services. However, it is doubtful whether either of the first two alternatives could be said to involve an 'economy' in the sense in which that term is widely used today (*e.g.*, in the financial and business media). In the third case, the identification of the notion of 'property' solely with the real-exchange economy is also questionable (as already discussed in *Lecture 1*). There would need to be a much more detailed discussion of the ontology of money, and social ontology in general, to effectively differentiate this mode of production.

Each system of provisioning is capable of change and adaptation, but perhaps only to a limited extent. In the case of the customary society, for example, change typically occurs only in response to external forces, such as environmental pressures or conflicts with rival groups. In the command based society, there can also be change, but in this case it occurs either on the initiative of the rulers, or *via* rebellion by the oppressed groups. Only in a market, or property-based, society is there an internal logic of development immanent in the system itself. But, again, to fully establish this point it would be necessary to give a much more detailed description of the *modus operandi* of the system than has been done so far.

What, then, would be required for a scientific understanding of the way in which each system functions? Heilbroner argues that there is no need for the particular skills of the economist *per se* outside of the institutional framework of capitalism and it is certainly true that there was no systematic economic theory before such a system existed.[13] When studying either a customary or command society, supposing a researcher had a grasp of the main cultural, political, and technological features, this would be sufficient to explain what is going on. There is nothing an economist would be able to add. In some examples of command economies (such as the state socialisms of the 20th century), problems of the management of large-scale enterprise do arise, but these involve only administrative, technical, or logistical issues, not specifically economic questions. What is different, in a property-based or market-type system (assuming we can make this identification), is that the 'players' must also deal with problems

---

[13] Robert Heilbroner, *Twenty-First Century Capitalism* (Toronto: House of Anansi Press, 1992).

of competitive strategy. This is a key point. Only in this type of system do economic issues recognizable as such (involving demand and supply, relative prices, competition, *etc.*) begin to arise.

The indifference of contemporary mainstream economics to any further investigation of the specific social structures needed for a property-based system to exist is thus a very strange twist in intellectual history. The rational choice theory simply takes for granted the existence of some such system, and sketches out an abstract theory of how rational agents *should* behave in a stylized version of it. There is no attempt at investigating how such a system came into being, how it is reproduced, or even how individuals actually do make decisions in reality. It is impossible to discover any coherent socio-economic vision in an exercise of this kind.


## 2.4  What Exactly *Should* be Studied?

In the above discussion, three different broad classes or types of social system were mooted. But it was also hinted that the distinctions are not really sufficiently detailed to fully distinguish one system from another. In fact, if we look at the actual literature on economic theory and policy that has developed over the years, it seems that at least *five* different methods of provisioning have been canvassed, not three. These are, (i) *the Crusoe economy*, (ii) a traditional society, (iii) a command economy, (iv) *a real-exchange economy*, (v) the method of enterprise (as in Weber). All of these have their own logic and principles. But it is indicative of the real interests of many mainstream economists that the two italicized in the list are essentially fictional. They can be used only for thought experiments about how things may work out in the assumed circumstances.

Command economies and traditional economics certainly can exist, have existed, and do still exist in various places today. The same thing can be said (*a fortiori*) about the method of enterprise. The definition of this system from Weber was given above, and there is no question of the reality of profit-driven systems involving business and markets. It really ought to be self-evident that these are what should be studied by economists to understand the sort of society in which most of us live. The key question raised by the definition is what exactly is this 'profit' that is supposed to provide the incentive for economic activity? Most obviously it is a sum of money. Hence, the importance of the ontology of money, the significance of credit and money creation by the banking system, the availability of initial and final finance, and so on. It is precisely the monetary element that is missing from standard characterizations of the market economy.

In contrast to the method of enterprise, the notion of the *Crusoe economy* is literally based on the 17th century fictional character Robinson Crusoe, from the novel by Defoe. Crusoe, shipwrecked on a desert island, has no use for money. Yet, this fable is often the preferred starting point for conventional economic analysis. The admittedly hard (but entirely hypothetical) choices that Crusoe has to make are presented as the paradigmatic example of the problem of resource allocation. But this sort of discussion makes no sense as social science. The decisions that Crusoe makes are not relevant to anyone but himself.[14] He is not participating in an economy at all.

Moving beyond the pathological case of the isolated individual, when it becomes necessary to make provision for more than one person, there remains a strong flavour of the fictional in almost all conventional economic discussion. This is clearly applicable to the notion of voluntary exchange in a free market (in principle conducted by barter), as in point (iv) above. And to be fair, this case *is* often put forward as a normative ideal rather than a historical case study. As all the trades are supposed to be made on a voluntary basis, the fundamental idea is that individual liberty will be maximized. The difficulty with the argument is not with this moral standpoint. Rather, it is that the concept of the market employed in the narrative is purely abstract. All of the social structure necessary for actual markets to exist (including money) is lacking. Indeed, the most rhetorically persuasive theoretical accounts are those of a system of exchange portrayed as functioning entirely without any of the financial, monetary, or legal paraphernalia of a real system. But the absence of social structure means that it is incorrect to identify the abstract pure exchange model as anything resembling capitalism or the method of enterprise. This is why the hypothesized pure exchange system should be given a separate label, such as the 'real-exchange economy' or similar, as already discussed. This moniker conveniently covers the cases both of pure barter and Keynes's 'neutral economy' (in which a sort of money

---

[14] In the novel, Crusoe does eventually encounter a second person on the island whom he calls 'Man Friday'. From this point on in the narrative we do have a social situation. The Crusoe economy *per se* ceases to exist. Friday becomes a sort of servant to Crusoe, a situation which inevitably involves some degree of coercion.

exists but only as a token medium of exchange). Neither describes any actual historical situation. Keynes plainly stated that '... [in]... the real world ... the conditions for a neutral economy are not satisfied'.[15]

In the final analysis, only the three remaining basic constructs, the traditional society, command systems, and the method of enterprise, have any historical verisimilitude. Only the last of these is amenable to economic analysis properly so called.

## 2.5  Some Existing Visions

Another way of arriving at some sort of vision of the capitalist/entrepreneurial economic system might be to consider the views of some of the great scenarists of the past, to recapitulate what they made of the 'capitalisms' of their day. Previously, David Barrows and I identified Adam Smith, Karl Marx, Joseph Schumpeter, J.M. Keynes, and Friedrich von Hayek as having been among the most significant of these writers.[16] In what follows, the main ideas of each of them are briefly sketched.

### 2.5.1  *Adam Smith (1723–1790)*

Originally, it was Adam Smith who was regarded in his own time and long after as the main expositor of the workings of the price mechanism. This is what seemed to him to be the most important feature of the nascent industrial capitalism of the 18th century. He attempted to demonstrate the power of market forces *via* the famous metaphor of the invisible hand, and advocated a 'system of natural liberty' rather than detailed regulation of industry.[17] It is debatable, in my opinion, whether Smith's view was actually a precursor of later arguments about optimal resource allocation, information, and self-organizing systems. At this stage, the argument seems simply to have been that the incentives provided by the market are what make things happen. Price and profit incentives ensure the provision of goods and services, that living standards rise, that people do not starve, *etc.* It is just how the system works.

---

[15] Keynes, 'The distinction ...'.
[16] David Barrows and John Smithin, *Fundamentals of Economics for Business*, second edition (Singapore: World Scientific Publishing, 2009).
[17] Smith, *Wealth of Nations*.

The most important consideration (at least for Smith the moral philosopher) was to explain how motives deprecated in conventional systems of morality, such as self-interest, nonetheless rebound to the overall benefit of society. The growth of wealth is attributed to the division of labour, that is, improvements in productivity *via* specialization as the volume of output increases. This is itself a market phenomenon, limited only by the 'extent of the market'. The main illustration was the well-known example of the Scottish pin factory.

Although Smith was certainly an advocate of free markets, he was not as naïve on questions of governance as some later advocates of economic liberalism. For Smith, government remained an integral part of the functioning of society. There was a clear role for government in national defence, the law, and to provide for those public works needed to support the infrastructure, but which are 'of such a nature that the profit could never repay the expense to any individual ...'. The system of natural liberty was not one in which government was absent, but simply one in which the authorities refrain from detailed regulation of the market so as not to interfere with its operation.

But there was one glaring omission from Smith's overall vision of capitalism, which would be obvious to anyone encountering such a system for the first time, but has somehow seemed perfectly natural to all the succeeding generations of classical, neoclassical, and mainstream economists. Smith was one of the originators of the tradition, later followed by almost all of orthodox economic theory, to deny the importance of money in determining economic outcomes. Dostaler and Maris summed up this attitude with the telling statement that '... orthodox economics wanted to create a science that ignored money'.[18] As explained in *Lecture 1*, underlying this stance is the idea that economics should focus mainly on the barter exchange of goods and services, not on financial or monetary matters. For Smith, a main preoccupation was apparently indignation at the perceived errors of his mercantilist predecessors, including the idea 'wealth consists in ... gold and silver' (the money of the time). He had to overlook the fact that it had presumably been that very same 'mercantilist system' that had led to Britain's rise to the status of the leading world power of the day. Logically, Smith's own influence, if any, must have

---

[18] Gilles Dostaler and Bernard Maris, 'Dr. Freud and Mr. Keynes on money and capitalism', in John Smithin, ed., *What is Money?* (London: Routledge, 2000).

come mainly after the publication of his famous book. In any event, Smith's lead on money has been followed by most economists ever since.

Aside from the fatal flaw with respect to money, the overall message that Smith conveyed about the burgeoning capitalist economy was optimistic. As long as market forces are left to operate unhindered, there will be a continual increase in prosperity. As living standards gradually rise, economic growth will tend to benefit all social classes. There will be no serious conflict between them.

### 2.5.2  *Karl Marx* (*1818–1883*)

Karl Marx, writing 90 years later than Smith, sent out the opposite message about the likely development of the capitalist system. In place of gradual and harmonious progress, Marx saw only class conflict, the increasing immiseration of the workers, and ultimately inevitable collapse. By Marx's time the landowning classes, on whom Smith devoted much attention, have dropped into the background. The remaining protagonists are the capitalists or 'bourgeoisie', and the workers or 'proletariat'. Like Smith, Marx does not make much of a distinction between the entrepreneurs/factory owners, who own or operate the means of production, and the financiers or rentiers who provide the money. They are all part of the same capitalist class, and their incomes ultimately arise from the same source. The relations between the two classes are solely those of power and exploitation.

In the Marxian theory, labour power is assumed to be the only source of value. The value of each commodity reflects the amount of labour power put into it. This is not just mindless effort. For example, simply digging holes in the ground and filling them in again would require exertion, but Marx is interested only in 'socially necessary labour time'. This means the time it takes, given average skill and the existing technology, to produce an item valued by the community. Marx's argument is that this attribution of value should logically also be applied to the commodity labour itself. But the value of labour power on this definition is only the effort needed for the workers to reproduce themselves (to pay for food, shelter, clothing, and so on). This only takes up some fraction of the working time available — which circumstance accounts for exploitation. For the rest of the working day, the value the workers create accrues to the capitalists. This is the so-called 'surplus value' which is the source of profit in the Marxian system.

The capitalists can extract the surplus because of their superior strategic position gained *via* the ownership of the means of production.

As a vision of capitalism, this is the polar opposite of Smith's benign system of liberty from which all benefit. The dominating principle is an unequal struggle over distributive shares. As seen by Marx in his own lifetime, the prognosis is fatal. The struggle will intensify over time. To prevent real wages from rising, capitalists will bring in labour saving machinery, and try to keep wages down by creating an 'industrial reserve army' of the unemployed. However, the rise in the 'organic composition of capital', as Marx calls it, only contributes to further declines in profitability. There will be an ever-worsening series of crises, and the eventual demise of the system is inherent in its own logic. Eventually, it will give way to the supposedly ideal system of socialism. As to how such a utopia will come about, and how it will function, Marx says nothing.

How does Marx handle the point on which Adam Smith was taken to task above, the question of integrating a coherent vision of money into the overall system? We can do no better than to once again quote Geoffrey Ingham, from the *Nature of Money*;

> The labour theory of value committed Marx and ... his successors, to a version of the commodity theory of money with all its ... errors. To this extent Marx's ... theory of money was mistaken, and the error ... [was] ... unequivocally stated, 'the principal difficulty ... is surmounted ...[if] ... it is understood that the commodity is the origin of money'.

Therefore, with due allowance for differences in terminology and outlook, if the orthodox real exchange theory has appeared increasingly anachronistic as the system has developed, the same logic must also apply to the Marxist conception of money. As already mentioned, however, there was one feature of Marx's monetary economics worth noting, even if Marx himself did not make good use of it, the idea of the circuit $M \to C \to C' \to M'$.

### 2.5.3 *Joseph Schumpeter* (*1883–1950*)

The Austrian school economist Bohm-Bawerk, a teacher of Joseph Schumpeter (the next in our list of visionaries) used to be described as the 'bourgeois Marx'. But according to a later editor of Schumpeter, J.E. Elliot 'the title better fits Schumpeter himself'.[19] The claim is that Schumpeter's work was comparable in method, analytical style, and scope to that of Marx. A main difference is that whereas Marx hated capitalism, and was its would-be nemesis, Schumpeter claimed to be an admirer and supporter of the system. After a period of neglect, Schumpeter's reputation underwent something of a revival at the end of the 20th century because some of the issues he raised, such as the role of the entrepreneur and the importance of innovation, once again became popular themes at the time. Schumpeter makes the entrepreneur the hero of the economic drama. Such a figure is to be distinguished from both the financial capitalist and the mere business manager as the driving force responsible for innovation in capitalism. According to Schumpeter, it is precisely innovation and entrepreneurship that are responsible for the emergence of profit opportunities within what would otherwise be a static environment, and thus for growth and development. Entrepreneurs are not so much a class as a group, a small elite within society blessed with unusual qualities of drive, courage, leadership, *etc.* In a different type of society they might have been military leaders or feudal lords, but in a commercial environment they content themselves with innovation in business. So long as the spirit of entrepreneurship remains strong, the capitalist system has no difficulty in delivering rising prosperity and living standards. Schumpeter is not worried about the tendency to monopoly that concerned both the neoclassical economists and Marx. If there is a monopoly in railroads, for example, some entrepreneur or another will have the incentive to get around this by inventing the automobile. Schumpeter refers to this as the 'perennial gale of creative destruction'.[20] New industries and processes are continually being created and old ones destroyed.

However, and this is a strange thing, Schumpeter finally agrees with Marx that the capitalist system is doomed. He poses and answers his own question, 'can capitalism survive? … no, I don't think it can'. But there is no real economic reason for the system to fail. Rather, it is the cumulative effects of broadly sociological trends and developments that will eventually bring it to an end. The intellectual and political climate turns decisively

---

[19] J. E. Elliot, 'Introduction to the *Transactions* edition', in Joseph Schumpeter, *The Theory of Economic Development: An Inquiry into Profits, Capital, Credit, Interest, and the Business Cycle* (New Brunswick, NJ: Transactions Publishers, 1983).

[20] Joseph Schumpeter, *Capitalism, Socialism and Democracy*, 1942 (as reprinted by Routledge: London, 1992).

against capitalism. In the end, nobody defends the system, not even the bourgeoisie themselves. The bourgeois intellectuals are particularly guilty of this betrayal. They cut off the branch they are sitting on. (They fail to understand that there would be no room for intellectuals to pontificate, certainly not to make a good living doing so, in any other type of system.) The critical rationalistic mentality of capitalism, initially responsible for its triumph over older forms of social organization, ends up working against itself. Given the mid-twentieth century intellectual climate, Schumpeter's analysis would no doubt have seemed *a propos* at the time, and perhaps rather wide of the mark forty to fifty years later around 1989–1991, after the collapse of communism in Europe. These things are cyclical, however. Today, similar sorts of ideas are again popular, and (at the precise time of writing) even dominant, in academia, the media, the entertainment industry, the popular culture, politics, and thereby in the boardrooms of corporate business itself.

No doubt influenced by the similar intellectual climate of his own day, Schumpeter was also on the wrong side of the interwar 'socialist calculation debate' involving Mises, Hayek, Lange, and others. He asks, 'can socialism work?' and responds, 'of course it can'. A main reason for this seeming error is that Schumpeter, in spite of his own ideas about creative destruction, *etc.,* vastly overrates the purely formal general equilibrium system of economics pioneered by Walras. He thinks that this mathematical algorithm can be applied just as well to socialism. On this view, there is no difficulty for socialist managers to solve the general equilibrium problem and institute a system of shadow prices as a perfect substitute for the market. This is an argument that could only pass muster within the ivory tower of academia. It entirely misses the point about what makes capitalism a dynamic system. It is not 'information' that is lacking in socialism, but incentives. Nor did the ostensible winners of the calculation debate clearly understand the issue, and have not done so down to the present day.

On the contentious question of money and credit, some writers have praised Schumpeter for recognition of the role played by bank financing and endogenous credit creation. In Schumpeter's view, again according to Elliot[21];

---

[21] Elliot, 'Introduction …'.

> ... the provision of credit ... to entrepreneurs to finance innovations is a
> vital function in a capitalist economy ... [and credit creation is important
> enough] ... to serve as its [capitalism's] *differentia specifica.*

There is an important caveat, however, because Schumpeter thinks that credit financing is only relevant in periods of innovative change. He also has a concept of a static circular flow of income, the background from which innovation erupts. In this phase, credit creation is thought to be unnecessary. The rate of interest on money falls to zero and for as long as equilibrium persists we are safely ensconced back in the world of barter exchange. All of this validates a pertinent remark by Ingham that 'Schumpeter was only a reluctant and equivocal creditist'.[22]

### 2.5.4  *John Maynard Keynes (1883–1946)*

Keynes put forward yet another version of the essence of capitalism. Unlike the majority of other writers, before and since, his theory of effective demand focuses on the very real difficulties that capitalist entrepreneurs face in marketing their output. The term 'effective' seems to me clearly to imply that the demand must correspond to actual purchasing power in terms of money, not merely notional wants derived from the perceived value of output before it is sold. Keynes denied the presumed automatic self-adjusting mechanism that most other writers (except Marx) had attributed to the market system. If aggregate demand is deficient, there can be a state of permanent widespread unemployment in the long-run, not just in the short-run. This argument was highly relevant to the period when Keynes was writing in the 1930s as opposed to the views of Schumpeter and most others at the time. A corollary is that if there is to be economic growth, there must be demand growth, but recognition of this basic point has now disappeared almost entirely from the economics mainstream.

Perhaps the most significant element of Keynes's new vision in the 1930s was the notion of a monetary theory of production. Ultimately, however, this was only a partial success in challenging accepted views. The basic idea of monetary production is that the commercial system, which has existed in one form or another since the Italian renaissance, is

---

[22] Ingham, *Nature of Money.*

pre-eminently a monetary system. Those responsible for setting production in train, entrepreneurs or corporations, must first acquire the necessary financial resources to do so. And at the macroeconomic level, as argued in *Lecture 1,* new monetary resources can only be generated by bank credit creation. The proceeds from the sale of goods are also sums of money. In such an environment, contrary to the view 'money does not matter', the monetary system takes on major significance. In particular, 'the terms on which'[23] the monetary resources necessary for production are obtainable (that is, the rate of interest) are of vital importance.

As previously mentioned, Keynes had earlier made a distinction between a 'co-operative economy' and a 'money-wage or entrepreneur economy'.[24] The former involves barter in the sphere of production as well as exchange, the factors of production agreeing to receive rewards as a pre-determined share of output produced. For Keynes, the fault in orthodox economic theory was to confine itself to the study of this kind of system (or to one that replicates its properties with a token money). But, in an entrepreneur economy production and employment decisions are made by those hiring productive factors with money payments, and whose receipts from the sale of output are also sums of money. For Keynes, this was a better description of an actual economy than the imagined world of the co-operative economy. Output and employment outcomes depend upon expectations of money receipts relative to money cost, and monetary conditions matter in an essential way for economic performance.

### 2.5.5 *Friedrich von Hayek* (*1899–1992*)

Hayek was the leader of the intellectual reaction against Keynes in the later 20th century. However, it is one thing, as Hayek certainly did, to point out *The Fatal Conceit*[25] of socialism, and quite another to lead the 'fight' (as it seems he was explicitly recruited to do)[26] against the only

---

[23] Keynes, *General Theory.*

[24] A. Asimakopolous, 'The aggregate supply function and the share economy: some early drafts of the *General Theory*', in Omar Hamouda and John Smithin, eds., *Keynes and Public Policy After Fifty Years*, vol. 2 (Aldershot: Edward Elgar, 1988).

[25] Friedrich Hayek, *The Fatal Conceit: The Errors of Socialism* (Chicago: University of Chicago Press, 1988).

[26] Friedrich Hayek, *Hayek on Hayek*, S. Kresge and L. Wenar, eds. (Chicago: University of Chicago Press, 1994).

possible remedy which could make the method of enterprise function. It is significant that this contrary vision redirected attention once again to the *minutiae* of detailed market processes, rather than to the social ontology which makes a market system feasible. Hayek myopically focused on how changing market prices are supposed to provide the 'information' by which a vast economic network may be coordinated, even though each participant has limited knowledge of the whole. It is an up-dated version of Smith's invisible hand, with the market now conceived of *via* an analogy to a self-organizing system in the biological or neurological sciences. With this move, Hayek is searching for a model of social process outside society itself, in the physical or natural world. In this case the analogy is to biology, just as the neoclassical economists sought their inspiration in physics. According to Hayek, it is this quasi-natural mechanism, rather than any form of human intentionality, that is responsible for the development of the system. A market system is believed to be spontaneously generated without conscious design, and is supposedly too complex for any one individual to be able to comprehend. Therefore any attempt to interfere with its operation is thought to be damaging. It is deemed impossible to devise any policy measures to improve, modify, or ameliorate the system without killing the goose that lays the golden eggs. There are caveats regarding the provision of some minimum level of social services, but it is not unreasonable to identify this position as the main argument. Hence, Hayek's opposition to anything that he thinks resembles socialism. He held that the adoption of socialism, or communism, will cause economic stagnation, societal decline, and mass privation — which judgement, moreover, seems to be correct, at least as applied to the historical examples of state socialism observed in the 20th and 21st centuries. Hayek lived long enough (died 1992) to witness events that seemed at the time to vindicate his theories, such as the collapse of communism and the earlier *volte face* in attitudes to economic theory and policy in the West that was known (prematurely as it turned out) as the 'Conservative revolution'.[27]

Nonetheless, even granted the empirical failures of socialism and communism in the 20th century and thus the putative superiority of capitalism/enterprise in that respect, the idea that the system evolved entirely without human intentionality, and that no type of 'policy' can ever contribute to its betterment and preservation, remains untenable both logically

---

[27] John Smithin, *Macroeconomics After Thatcher and Reagan: The Conservative Policy Revolution in Retrospect* (Aldershot: Edward Elgar, 1990).

and historically. It ignores all of the actual legislation, policy initiatives, different systems of governance, land grants, bank acts, trade agreements, company law, labour legislation, *etc.*, that have ever been in place. Historically, there can be no doubt that questions of government and governance, and the evolution of societal norms in general, have played a major role in the creation of an environment *within which* a market economy can emerge and continue to be viable. Hayek can certainly be credited with one of the most forceful statements of the anti-statist position, and had he contented himself with the statement that a particular style of governance is required for capitalism to function (*e.g.*, that to overburden the society with regulations and punitive taxation will cause the system to collapse) he might have been on unassailable ground. But there is very much more to the study of social ontology, economic sociology, and political economy than this.

The most telling instance of the neglect of social ontology is that although Hayek began his academic career as a specialist monetary economist, the role of money itself in his final system is deeply problematic. According to Hicks,[28] who was a colleague of Hayek's at the *London School of Economics*, Hayek;

> ... [did] ... introduce ... an important qualification –that money must be kept 'neutral', in order that the [price] mechanism should work ... [but] ... claimed that if there was no monetary disturbance the system would remain in equilibrium.

I have read that Hayek's admirers apparently thought of him not only as the 'Anti-Lenin' of the 20th century, but also as the 'Anti-Keynes'. But this conflation of Hayek's two enemies indicates the central weakness of his system, notwithstanding its political appeal in some circles. Socialism and Keynesianism are by no means the same thing, politically or economically. However, Hayek and others consistently failed to treat Keynes with the respect he deserved. Keynes thought he was 'knocking away the Ricardian foundations of Marxism', but to the critics, his arguments were seen as just the thin end of the socialist wedge, a first step along the road to serfdom. The main problem is precisely the lack of understanding of the role of money. Consider a very revealing statement made by Hayek about

---

[28] John Hicks, *Money, Interest and Wages: Collected Essays on Economic Theory*, vol. II (Oxford: Basil Blackwell, 1982).

the supposed 'inflationary boom' of the 1950s and 1960s. Hayek is asked to explain the economic growth of that period on the principles of the Austrian School, and unconvincingly replies[29];

> The particular form I gave was connected with ... the gold standard, which allowed a credit expansion up to a point and then made a ... reversal possible. *I always knew that in principle there was no definite limit* ... But I just took it for granted that there was a built-in stop in the form of the gold standard ... in that I was a little (sic) mistaken in my diagnosis of the postwar development. I knew the boom would break down, but I didn't give it as long as it actually lasted ... My expectation was ... five or six years ... *it has lasted very much longer* ... The end result was the same ... (emphasis added)

There is no explanation of why the end result *must* be the same. Nonetheless, the rest of the passage seems backhandedly to concede the essence of the Keynesian and Hicksian approaches to monetary economics. The constraint whereby expansionary policies are always supposed to lead to disaster, artificially stimulating the economy and causing 'over-investment', was itself a social artifact.

## 2.6  Toward a Synthesis?

A more succinct device to illustrate the variety of different existing visions of the economic system may perhaps be to list just a few of the different labels that have been attached to it, including the 'entrepreneur economy', the 'extended order', 'free-market capitalism', 'laissez-faire capitalism', the 'market economy', the 'property-based society', and so forth. It seems that each writer picks out just one of the outstanding characteristics of the social system, the market, entrepreneurship, property rights, or whatever, and focuses on that to the exclusion of the others. As opposed to this, David Barrows and I have argued that the method of enterprise is a layered system based on the following five underlying social structures[30]; (A) a political settlement, (B) money, (C) private property, (D) markets, and (E) entrepreneurial business. The social, legal, and governance systems must

---

[29] Hayek, *Hayek on Hayek.*
[30] Barrows and Smithin, *Fundamentals.*

be such as to let these institutions function effectively, and also generate sufficient effective demand for the products of capitalist innovation.

The expression money does not just mean notes and coins, but rather the entire system of social relations covered by that rubric. These would include, firstly, a money of account. Second, a well-identified asset, not necessarily a physical asset, denominated in the unit of account, that serves as the final means of settlement or payment. Third, a developed banking and financial system that enables secure credit relations. These are the prerequisites for the existence of such things as price lists and rational accounting frameworks. They are required for the very feasibility of a system of production that entails taking a long position in goods and services, and functions *via* the generation and realization of monetary profits. Property rights are important for such a society because in a system centered on the profit motive (and the receipt of wages for services rendered) it is important that income recipients be able to control their final disbursement. They are important for *incentives*. For the system to work, those remunerated should be able to retain their rewards and dispose of them as they see fit, and not be subject to arbitrary confiscation. As already discussed, this does not in itself de-legitimize taxation, particularly when conceived of as an act of sovereignty rather than appropriation. Indeed, following the modern monetary theory (MMT) school it can be argued that the existence of some such authority is itself required for the establishment of a commercial society in the first place.[31] However, the concept of private property does mean that if the system is to function, there is a definite set of economic and legal principles that sharply delimit the scope of taxation.

The idea of market appears only in fourth place in the list which would no doubt seem strange from the viewpoint of orthodox economic theory. From that perspective, market exchange is co-extensive with economic activity. The market is supposed to be the mainspring of the whole system, based on a supposed natural propensity to 'truck, barter and exchange', as in Adam Smith. On this view, markets as such perform all the functions of providing information, coordinating activity, and ensuring productive efficiency. Moreover, money need not really be involved, in principle all that is going on is barter. The information content is supposed to consist of just these barter exchange ratios rather than accounting notions of profit. As against this belief in the supremacy of pure exchange, in actual social systems things are more complicated. Each set of social

---

[31] Recall the slogan of the MMT school that 'taxes drive money', as discussed in *Lecture 1*.

institutions builds on those existing at an earlier level, in a process known as 'iteration'.[32] Markets themselves are built upon the prior institutions of money and private property, and thus also on 'government', in the most basic sense, as already explained.[33]

Monetary exchange comes in simply because if there is to be a system in which the incentive for production is profit, quantifiable in monetary terms, there must exist a number of actual or virtual locations where the output of production can be sold. This is the most obvious function of markets in reality, hence the vital importance of marketing and advertising in actual business. If the output cannot be sold, there can be no profit. That said, markets do also to some extent serve the regulatory/validating function implicit in both the Marxian notion of 'socially necessary labour time' and neoclassical 'utility'. If someone, somewhere, buys the output, the effort that went into its production presumably was socially necessary, at least in the opinion of the purchaser at the time of sale.

The role of business is to organize productive activity in pursuit of profit. The term business is here used generically, including all types of business organizations, such as individual proprietors, partnerships, and all corporate forms. In point (E) the qualifier 'entrepreneurial' is used to emphasize the point recognized by Schumpeter and Keynes that, given an accommodative institutional framework, the essence of the system is the impetus for innovation and dynamic change.

Compare the account of social structure given here to the original six-fold schema of Weber's *General Economic History*.[34] In Weber, the structure of 'modern capitalism' is supposed to consist of (1) rational capital accounting, (2) freedom of markets, (3) rational technology, (4) calculable law, (5) freedom of labour, and (6) commercialization of economic life. Weber does not seem to have paid any attention to the notion of iteration as described above. The categories are not presented in any particular order, and this might explain why Weber's item (3), in particular, does not fit. In the present argument, 'rational technology' is seen as an *outcome* of capitalism, rather than its pre-condition. Otherwise, there are several points of correspondence between Weber's remaining items and those mentioned above. For example, item (1) is subsumed in the earlier point (B) about the

---

[32] Searle, *Construction of Social Reality*.

[33] Robert Skidelsky, *Money and Government: The Past and Future of Economics* (New Haven and London: Yale University Press, 2018).

[34] Max Weber, *General Economic History*, 1927 (as reprinted by Dover Publications: Mineola NY, 2003).

importance of money, and items (2) and (5) are covered by point (D). Item (4), on calculable law, is implicit in points (A), (B), and (C). Both money and private property require a legal system for the enforcement of contracts. Money is intimately involved in the system of debts and credits, and it is in this field that specifically legal considerations apply. Finally, item (6) is closely connected with point (E).

## 2.7   The *'Differentia Specifica'*

This section heading refers back to the quote from Elliot about Schumpeter cited above. In that Aristotelian idiom, credit creation is the identifying characteristic of the *species* 'capitalism' within the *genus* 'economic systems'. This same point came up time and time again in our discussion of the various visionaries. It was notable both by its presence in some cases and absence in others. In terms of Marx's $M \rightarrow C \rightarrow C' \rightarrow M'$ the capitalist production process is seen as one of transforming an initial amount of money, $M$, into commodities, $C$, then *via* production into a more valuable set of commodities, $C'$. Finally, into a greater amount of money, $M'$. But Marx did not explain where the additional money $(M' - M)$ was supposed to come from. Many of the issues at stake can be resolved into the question of just how the necessary increase in money is supposed to happen. (Not just for an individual firm but for the economy as whole, in aggregate or on average.) The answer is simply that monetary profits must be generated by credit and money creation over and above the initial costs of production. For there to be money profit for others, one sector or another of the economy must be continuously willing to go into debt. Among the possible candidates in the real world are (*e.g.*) the government budget deficit, consumer debt, borrowing by the foreign sector, or the 'animal spirits' of other entrepreneurs. However it happens the point is that credit creation is an integral part of the productive process, not merely an adjunct to it. The realization of profit, first in its initial monetary form and subsequently in real form, could not occur otherwise.

It might be useful at this point to provide (a simplified and stylized) numerical illustration of what is going on, based on some arithmetical exercises I have worked out in previous publications. Suppose, therefore, that in a system which has previously had no money a new institution is created and given a charter to be a monopoly bank. It will be the only entity with the right to grant credit and accept deposits denominated in a new unit of account. Immediately after the charter is granted the financial balance sheet of the bank will not be very informative. There will be zero assets and zero liabilities. (The owners of the bank will obviously not have been able to contribute any financial capital to the enterprise, as there was no such thing as financial capital before.) Next, suppose that an entrepreneur borrows $1,000,000 from the bank to make a product called '*widgets*'. The widgets take one year to produce, and the entrepreneur hires the workers at the start of the process, paying out the whole sum of money as wages in advance. Having received the money, the workers have nowhere else to put it but in the bank. (No items are available for sale as yet.) After the first loan, the bank's balance will therefore be as shown in *Table 2.1*.

The bank charges 10% simple interest, but will not insist on the repayment of principal or interest until after the production period is complete and sales are made. It does not pay interest on deposits. We then need to make some behavioural assumptions about how people are going to behave in this new environment. Let us suppose that whenever goods are available for sale, deposit holders among the non-bank public (workers or anyone else) will try to spend 80% of their money holdings and save 20%. On the other hand, all bank profits will be retained by the bank owners as they try to build up their 'capital'.

Time rolls on, a year passes, and the widgets are ready for sale. But as can be seen from *Table 2.2,* the firm cannot possibly make a profit in these circumstances. This is, in fact, the *essential* problem that always has the potential to cause difficulty in a monetary system. In this case, the only money in existence and available to be spent is the wage bill itself, and the workers or other consumers are only willing to spend 80% of it. There is not

*Table 2.1*: Monopoly Bank Initial Balance Sheet (After the First Loan)

| Assets | Liabilities |
|---|---|
| Loans: 1,000,000 | Deposits, Non-Bank Public: 1,000,000 |
| 1,000,000 | 1,000,000 |

*Table 2.2*: Income Statement of Widget-Maker #1 (With No New Borrowing)

| | | |
|---|---|---|
| Receipts: | $(0.8) \times (1,000,000)$ ... | 800,000 |
| (*minus*) | | |
| Repayment of Principal + Interest: 1,000,000 + 100,000 ... | | 1,100,000 |
| | **(Loss)** | **–300,000** |

enough money to pay back principal and interest, let alone make a profit. This is what is shown in the widget-makers income statement in *Table 2.2*.

There will be a crisis and the firm and the bank will both fail. How can this situation be avoided? As we have already seen, the answer is that some other sector of the economy must also be willing to become indebted, such that current producers can make money profits. In this particular case, we can let a second widget-maker (a 'second mover') become active and borrow $1,000,000 just before the original widgets come to market (before the end of year 1). If that happens, the bank's balance sheet will momentarily look as it does in *Table 2.3*.

Now enough money *is* available. The widget-maker can sell the widgets, pay off principal and interest, and still have a profit of $500,000 just as shown in the new income statement in *Table 2.4*.

However, it is also important to realize that when the loan is paid off, the supply of money will fall once again. (Money can be destroyed, as well as created, *via* these balance sheet operations.) As shown in *Table 2.5*, the effective money supply has actually fallen to $900,000, as

*Table 2.3*: Monopoly Bank Second Balance Sheet

| Assets | Liabilities |
|---|---|
| Loans: 2,000,000 | Deposits, Non-Bank Public: 2,000,000 |
| 2,000,000 | 2,000,000 |

*Table 2.4*: Income Statement of Widget-Maker #1 (With New Borrowing)

| Receipts: | (0.8) × (2,000,000) ... | 1,600,000 |
|---|---|---|
| (*minus*) | | |
| Repayment of Principal + Interest: 1,000,000 + 100,000 ... | | 1,100,000 |
| | (**Profit**) | **+ 500,000** |

*Table 2.5*: Monopoly Bank Third Balance Sheet

| Assets | Liabilities |
|---|---|
| Loans: 1,000,000 | Deposits, Non-Bank Public: 900,000 |
| _____ | Bank Capital: **100,000** |
| 1,000,000 | 1,000,000 |

by assumption the bankers are not going to spend any of their own $100,000 in bank capital that they have acquired from the receipt of interest payments.

If things stay like this, the second mover in the widget industry will also not be able to make a profit. There will have to be a third mover, for example, to come in and borrow another $1,000,000 before the second batch of widgets is ready. If this happens, the second mover can breathe a sigh of relief. They can then make a profit of $420,000, as *per Table 2.6*.

As a cautionary note, however, we can see that profits have already started to fall again. Profits have now declined from $500,000 last year to $420,000 currently. From the bank's balance sheet after the second round, in *Table 2.7*, we also see that the effective money supply has decreased once again.

There is going to have to be a fourth mover, a fifth mover, and so on. Even so, clearly a time will come when there will not be enough money to spend, and there will be another crisis. Ironically, this comes about precisely because the bank is following the advice sure to be given them by real-world financial regulators! That is, they are told *not* to spend their profits but to build up their capital–asset ratios. In fact, the solution would be exactly the opposite. The bank owners should try to spend their income at the same rate as everyone else, not save all of it.

If the basic arithmetic of the situation is so straightforward, why has the point been missed by so many professional economists, generation after generation? Part of the answer must be the historical emphasis on barter

*Table 2.6*: Income Statement of Widget-Maker #2 (With New Borrowing)

| Receipts: | $(0.8) \times (1,900,000) \dots$ | 1,520,000 |
|---|---|---|
| (*minus*) | | |
| Repayment of Principal + Interest: 1,000,000 + 100,000 ... | | 1,100,000 |
| | **(Profit)** | **+ 420,000** |

*Table 2.7*: Monopoly Bank Final Balance Sheet

| Assets | Liabilities | |
|---|---|---|
| Loans: 1,000,000 | Deposits Non-Bank Public: | 800,000 |
| _____ | Bank Capital: | **200,000** |
| 1,000,000 | | 1,000,000 |

exchange as the template. The means by which mainstream economics has usually tried to evade the issue is the *equation of exchange* from the quantity theory of money, namely $MV = PY$, where $V$ is 'the velocity of circulation'. The idea is that even if there is only (say) one 20 dollar bill in existence, it is possible for it to change hands so rapidly as to support any dollar value of business transacted. So it is, *if* all we are interested in doing is trading existing goods and services, as in barter. But this clearly does not solve the problem where monetary profit is to come from.[35]

## 2.8  Conclusion

The mainstream approach to economics interprets the discipline as a mathematical theory of rational choice applied to individual atomistic agents. The inference is that the disposition of economic resources should be mediated by these choices *via* a system of market exchange. This approach, however, provides only a highly attenuated vision of the complex set of social institutions that make up the system conventionally labeled 'capitalism'. These remarks apply in particular to the roles of rational accounting, calculation in terms of money, and debt and credit relations, that are at the heart of the system. Money in this sense logically precedes the idea of private property in the legal arena (as opposed to mere possession). It is therefore a pre-requisite for markets themselves, as they actually function in capitalist economies, and thus for the exercise of business operations and the entrepreneurial function in that context.

The field of monetary macroeconomics, founded by Keynes in the mid-twentieth century, did potentially represent progress in dealing more coherently with institutional and sociological factors than the earlier neoclassical microeconomics. However, any forward momentum was lost in the second half of the twentieth century. Over this period, the mainstream project has been described as re-establishing the 'micro-foundations of macroeconomics'. The aim was to reduce the discussion once more to the limits defined by the preferred choice theory. In *Rethinking,* I suggested, to the contrary, that it would be better;

> ... (a) to use explicitly macroeconomic methods, (b) to take seriously the notions of bank credit creation and endogenous money, (c) to restrict

---

[35] Smithin, *Rethinking.*

attention to relatively small and hence intelligible models, (d) 'make use of only two fundamental units of quantity, namely, quantities of [real] money value and quantities of employment'.[36]

I hope that the analysis of that book, and now in the present set of *Lectures*, has been able to fulfill these *desiderata*, at least to the extent possible in the current state of knowledge.

---

[36] This last phrase is a direct quote from the *General Theory*.

# Lecture 3

# A Teachable Macroeconomic Model of 'Modern Capitalism' (*aka* 'The Method of Enterprise')

## 3.1 Introduction

At the end of *Lecture 2*, I suggested that there are four key principles that seem to be necessary if we are ever to be able to construct a usable, relevant, and teachable model of the operations of an economy whose nature is that of the method of enterprise.[1] The purpose of *Lecture 3*, therefore, is to now put these principles into action.

The first principle was to use only specifically macroeconomic methods. As already discussed in previous *Lectures*, the nature of money both *necessitates* and therefore *justifies* a macroeconomic approach. However, for some time now within the economics profession there has unfortunately been a pronounced tendency, for example on the part of some mainstream economists and members of the Austrian school, to actively disparage macroeconomics on the spurious grounds that these methods involve only the mechanical manipulation of 'aggregates and averages'.[2] As discussed in *Lecture 2*, the aim is to once again reduce the discussion

---

[1] See Corrado Andini, 'Teaching Keynes's principle of effective demand within the real wage *vs.* employment space (*Forum for Social Economics* 38, 2009), and Andini, 'Marx meets Keynes in the classroom: Teaching a simple model of modern capitalism' (*Review of Political Economy* 32, 2020).

[2] Hayek, *Hayek on Hayek*.

to the limits defined by the pure theory of choice. However, if the ultimate objective is, as it should be, to study a genuinely monetary system, it seems to me that this attitude is totally off the mark. Only the social institution of money itself bestows sufficient organic unity on the system to make any kind of rational decision-making feasible, much less a scholarly analysis of that decision-making. The alternative strategy, of reductionism and atomism as applied to a barter economy or neutral economy, is rather the equivalent of 'nonsense as game'.[3] It has to do mainly with bolstering the psychological well-being and self-esteem of the analyst rather than actual research in the sense of finding things out. Anyone acquainted with the contemporary mainstream economics literature will easily recognize the parallels that are intended to be drawn here with the conduct of such research programs as neo-Walrasian general equilibrium theory, the 'micro-foundations of macroeconomics' approach, the dynamic stochastic general equilibrium (DSGE) model, and the whole can of worms opened up by the very idea of 'game theory' itself. To the contrary, the significance of *monetary* macroeconomics is that it is the only way to make a genuine behavioural analysis possible. It is definitely not just a question of appealing to mathematical aggregation and statistical averages.

The second important principle was to take seriously the importance of endogenous money and bank credit creation, which follows logically as soon as the difference between real and monetary analysis is recognized. As explained in *Lectures 1* and *2,* a critical examination of Marx's notion of the monetary circuit, $M \to C \to C' \to M'$, leads directly to the insight that unless there *is* bank credit creation, such that $M'$ can be greater than $M$, there can be no monetary profit. Therefore, there can be no real profit and no incentive for production. Among the historical figures in economics mentioned in *Lecture 2*, both Keynes and Schumpeter (but not actually Marx) did address this important issue, at least to some extent. However, in neither case did they succeed in unambiguously establishing the point for future generations of economists. Most of the latter either quickly forgot the issue or have never been aware of it.

The third principle was to insist on the importance of relatively small and hence intelligible models of both closed and open economies. The expression 'closed economy' refers to a hypothetical polity in a thought experiment which does not trade with the rest of world. It is therefore useful

---

[3] John Smithin, Review of Fletcher, *Understanding Dennis Robertson: The Man and His Work* (*Eastern Economic Journal* 28, 2002).

primarily for discussion of the basic theoretical issues in a focused manner, as will be done for the most part in the pages that follow in the next two chapters. In the real world, most economies are open to one degree or another, and therefore it is the open economy model that must ultimately be applied for practical policy analysis. *Lecture 5* of the present volume deals with the case of the open economy in full detail. In both cases, relatively small models are required to ensure that their logic is fully comprehensible, not only to those who are constructing the models, but just as importantly to those who are using them. There should be no 'black boxes'. In these days of almost infinite computer power, models with dozens or hundreds of equations may well be easy to manipulate and they can seem superficially impressive when simulated on a computer screen. However, they are quite useless from the point of view of gaining economic understanding.

Our fourth principle, to make use of only two fundamental units of quantity — quantities of real money value and quantities of employment — is necessary because of the failure and (in truth) the incoherence of any and all attempts that have been made at deriving capital theory. Joan Robinson, writing in the early 1950s,[4] explained the problem in the following way.

> ... the production function has been a powerful instrument of mis-education. The student of economic theory is taught to write $Y = f(K, N)$ where $N$ is a quantity of labour, $K$ a quantity of capital and $Y$ a rate of output of commodities.[5] He is instructed to assume all workers alike, and to measure $N$ in man-hours of labour; he is told something about the index-number problem in choosing a unit of output; and then he is hurried on to the next question, in the hope that he will forget to ask in what units $K$ is measured. Before he ever does ask, he has become a professor, and so sloppy habits of thought are handed on from one generation to the next.

But the capital theory debate between the 'two Cambridges' petered out by the end of the next decade, never to be revived. In a sense it might be argued that Robinson and her colleagues at the University of Cambridge, UK, eventually won the purely intellectual argument against

---

[4] As quoted by Avi Cohen and G.C. Harcourt, 'Whatever happened to the Cambridge capital controversies' (*Journal of Economic Perspectives* 17, 2003).
[5] The original notation has been changed to conform with the usage in these *Lectures*.

their rivals in Cambridge, USA, at the Massachusetts Institute of Technology (MIT). As a practical matter, however, this made no difference to the way in which economic research was actually conducted. The 'sloppy habits of thought' have persisted, and continue to vitiate any type of economic theory derived on the basis of capital-theoretic arguments. In these circumstances, the principle of only using two fundamental units of quantity, as originally suggested by Keynes, is an essential device to avoid the 'quagmire of capital theory' as I have previously called it.[6]

At the end of the day, I would argue that there are ultimately only two main alternative ways of characterizing the theory of production in macroeconomics, and that they are mutually exclusive. Either we can relate the level (*i.e.*, the annual rate) of GDP to labour input, or to some measure of 'capital'. If we write down something like $Y = AN$ (where $A$ stands for average productivity and $N$ for employment), this is easily measurable. For example, rather than Robinson's 'man hours', we could simply use the standard definition of persons employed in the official statistics (see *Lectures 7* and *8* that follow). Meanwhile, the definition of real GDP, taking account of Robinson's 'index number problem', has already been given in *Lecture 1*. The average product of labour in this sense (*per* employed person) is then given by $A = Y/N$. By no means does this procedure imply that we are ignoring all the contributions of the machines, raw materials, and so forth that go into production, or such questions as the difference in hours worked and skill levels of the persons employed. All these are simply rolled up in the catch-all term $A$. On the other hand, to write $Y = AK$ (where $A$ is now supposed to be the 'average product of capital') is simply meaningless. There is no way to give any concrete meaning to the term $K$. And, precisely for that reason, the different approaches cannot be reconciled, neither by the standard neoclassical production function $Y = F(K, N)$ as mentioned by Robinson, nor by a two-sector or multi-sector approach such as one sometimes sees in the literature. The different ways of characterizing production lead to quite different conclusions about the sources and mechanisms of economic growth. They cannot successfully be mixed. Moreover, it is not true, as is sometimes claimed, that using the $Y = AN$ approach restricts the discussion of macroeconomics only to the 'short-run'.[7] As will be shown in what follows, it is entirely possible to construct

---

[6] Smithin, *Rethinking*.

[7] I think that Keynes himself (wrongly) did much to encourage this view by various references in the *General Theory* about 'taking as given' such factors as 'the existing quality

a relevant and useful macroeconomic theory that is well able to cope with important long-run questions about growth, development, and technical change (as well as those of short-run stabilization policy), without recourse to the dead-end of capital-theoretic reasoning.

The reader will recall that one of the topics discussed in *Lecture 2* was about how some of the famous historical figures in the development of economic theory either were, or were not, able to cope with each of the several problems just identified. Neither Adam Smith nor Friedrich Hayek, for example, would have been at all comfortable with the distinction between real and monetary analysis, crucially important though that is. Nonetheless, both of these writers in their different ways did draw attention to at least two other important topics in macroeconomics, which will also need to be taken into account in any complete analysis of macroeconomic issues.

As already discussed in *Lecture 1,* Smith did notice one important fact about the operations of the capitalist or enterprise economy, which in my view is still true today, but has all too frequently been overlooked in the ensuing two-and-a-half centuries. This is that the *level* of real wages depends positively on the *rate* of economic growth. Therefore, if the economic position of the working and middle classes, in particular, is ever to be improved, this does require 'rapid economic growth' in one sense or another. As pointed out in *Lecture 1*, this proposition seems actually to have been something of an embarrassment to both the conventional right and conventional left in contemporary politics, each for their own reasons. Nonetheless, it is a factor that must be taken into account in any coherent representation of the total system. Here is what Smith said about the matter in the *Wealth of Nations*:

> It is not the actual greatness of national wealth, but its continual increase which occasions a rise in the wages of labour. It is not accordingly in the richest countries, but in the most thriving, or in those which are growing rich the fastest, that the wages of labour are the highest.

He was clear that the hypothesis was about *real* rather than money wages. The example given was that wages were higher in the fast growing

---

and quantity of available equipment'. The whole idea of the different 'runs' in economic theory, based on whether or not there are changes in capital equipment, was originally due to his teacher Alfred Marshall. It seems that in this, and in other matters, Keynes was never able wholly to shake off the Marshallian influence.

North American colonies, at his time of writing in 1776, than in England, even though England was clearly the wealthier country at the time. At the same time, Smith plainly stated that 'the price of provisions is everywhere much *lower* (emphasis added) in North America than in England'.[8] Ironically, we might note that 1776, the year of the publication of the *Wealth of Nations*, was also the year of the American *Declaration of Independence*. Evidently, the recipients of the high American wages objected to them being redistributed by taxation to the future employees of the British state, such as Adam Smith himself.[9]

Another very important issue that needs to be taken into account in macroeconomics is the significance of the so-called forced saving effect (or Mundell–Tobin effect), which we have interpreted as the existence, in principle, of a negative relationship between the inflation rate and the real rate of interest. Among the different economists whose views were discussed in *Lecture 2*, Hayek was prominent in paying particular attention to this issue, but not in any positive light. In fact, he seems to have seen it (I think correctly) as a major threat to the system that he himself was trying to construct, and was therefore at pains to deny any such thing. As we have seen in *Lecture 1*, however, in the real world of banking and finance, given the way commercial banks react to any changes in the policy rate of interest set by the central bank, this relationship is already implicit in the very idea of the monetary policy transmissions mechanism. It cannot be avoided.

## 3.2   Alternative Explanations of Economic Growth

In this section, we will go on to discuss the two main alternative approaches to the theory of economic growth. These are (a) what I have previously called a '*Keynes-type*' theory.[10] This validates three important ideas, (i) that fiscal expansion leads to growth, (ii) that investment drives saving (an idea which Keynes called the *paradox of thrift*), and (iii) that a trade surplus leads to growth. The latter proposition has sometimes been

---

[8] Smith, *Wealth of Nations*.

[9] Ian Simpson Ross, *The Life of Adam Smith*, second edition (New York: Oxford University Press, 2010).

[10] John Smithin, 'Economic growth, free trade, public finance, and the paradox of thrift' (*Review of Keynesian Economics* 4, 2014).

called *monetary mercantilism*, or *economic nationalism*, or similar. There is also (b) a *'Classics-type'* theory. This yields anomalous results and does not provide a solid foundation for the classical theories of trade, savings, and public finance.

To develop the two generic growth equations, recall that the definition of real value-added (real GDP) in the economy for a given accounting period is simply;

$$Y = C + I + G + (EX - IM). \tag{3.1}$$

Here the symbols continue to have the same meanings that were assigned to them in *Lecture 1*. We are primarily interested in the growth rate of real GDP (lower case $y$), given by;

$$y = (Y - Y_{-1})/Y_{-1}. \tag{3.2}$$

The Keynes-type growth equation can be then be derived by specifying a lagged consumption function, which is an idea originally due to Sir John Hicks.[11] For example;

$$C = C_0 + c(Y_{-1} - T_{-1}). \quad 0 < c < 1 \tag{3.3}$$

The new variables appearing in equation (3.3) are $C_0$, the intercept term in the consumption function, $c$ the marginal propensity to consume out of (lagged) disposable income, and $T$ which is total real tax collection. Using equations (3.1) and (3.3), we can then write;

$$Y - I - G - (EX - IM) = C_0 + c(Y_{-1} - T_{-1}). \tag{3.4}$$

Next, define the total *autonomous expenditure* of the private sector, $X$, as;

$$X = C_0 + I. \tag{3.5}$$

This notion of autonomous spending was frequently used in the original 'Keynesian' textbooks that appeared in the quarter century after WW2, and was originally taken to mean those expenditure decisions that are *not* dependent on the spender's current income.[12] (As we have already

---

[11] Hicks, *Money, Interest, and Wages.*

[12] Paul Davidson, *Post Keynesian Macroeconomic Theory*, second edition (Cheltenham: Edward Elgar, 2011).

seen, at the macroeconomic level the total of these expenditures must presumably be financed by credit creation, but this point was not usually made explicit in the standard treatments.) Clearly, therefore, the $C_0$ term, the intercept term in the consumption function, is a component of autonomous expenditure in this sense. At this stage in the exposition, we are also treating the whole of spending by business firms, $I$ ('investment spending'), as dependent on Keynes's 'animal spirits' (business confidence) and not primarily on objectively calculable factors such as the level of income itself, interest rates, or realized profit. This was also an assumption often made in the first generation of Keynesian textbooks,[13] to emphasize Keynes's point about the potential volatility of investment resulting from swings of optimism and pessimism.[14] Such an assumption will eventually need to be relaxed in more advanced expositions later on in the present book (for example, in *Lecture 4* that follows), but it raises a sufficiently important point to be the primary focus of attention at this stage.

Using equation (3.5) in (3.4), dividing through by the lagged level of real GDP, re-arranging, and noting that $c = 1 - s$ (where $s$ is the marginal propensity to save), we obtain;

$$Y/Y_{-1} - (Y/Y_{-1})[X/Y + G/Y + (EX - IM)/Y] = (1 - s)[1 - (T_{-1}/Y_{-1})]. \quad (3.6)$$

The ratio $T_{-1}/Y_{-1}$ is the average tax rate, $t$, and also let $g = G/Y$, $x = X/Y$, and $ex - im = (EX - IM)/Y$. The ratios $g$ and $x$ are government spending and total autonomous expenditure as percentages of GDP, and $ex - im$ is the trade surplus as a percentage of GDP. Therefore,

$$(1 + y)[1 - x - g - (ex - im)] = (1 - s)(1 - t). \quad (3.7)$$

Finally, taking natural logarithms, using approximations such as $ln(1 - s) = -s$ (*etc.*), and re-arranging, yields the Keynes-type growth equation we have been looking for. This is;

$$y = (x - s) + (g - t) + (ex - im). \quad (3.8)$$

---

[13] Paul Samuelson, *Economics: The Original 1948 Edition* (New York: McGraw-Hill, 1997).

[14] Keynes, *General Theory*.

In *Rethinking the Theory of Money, Credit, and Macroeconomics*, I summed up what I think are these *very* important results in the following terms[15];

> … real GDP growth will occur when, [1] … there is a trade surplus as a percentage of GDP (hence the expression 'monetary mercantilism'), [2] … the total autonomous spending of the private sector as a percentage of GDP is greater than the marginal propensity to save, [3] … there is a primary budget deficit as a percentage of GDP.

These are not just accounting identities but genuine causal relationships, the ultimate exogenous variables being things like the parameters of monetary and fiscal policy, both at home and abroad, productivity shocks, national and international liquidity preference, *etc.* Equation (3.8) obviously does not mean that growth cannot possibly occur in the presence of a budget surplus, a trade deficit, or a high propensity to save. It does mean, however, that at least one of the above terms must be positive, and sufficiently large to outweigh the other two, if there is ever to be economic growth. This statement runs contrary to the usual advice given to policymakers from all sides. Policymakers are typically told that they should always aim for trade balance and pursue a 'sound' fiscal policy (balance the budget). Failure to grasp the basic difference between a monetary analysis and a real analysis thus continues to be a major weakness in our contemporary understanding of economic problems. Keynes did try his best to explain some of the issues almost a century ago. But in the long-run insufficient attention was paid to what he was saying, and these sorts of ideas were eventually forgotten.

## 3.3 Reconciliation of the Growth Equation and the Sectoral Balances Identity

How does the causal growth equation above relate to the familiar 'injections equals withdrawals' version of the GDP identity? If the term $S$ stands for saving, the identity is the familiar;

$$I + G + EX = S + T + IM. \tag{3.9}$$

---

[15] Smithin, *Rethinking.*

Dividing through by *Y*, and also introducing new notation such that *inv* = *I/Y* and *sa* = *S/Y*, this gives;

$$0 = (inv - sa) + (g - t) + (ex - im). \tag{3.10}$$

Comparing this expression to the growth equation in (3.8), it is clear that both (3.8) and (3.10) are indeed consistent with one another. The reason is simply that the terms *inv* and *sa* are not the same things as *x* and *s*. To put it another way, the sectoral balances identity must always sum to zero, but this is not so in the case of the growth equation.

## 3.4   The Harrod–Domar Growth Formula

What then would be the alternative Classics-type growth equation, and how to derive it? In *Rethinking,* I argued that the most convenient starting point is actually the famous Harrod–Domar growth formula from the 1940s, which (translated into my notation) is[16];

$$y = s/O. \tag{3.11}$$

Here, *y* stands for the real *GDP* growth rate*, s* for both the marginal and average propensity to save (in this case *s* is, in fact, the same concept as *sa* above), and *O* is the capital/output ratio. This last definition obviously does presume, with neoclassical and mainstream economics, that it is possible to somehow quantify the notion of the capital stock, and make it commensurate with the way in which GDP is measured. We have already seen that this is false, which immediately gives a very strong clue towards explaining why the 'Classics-type' approach ultimately does not work.

Reading the literature of the time, however, one gets the impression that Harrod and his followers actually thought that the formula was a contribution to the Keynesian economics of the day, rather than classical economics, *via* their argument that the equation is unstable. This was the celebrated 'knife-edge' problem in growth theory. In my view, however, this line of argument does not really fit with the general tenor of Keynesian economics, and seems to have been something of a misunderstanding of Keynes. What Keynes had, in fact, argued was that the

---

[16] Amartya Sen, 'Introduction', to Sen, ed., *Growth Economics* (Harmondsworth: Penguin, 1970).

economy could become stuck in some low-level equilibrium which could prove difficult to get out of. The expression used was *underemployment equilibrium*.[17]

Harrod's treatment of the stability issue was also something of a special case, in the sense that he and others relied on assumptions about the formation of short-term expectations that were different to those made by Keynes. Keynes himself was more interested in long-term expectations, as he made clear in a famous article in the *Quarterly Journal of Economics* in 1937.[18] For the purposes of developing the theory of effective demand, he was often content to assume that short-run expectations would be fulfilled. But, if this appeal to the special case of knife-edge growth does *not* hold up, the Harrod–Domar formula makes a big step backward from Keynes to the domains of classical economics and capital theory. In that case, the implication of equation (3.11) is simply that when the propensity to save increases, growth increases. This is the opposite to Keynesian views about the paradox of thrift, and reverts to the classical idea that savings precede investment.[19] In these circumstances, the formula may then legitimately be used as a general template to describe the Classics-type theory itself.

## 3.5  The 'Classics-type' Theory of Economic Growth

In the late 1940s, and through the 1950s and 1960s, a popular modification of the Harrod–Domar framework was to add an explicit investment function known as the '*accelerator*'. This idea relied not only on the assumption that it is possible to quantify the capital stock, but also that all firm spending on 'investment' adds directly to this stock (that none of it misfires, or is simply disguised consumption spending). It is assumed therefore, in whatever units it is measured, that;

$$I = K_{+1} - K. \tag{3.12}$$

---

[17] Keynes, *General Theory*.

[18] John Maynard Keynes, 'The general theory of employment' (*Quarterly Journal of Economics* 51, 1937).

[19] On this point, see Robertson's discussion of the views of Michael Kalecki in Dennis Robertson, *Essays in Monetary Theory* (London: P.S. King, 1940).

Thus, as $O = K/Y$, the final accelerator function for investment turns out to be;

$$I = O(Y_{+1} - Y). \tag{3.13}$$

Next, use this definition in (3.9), noting that in this case we must have $S = s(Y - T)$, as there is no intercept in the consumption function and the function is not lagged. We obtain;

$$O(Y_{+1} - Y) = s(Y - T) + (T - G) + (IM - EX). \tag{3.14}$$

Then divide through by $Y$, which in our lower-case notation gives

$$y = s(1 - t)/O + (t - g)/O + (im - ex)/O. \tag{3.15}$$

This, therefore, is the 'Classics-type' growth equation. However, when written out in full like this (which is not usually done), it evidently gives very strange results. It says not only that an increase in the saving propensity leads to growth, but also that a budget *surplus* and a trade *deficit* lead to growth. The argument that savings leads to growth is usually made on the grounds that saving is necessary to finance investment. We have already seen that this is not accurate, but from the point of view of mainstream or neoclassical economics it traditionally had at least some superficial plausibility. On the other hand, there is no sound rationale for the other two propositions. The classical theory also states that tax cuts lead to growth, which is also true in the traditional Keynesian case (and for my AMM) albeit for different reasons. There will be further discussion of this important point later in the present volume, in *Lecture 4*.

## 3.6  Real World Political Economy?

In reality, the conventional wisdom on economic policy does not actively argue for a trade deficit, nor for a budget surplus *per se* (just to avoid deficits). Rather, in policy discussion it is simply taken for granted that budget balance ($g = t$) is a good thing in itself, and that trade balance or external balance ($ex = im$) is also a good thing. The basic point of the standard argument for free trade, for instance, is that both sides benefit from the supposed gains from trade even when exports *are* equal to imports. What therefore tends to happen is that the final two terms on the right-hand side (RHS) of equation (3.15) simple disappear from the discussion. What then emerges is nothing other the so-called 'supply-side' argument for economic growth, which came to prominence in the public policy debate of the 1970s and 1980s. If we eliminate the two RHS terms, the Classics-type growth equation reduces to;

$$y = s(1 - t)/O. \tag{3.16}$$

Thus, the expression in (3.16) is the supposed 'natural rate' of growth which, according to the supply-siders can only be improved by productivity improvements or tax cuts to provide incentives. In none of these discussions, however, was any argument offered as to why the seemingly perverse logic of budget surpluses and trade deficits should not apply.

Comparing the two equations (3.15) and (3.16) clearly exposes the underlying problems with the classical approach to thrift. Equation (3.15) is a *reductio ad absurdum*. The bedrock of the underlying worldview is that saving is always supposed to be a good thing. It is the route to virtue, prudence, and prosperity. If so, why not take this idea to its logical conclusion and save 100% of income? But then there would be no spending at all, and no economy. To firmly establish their own views about economic progress, it would have been necessary for the supply-siders and mainstream economists to come up with some sort of solution to this paradox, but they have never properly done so.[20] The technique of simply eliminating the two RHS terms in (3.15) does nothing to achieve this.

Although the policy recommendations implicit in equation (3.16) have often been influential in practice, we can now see that they really have only been arrived at by hopelessly confusing the separate concepts of demand and supply as applied to things like investment and savings, money, and goods. The item which is labelled 'investment' in the above set of equations starts life as referring to a sum of money (real purchasing power) which can then be spent on a number of different things, including orders for machinery and suchlike. In this guise it does genuinely represent effective demand and as such can and does stimulate the production of actual things to satisfy the demand. But, of course, production takes time. The 'things' do not exist as yet. They will do in due course, but only after the production process has taken place. This is why Keynes talked about a monetary theory of *production*. What is not reasonable, however, is to imagine that those goods which do currently exist and were originally destined for consumption purposes can be 'saved' (not consumed), and somehow converted without effort into investment goods. But that is

---

[20] Joan Robinson, *Economic Philosophy* (Harmondsworth: Penguin, 1964).

essentially what *is* supposed to happen in orthodox theory. The intelligible notion of financial investment gets somehow transformed into the actual things themselves, even before any more production is stimulated. Instead of being a sum of money, the term *I* turns instantaneously into a collection of things with actual physical properties which can be directly added to an existing stock of other physical things, also with determinate properties. This is incoherent. We are asked to imagine that the public physically saves by eating less food, for example, and then a mathematical economist is able to wave a magic wand and convert the unconsumed edibles into machinery. 'Savings' precedes 'investment' in the algebra, but the production process itself is ignored. In the actual financial world, as we have seen, the logic is quite otherwise. 'Loans create deposits' not the other way around. Production is the outcome, or result, of the preceding financial process. The role of finance is to provide the *money* to stimulate the actual production of new *things* which eventually do satisfy the demand.

So much for what we have called the 'classical' or 'supply-side' approach. On the other hand, a superficial counter-argument might be made that the Keynes-type theory itself only takes account of demand and does not deal with supply at all. This is not accurate either. It may perhaps have been true of some of the early textbook distillations and interpretations of Keynes, such as Samuelson's famous *Economics* cited above, but it is not inherent in the Keynesian approach *per se*. Keynes himself paid equal attention to what he called the 'aggregate supply function'.[21] The next section will elaborate on this point, specifically on the role potentially to be played by the supply side of the economy in determining the growth rate *via* feedback effects on the distribution of income and on profitability.

## 3.7   The 'Supply Side' of the Economy and the Distribution of Income

In previous contributions, using a variety of different approaches, I have shown that a synthetic theory of profit may usefully be derived from the following two equations[22];

---

[21] Sidney Weintraub, *Classical Keynesianism, Monetary Theory, and the Price Level* (Philadelphia: Chilton Company, 1961).

[22] John Smithin, *Essays in the Fundamental Theory of Monetary Economics and Macroeconomics* (Singapore: World Scientific Publishing, 2013).

$$Y = AN_{-1} \qquad\qquad \text{production takes time} \quad (3.17)$$

$$PY = (1 + K)(1 + i_{-1})W_{-1}N_{-1}. \qquad \text{nominal revenue} \qquad (3.18)$$

I have experimented with a number of different ways of making this point in the past, but these two expressions are perhaps the simplest ways to explain the underlying ideas. The underlying premise is a one-period production lag, which is the easiest way whereby we can conveniently introduce the crucial element of time into the production process. The symbol $Y$, therefore, stands for the level of output that is sold currently but was actually produced in the previous period. As $P$ is the current price level, the term $PY$ stands for nominal revenue in the case of an individual firm, or for nominal GDP in aggregate.

In equation (3.18), the total money value of the output is expressed as a multiple of the original investment in the nominal wage bill. The multiplicative factor must cover the three main elements in the accounting scheme, the interest charge, user cost (including depreciation on fixed capital), and net profit. The nominal interest charge levied on the wage bill is based on the nominal interest rate that was prevailing at the start of the production period. Taking equations (3.17) and (3.18) together, we can see that the basic reality that production takes time is what accounts both for the interest charge and also the necessity for entrepreneurs to form expectations of future sales receipts *before* they decide to undertake production. As already explained, although the formulation in (3.1) only explicitly shows the relation between output and labour input, it does not ignore the other factors of production. The contributions of the various machines, technical knowledge, raw materials, *etc.*, are all rolled-up in the term $A$. As usual, nominal quantities such as $PY$ (nominal revenue) and $W_{-1}N_{-1}$ (the lagged nominal wage bill) should be taken as referring to actual flows of funds. Moreover, as we have eliminated the ambiguous notion of 'capital' entirely from the description of the production process, we are now free to appropriate the symbol $K$ (upper case) to stand for the gross entrepreneurial mark-up.[23] Even though we have not specified a term for capital or raw materials in the production function itself, the mark-up factor $(1 + K)$ evidently must include financial allowances for both depreciation on

---

[23] This move was often made in the early Post-Keynesian literature. See, for example, Sydney Weintraub, *A General Theory of the Price Level, Output, Income Distribution and Economic Growth* (Philadelphia: Chilton Company, 1959).

physical capital and user cost, including the money value of raw materials used up in the production process, as well as net profit. The mark-up is 'gross' in that sense, but at the same time is 'net' of the nominal interest charge which enters as a separate element in the income statement.

We next take natural logarithms of each of the variables in (3.17) and (3.18) where (lower-case) $k = ln(1 + K)$, and once again employ the widely-used approximation(s) that $ln(1 + i) = i$, *etc.* Substituting (3.17) into (3.18), this yields;

$$lnP = k + i_{-1} + lnW_{-1} - lnA. \tag{3.19}$$

Now subtract $lnP_{-1}$ from both sides of the equation and re-arrange. The result is;

$$k = lnA - [i_{-1} - (lnP - lnP_{-1})] - (lnW_{-1} - lnP_{-1}). \tag{3.20}$$

The term in square brackets is the lagged real interest rate, $r_{-1}$. Therefore, if lower-case $w$ stands for the natural logarithm of the average real wage rate *per* employed person, and lower-case $a$ for the natural logarithm of labour productivity, the basic theory of profit can be written as;

$$k = a - r_{-1} - w_{-1}. \tag{3.21}$$

This is an 'adding-up' theory of the functional distribution of income, expressed in terms of logarithms or percentages. In equilibrium, the breakdown of the income distribution is thus;

$$k = a - r - w. \tag{3.22}$$

To complete our description of the supply side of the macroeconomy, we next draw on the insight, attributed above to Adam Smith, that real wages tend to increase with the rate of economic growth. Equation (3.23) therefore specifies an empirically plausible 'wage function'[24] for the closed economy case which suggests that there are two main influences on the macroeconomic behaviour of after-tax real wages. First, after-tax real wages will increase with economic growth, because this will increase the bargaining power of labour. Second, regardless of whether or not the economy is growing, there can be changes in real wages due to political,

---

[24] See, for example, Collis, *Three Essays.*

sociological, or institutional considerations, such as collective bargaining or labour legislation;

$$w - t = h_0 + h_1 y. \qquad h_0 > 0, \ 0 < h_1 < 1 \tag{3.23}$$

The term $w - t$ is the natural logarithm of after tax real wages *per* employed person, and $h_0$ is an index of the cumulative effect of such things as labour legislation, social attitudes, and the strength or otherwise of labour unions. The term $h_1$ is the sensitivity of the after-tax real wage *per* employed person to the growth rate of real GDP.

## 3.8 A Simple Diagrammatic Exposition of the Macroeconomic Model of the 'Method of Enterprise'

We now are in a position to be able to sum up the basic outlines of our macroeconomic model in a simple diagram, which has average labour productivity on one axis and the growth rate of real GDP on the other, as in *Figures 3.1* and *3.2*. The gross real wage rate can be depicted in the diagram as follows;

$$w = t + h_0 + h_1 y. \qquad h_0 > 0, \ 0 < h_1 < 1 \tag{3.24}$$

We will also take it that the real rate of interest is predetermined by conditions in the financial sector of the economy, including the policy decisions of the central bank. In such circumstances, the profit mark-up $k$ is the residual component of income after the other shares have been decided. This is the situation depicted in *Figure 3.1*. The rate of growth itself is proximately determined by effective demand growth, as in the Keynes-type equation. In the closed economy version of the model, this reduces to;

$$y = (x - s) + (g - t) \tag{3.25}$$

This is depicted as a vertical straight line in the diagram. *Figure 3.1*, therefore, illustrates the functional distribution of income for a given rate of effective demand growth.

As simple as this diagram is, it immediately answers an extremely important question about the relationship between interest and profit. A major problem in economic theory is that these two notions are often erroneously conflated, even to the extent of leaving the impression that they are more or less the same thing. They are treated as part of the generic return to 'capital' in some sense. On the contrary, we have insisted that there is actually a three-way distribution between wages, interest, and profit and it is misleading to think of the entrepreneurs and rentiers being lumped together in a monolithic single class of 'capitalists'. The pecuniary interests of Main Street and Wall Street (to use the American parlance) frequently diverge.

*Figure 3.1* illustrates this point in the case of an increase in the real rate of interest. An increase in real interest rates, shown by an upward shift of the *r* schedule, unambiguously cuts into profits, and *vice versa*. Otherwise, there is not much else going in the diagram. Note, in particular, that the fall in profits does not have any effect on the growth rate itself. The reason for this, as already explained, is simply that in the basic model all firm expenditure (so-called investment) has been denoted as 'autonomous expenditure' and therefore the effective demand growth schedule is a straight line. In a more detailed treatment, such as my AMM for example, the likely feedback effects, from the fall in the mark-up on firm spending, will also need to be taken into account. This would then validate the earlier statement that these feedback effects are one of the main ways in which supply-side considerations affect the rate of economic

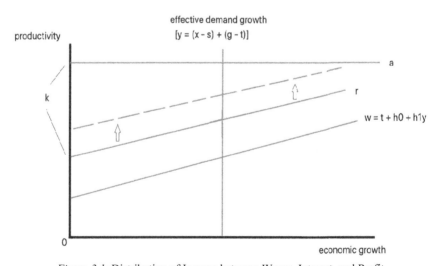

*Figure 3.1*: Distribution of Income between Wages, Interest, and Profit

growth. These and similar issues are further explored in *Lecture 4* to follow.

*Figure 3.2* then shows the effect of an increase in the rate of demand growth itself. This is the key diagram to illustrate how the underlying monetary macroeconomic model works. Fundamentally 'Keynes-type' results carry through to the growth context just as well as they did in the static models of the older textbooks.

However, with this specification of the wage function note that although a demand expansion definitely improves the overall economic situation, the mark-up earned by entrepreneurial business is likely to fall in the aggregate and on average. Real wages are rising as the growth rate and the level of employment increase. But, as productivity and the real interest charge stay constant, the mark-up is reduced. This is not quite the same thing as Marx's 'falling rate of profit', but is a similar sort of idea.

The next obvious question to be asked therefore is whether this will make any difference to the political economy of the situation. Does it call into question the viability of a Keynes-type solution? In my own view it need not do. The mark-up does not actually fall to zero, and all the various firms and entrepreneurs will still be 'making money' in the new situation even if the mark-up is lower. More generally, there is the possibility that productivity itself (the *a* term) may not stay constant, and may well also be increasing as the rate of growth increases. In those circumstances, the mark-up need not fall. These and similar issues about income distribution

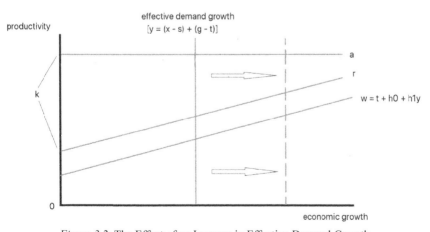

*Figure 3.2*: The Effect of an Increase in Effective Demand Growth

and incentives during the growth process will be addressed in more detail in *Lecture 7* that follows, on 'Interest Rates and Income Distribution'.

## 3.9  The Determination of the Inflation Rate and Real Interest Rates

In the previous section, we sketched out the basics of the underlying macro-monetary model to help to understand the main issues in the theories of economic growth, employment, and real wages. A next step is to go on to explain some of the interactions between the other economic variables that are involved in the macroeconomic process, such as the inflation rate and the real rate of interest. These are important topics both in their own right and also because, as mentioned, we will eventually need to take into account any feedback effects of the changes in profitability on firm spending (see *Lecture 4*).

An obvious starting point for the discussion of interest rates and inflation is to inquire into the factors determining the demand for and supply of money. But, remember that in a modern banking system the money supply in a modern system consists almost entirely of bank deposits of some kind, and is therefore endogenous. It may well be impossible therefore to count the actual number of dollars in the money supply at any one time. Nonetheless, in one way or another it is still going to be necessary to take account of both the supply of endogenous money and the voluntary demand for it.[25]

In current conditions, it might perhaps be reasonable to write down simple proportional relationships describing money supply *Ms* and money demand *Md*, as follows;

$$Ms = \phi W_{-1} N_{-1}, \qquad \phi > 1 \qquad\qquad (3.26)$$

$$Md = \psi PY. \qquad 0 < \psi < 1 \qquad\qquad (3.27)$$

The term $\phi$ expresses the supply of money as a multiple of the lagged nominal wage bill. As shown in the numerical example in *Lecture 2* loans create deposits (and hence money), and we can therefore think of the

---

[25] Sir John Hicks has made clear the distinction between, and the significance of, the 'voluntary' and 'involuntary' demands for money in *Critical Essays in Monetary Theory* (Oxford: Clarendon Press, 1967).

entrepreneurs borrowing from the banks to pay for the wage bill, thereby creating precisely the amount of money needed for the purpose. But, as also discussed in *Lecture 2*, notice that for the system to be viable — in the sense of generating sufficient money to purchase the full value of output — the coefficient $\phi$ must actually be greater than one. If only the wage bill were to be borrowed, and that is all the money there is to spend, the entrepreneurs are never going to be able to make a profit, or even to pay interest on the loans. It is for this reason that equation (3.26) expresses all other borrowing, whether for capital spending, consumer spending, or anything else, as a multiple of the wage bill. This assumption makes good sense, in fact, as the majority of loans granted are indeed likely be calibrated in some way to the income of the borrowers. If $\phi > 1$, then there will be enough money in existence to allow, in principle, for the generation of monetary profits (that is, to allow for $M' > M$, a necessary condition).

Thus, the money supply in existence in the current period is a multiple of the wage bill paid out in the previous period. The money demand equation in (3.27) goes on to suggest that the voluntary demand to hold that money (for the public to voluntarily hold on to the bank deposits created in the previous period throughout the current period) is some fraction of the nominal value of GDP. This specification is somewhat similar to what Keynes, in the *General Theory*, called the 'transactions demand' for money. However, here money demand is related to income (nominal GDP), rather than to transactions *per se*. Unlike some of the specifications in the older textbooks, there does not need to be an explicit interest rate argument in the demand for money function. This is because money in the modern world, in the form of bank deposits, is in principle itself an interest-bearing instrument.[26] Given the structure of production, and the timing of the borrowing and lending operations needed to finance it, there evidently must also be an involuntary demand for the deposits to be held over the turn of each period. This, however, has no economic significance.

---

[26] Hicks, *Market Theory of Money*. Note that in *Lecture 6*, which follows, another form of interest rate argument will be re-introduced to take account of Keynes's idea of the 'speculative demand' for money, also from the *General Theory*. This was a somewhat different twist on the idea of liquidity preference from that presented in the *Treatise on Money*. However, that would be an unnecessary complication here.

In his *Treatise* and also in the *General Theory*, it was Keynes who first introduced the concept of *liquidity preference*. In general terms, this means the propensity for wealth owners to leave some of their holdings in the form of money (a preference for liquidity) rather than to acquire other assets such as bonds or stocks. Keynes seems to have thought that this idea only applies to money *demand*. It is clear from (3.26) and (3.27), however, that under endogenous money the same principles apply on both sides of the money market. Some people are usually willing to incur debt for the express purpose of buying other assets. If there is an increase in liquidity preference, they are less likely to do so. On the supply side, therefore, an increase in the parameter $\phi$ represents a *reduction* in liquidity preference, in the sense of an increased willingness to borrow. An increase in $\psi$, on the other hand, means an *increase* in liquidity preference in the sense that the public is now more likely to hold on to their bank deposits rather than spend them. Combining equations (3.26) and (3.27), and setting $Md = Ms$ (true by definition in a banking environment), yields the following expression for the aggregate price level;

$$P = [(\phi/\psi)]W_{-1}]/A. \tag{3.28}$$

Taking natural logarithms of (3.27), we can thus obtain;

$$lnP = ln\phi - ln\psi + lnW_{-1} - lnA. \tag{3.29}$$

Then, subtract $lnP_{-1}$ from both sides and define a new variable, $p_0$, as $p_0 = ln\phi - ln\psi$. As the rate of inflation is given by $p = lnP - lnP_{-1}$ and the natural logarithm of the real wage rate is $w = lnW - lnP$, equation (3.28) can therefore be rewritten as;

$$p = p_0 + w_{-1} - a. \tag{3.30}$$

In steady-state equilibrium, we will therefore have;

$$p = p_0 + w - a. \tag{3.31}$$

The above is therefore a reasonably comprehensive theory of equilibrium inflation in an economy with endogenous money. Cost push and conflict inflation influences are relevant, as are productivity changes, but so also is liquidity preference itself *via* the parameters of the explicit money demand and supply functions. The former two influences have been well represented in the past in the various 'Post-Keynesian' approaches to inflation under endogenous money.[27] However, the liquidity preference aspect has typically been neglected, or so it seems to me, at least as far as any influence on inflation is concerned.[28] Recall that $p_0$ is an inverse measure of overall liquidity preference on both sides of the money market. It captures those changing sentiments in the money market that fall under the heading of 'bullishness' and 'bearishness' from Keynes's *Treatise*.[29] Therefore, when liquidity preference increases, either through an increase in $\psi$ on the demand side of the money market, or a fall in $\phi$ on the supply side, $p_0$ will fall and the inflation rate will fall, and *vice versa*.

## 3.10 Nominal and Real Rates of Interest Revisited

There was another lengthy debate in the Post-Keynesian literature of the 1980s and 1990s between rival schools who were labelled as 'horizontalists' and 'structuralists'.[30] The debate was mainly about the need to reconcile the notions of endogenous money, the actual interest rate operating procedures of real world central banks, and the idea from Keynes that liquidity preference also matters for the determination of interest rates. As we will see, all of these things are in fact quite compatible.

In the absence of any such thing as a natural rate of interest, however, it is important to move beyond the strict terms of reference of the various 20th century debates, and to recognize that the most important point at issue is about the determination of real interest rates, not just nominal rates. Given the way in which we have defined real and nominal interest rates in *Lecture 1*, the relationship between the two concepts is straightforward. In what follows, we will focus on the so-called *ex-post*, or inflation-adjusted, real rate of interest. Defining terms as in *Lecture 1*,[31] it

---

[27] John Smithin, 'Inflation', in John King, ed., *The Elgar Companion to Post-Keynesian Economics,* second edition (Cheltenham: Edward Elgar, 2012).

[28] The focus has been mostly on liquidity preference in the context of interest determination, on which more follows.

[29] As already mentioned, there will be further discussion of Keynes's 'speculative demand' for money in *Lecture 6* that follows.

[30] Louis-Philippe Rochon, *Credit, Money and Production* (Cheltenham: Edward Elgar, 1999).

[31] That is, $i$ = the nominal market rate of interest, $i_0$ = the nominal policy rate, $m_0$ is the mark-up between commercial bank deposit rates and lending rates, and $m_1$ is the pass-through co-efficient.

was there suggested that the monetary policy transmissions mechanism in nominal terms may be represented as;

$$i = m_0 + m_1 i_0. \qquad m_0 > 0, \ 0 < m_1 < 1 \qquad (3.32)$$

We can then use the simple device of subtracting the observed inflation rate, $p$, from both sides of the expression. This will give;

$$i - p = m_0 + m_1 i_0 - p. \qquad (3.33)$$

And;

$$r = m_0 + m_1 r_0 - (1 - m_1)p. \qquad (3.34)$$

where $r_0$ is the real (inflation-adjusted) policy rate of interest.

If the central bank is following a real interest rate rule for the policy rate, equation (3.33) shows that there is a negative relationship between the inflation rate and the general level of real interest rates. (This is the so-called 'forced saving effect' or Mundell–Tobin effect.) The inflation rate itself, $p$, in turn depends on $p_0$, which is an inverse measure of liquidity preference. An increase in liquidity preference thus causes a fall in $p_0$, and therefore a fall in $p$. Hence, an increase in the real rate of interest. A decrease in liquidity preference causes the real rate of interest to fall. The results are strongly reminiscent of Keynes's original arguments about liquidity preference and interest rates, but now with the emphasis shifted to real rather than nominal rates. At the same time, the real policy rate set by the central bank also feeds through to affect real interest rates in general. There is no contradiction between these two statements.

## 3.11  A Simple Two-Equation Model of the Real Rate of Interest

It is now possible to put together a simple formal model jointly explaining the determination of the real interest rate and the inflation rate. From equations (3.31) and (3.34), we have;

$$r = m_0 + m_1 r_0 - (1 - m_1)(p_0 + w - a). \qquad (3.35)$$

The real rate of interest therefore depends positively on the real policy rate, positively on liquidity preference, negatively on the real wage rate, and positively on labour productivity.

The equilibrium can also be depicted in graphical form as in *Figure 3.3*, which brings together the equation for equilibrium inflation and the Mundell–Tobin/forced saving effect. The symbol $r_0$ stands for the real policy rate of the central bank, and if the central bank is behaving sensibly, it will be trying to stabilize that rate at some given level. However, if the central bank neglects this advice, and either makes a deliberate change in the real policy rate or passively allows such a change to happen, these policy errors will be reflected in changes in real interest rates generally.

An increase in the real policy rate, illustrated in the diagram by a vertical upward shift of the downward-sloping schedule, will increase the overall level of real interest rates, leaving the inflation rate unchanged. A reduction in the real policy rate will cause the overall level of real interest rates to fall. Also, as already mentioned, something like the original Keynesian argument about liquidity preference and interest rates continues to have relevance. An increase in liquidity preference or 'bearishness' (a fall in the $p_0$ term), shown by a shift to the left of the vertical line, will increase the real interest rate and cause the inflation rate to fall. The opposite would be true for a fall in liquidity preference (that is, an increase in 'bullishness').

Changes in labour productivity (shown by changes in term $a$) also cause changes in the real interest rate. An increase in $a$ shifts the vertical schedule back to the left, reducing the inflation rate and raising the real rate

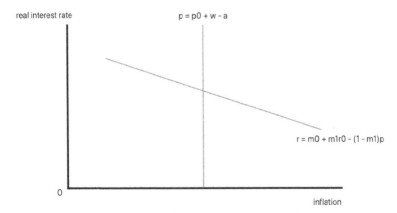

*Figure 3.3*: Real Interest Rates and Inflation Rates

of interest. A fall in labour productivity has the reverse effect. Arguments to the effect that changes in productivity cause changes in real interest rates are not uncommon in the mainstream literature. In this case, however, there is a quite different mechanism at play than in orthodox theory. It involves not only changes in productivity *per se* but also, most importantly, the attendant financial considerations. When there is an improvement in productivity, there is first a fall in the inflation rate. Then *via* the forced saving effect there is an increase in the real rate of interest. An increase in real wages with no change in productivity has the opposite effect. It will cause the inflation rate to rise, and real interest rates to fall. A real wage cut on the other hand causes inflation to fall, and the real rate of interest to rise.

Many years ago, Hicks had already addressed this question of the effect of real wage changes on interest rates, and found it something of a puzzle.[32] He could come up not only with an argument that a rise in wages leads to a fall in interest rates but also the opposite, and could only reconcile them (somewhat unconvincingly) by suggesting that the one effect applies in the short-run and the other in the long-run. Here, the final answer is definitive. There is a negative relationship between real wages and real interest rates in both the short-run and the long-run.

## 3.12   Conclusion

This *Lecture* has set out the main elements that I have argued should be present in any monetary or macroeconomic theory that aims for some degree of realism. In *Lecture 4* to follow, the aim will also be pedagogical to some extent, that is, to compare the approach put forward in these *Lectures* with that which has usually prevailed in the standard textbooks.

---

[32] Hicks, *Money, Interest and Wages.*

# Lecture 4

# Comparing Textbook Macroeconomics and the Alternative Monetary Model (AMM)

## 4.1 Introduction

The evolution of the textbook treatment of macroeconomics and monetary economics would be a fascinating subject in its own right, for anyone with the time and energy to pursue it. From the publication of the first modern textbooks in the late 1940s, through the 1950s and 1960s, so-called 'Keynesian' models stressing the importance of aggregate demand were the order of the day, even if some of them bore little resemblance to anything to be found in the writings of J.M. Keynes. The *locus classicus* of this genre was Samuelson's *Economics: An Introductory Analysis*.[1] A later influential competitor from the United Kingdom was Lipsey's *An Introduction to Positive Economics*.[2] The emphasis in these books (quite rightly so, whatever their other failings) was on how such things as changes in aggregate demand or 'effective demand' could affect output and employment. Perhaps not coincidentally, economic performance at this time did turn out much better than it had been in (say) the 1930s.

---

[1] Samuelson, *Economics*.

[2] Richard G. Lipsey, *An Introduction to Positive Economics* (London: Weidenfield and Nicholson, 1963).

Then, from roughly the late 1970s through the mid 1990s, the standard textbook fare was based on a kind of compromise between this supposedly Keynesian approach and the rival school of monetarism. The latter was the twentieth century version of the quantity theory of money and has long been associated with the name of the late Professor Milton Friedman of the University of Chicago. The essence of the compromise was to keep some remnant of the discussion about the influence of effective demand, but to restrict its operation mainly to the short-run. In the long-run (or so it was thought), a market economy would automatically reach full employment simply through the operation of the ubiquitous 'market forces'. Thereafter, changes in demand would have no further effect except on the price level. As far as economic growth was concerned, it was believed that there was a 'natural rate' of growth analogous to the supposed natural rates of interest and unemployment. This could not easily be altered except by hard-won improvements on the supply-side. Here is what the textbook authors Dornbusch and Fischer had to say about the compromise in the late 1970s, in a work entitled *Macroeconomics*[3];

> ... macroeconomics is often seen as the battleground for conflict between two implacably opposed schools of thought — monetarism, represented by its champion Milton Friedman and '[K]eynesianism' ... represented by economists such as James Tobin ... This is ... misleading. There are indeed conflicts of opinion ... and theory between monetarists and non-monetarists, but much more there are major areas of agreement: there is far more to macroeconomics than the topics on which monetarists and ... [others] ... disagree.

They are clearly searching for some kind of consensus approach to avoid the hard intellectual choices that would otherwise have to be made. But did the compromise actually work? Here is what I said about the topic myself, in the first chapter of my *Rethinking*;

> ... after a hiatus in the mid-20th century in which it ... [seemed] ... that Keynes had won the intellectual battle the academic discipline of ... macroeconomics ... [went] ... totally off the rails. [In] ... 1969 a volume

---

[3] Rudiger Dornbusch and Stanley Fischer, *Macroeconomics* (New York: McGraw-Hill Book Company, 1978).

had ... [actually] ... appeared with the optimistic title *Is The Business Cycle Obsolete?*[4] Subsequently, however, the economics profession apparently collectively decided that if the business cycle no longer existed, it would be necessary to reinvent it.

Finally, in the early 21st century a new textbook orthodoxy developed in the form of a simple three-equation model which might properly be called 'neo-Wicksellian' after the Swedish economist of a century earlier, Knut Wicksell. This was the same person who had originally laid great stress on the importance of the supposedly non-monetary natural rate of interest, as already discussed in *Lecture 1*. Again, the term consensus might well be applied. Now there was a 'new consensus', albeit based on the conventional wisdom from more than a century in the past. This time, at a superficial level, it may well have seemed that some features of the new consensus were similar to what we described earlier as the four 'key principles' required to construct a genuinely monetary theory. For example, the new consensus accepted that the monetary policy instrument is a nominal interest rate (*i.e.*, the policy rate of the central bank), and that the supply of credit and money is endogenous. (By this time, it had really become impossible for textbook orthodoxy to go on making statements to the effect that central banks 'cannot control interest rates', *etc.*, when the central banks themselves were saying and doing the opposite.) But the conversion was no more than skin-deep. It was the Wicksellian element, as such, that was meant to be the face-saver. There was still supposed to be a natural rate of interest lurking somewhere in the model that eludes the control of the central bank. It might be admitted that this entity cannot be observed in reality, but it was nonetheless presumed always to be exerting a decisive influence behind the scenes. In practice, therefore, there was no real change in the underlying approach to macroeconomic policy problems, and this led directly to the negative real world economic consequences that are by now familiar to everybody.

In *Lecture 4*, the main objective is to provide a detailed comparison between the model of the new consensus and the alternative approach to macroeconomics as set out in *Lecture 3* earlier. To illustrate the latter, we will use my own 'alternative monetary model' (AMM).

---

[4]Martin Bronfenbrenner, ed., *Is the Business Cycle Obsolete?* (New York: Wiley, 1969).

## 4.2 The Lessons of Economics 101?

In previous work, I think I have made it clear that I am not a big fan of the standard 'principles of economics' curriculum (that is, neoclassical *micro*economics) as usually taught in 'Economics 101'. In general, I think that something more like a genuine economic sociology would be far more useful.[5] However, there is at least one instructive comparison to be made between Economics 101 and what has usually been taught as macroeconomics (for example, in Economics 201). This concerns the shape and slope of the short-run and long-run supply curves in microeconomics and macroeconomics, and will do much to help to explain the issues at stake.

A standard textbook example often given in microeconomics is that of the market for rental housing units in a particular town or city.[6] The short-run supply schedule is taken to be a vertical line, as in *Figure 4.1*. In the economics jargon, the supply of rental units is 'perfectly inelastic'. The point is that there are only so many rental units in existence at any given point in time. It will take time to put up new apartment buildings or to convert existing properties, *etc.* Therefore, if there is a sudden increase in demand for rental housing because many people have moved to the city

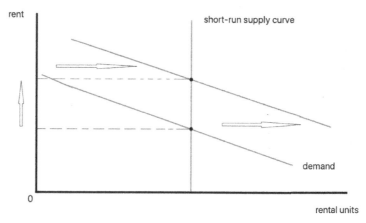

*Figure 4.1*: An Increase in the Demand for Rental Housing in the Short-Run

---

[5] Smithin, *Rethinking*.
[6] Barrows and Smithin, *Fundamentals*.

in search of work, the demand curve[7] will shift outward. In the absence of rent controls, the result will therefore be a relatively large increase in the price of housing (the rental rates). However, over a somewhat longer period of time, in the 'long-run', the argument is that the supply schedule will become considerably more elastic. By then there will have been enough time to complete more conversions and to put up new buildings. Given that demand has increased, there is clear incentive for property owners to provide more space, because of the high rents that can now be obtained. The eventual changes are illustrated by the much flatter supply schedule in *Figure 4.2*. The final result will be a greater supply of rental units, which (after all) was exactly what was needed, and in the end a far more modest increase in rents.

The depth of understanding of social ontology that might be gained from a study of microeconomics is probably quite limited, but it has to be admitted that this particular argument does make sense. It is an entirely understandable, if only a partial, explanation of economic activity. The basic idea is that if there are clear price incentives to do so, the necessary goods or services will indeed eventually be supplied, and then the price increases themselves will start to level off. But there is a contrast between this intelligible argument, which university students learn in their first year in Economics 101, and what they are told in their second year in Intermediate Macroeconomics. The contradictory message received in the

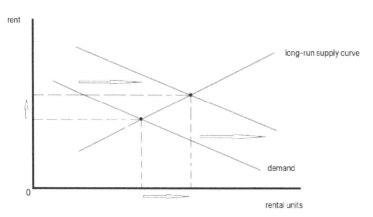

*Figure 4.2*: An Increase in the Demand for Rental Housing in the Long-Run

---

[7] This is again standard economics jargon. The 'curve' is actually a linear schedule in this particular diagram.

second course is illustrated by the diagram in *Figure 4.3* showing the aggregate demand and supply curves commonly used as the main analytical tools in macroeconomics.

*Figure 4.3* graphs the aggregate price level, *P*, on the vertical axis and real GDP, *Y*, on the horizontal axis. The aggregate demand curve (AD), or schedule, is downward-sloping, and the short-run aggregate supply function (SRAS) is upward-sloping. The long-run aggregate supply curve (LRAS), however, is vertical. As compared to microeconomics the roles of the short-run and long-run supply functions have been totally reversed. Not surprisingly this will lead to completely the opposite argument in macroeconomics to that made in microeconomics. *Figure 4.4* shows how the event of an increase in aggregate demand would be analyzed in a macroeconomic framework. The key idea is this. We are supposed to believe that in the long-run the level of real GDP cannot increase beyond the level $Y^N$ (which I have labelled in this way by analogy to the general notion of 'natural' rates). When I personally first encountered this idea, many years ago, the biggest puzzle to me was its seemingly obvious counterfactual nature. In reality, the *level* of real GDP never settles down to any single or constant level (I am not talking about the *growth* rate of real GDP here). Real GDP increases in most years *via* the phenomenon of growth itself. But it also sometimes falls, in a recession. It rarely, if ever, stays exactly the same. Furthermore, growth occurs in widely differing increments across different countries, and at different time periods. Some countries do well, and some do not.

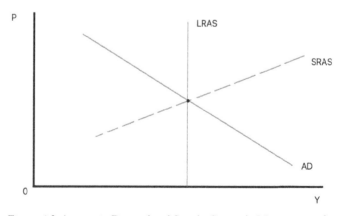

*Figure 4.3*: Aggregate Demand and Supply Curves in Macroeconomics

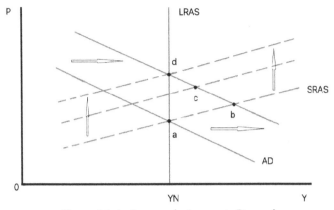

*Figure 4.4*: An Increase in Aggregate Demand

In fact, the same textbooks that have used diagrams similar to *Figures 4.3* and *4.4* for their basic theory seem always to have had great difficulty in incorporating the very idea of economic growth itself into their analyses. For example, one popular device was a so-called 'growth model' which did not actually determine the growth rate. The solution to the model was a static equilibrium capital/output ratio.[8] The growth rate itself then had to be explained by various exogenous factors. In my own work, as the reader of this book can attest, I have always tried to frame macroeconomic theory in such a way as to be able easily to incorporate the phenomena of growth, inflation, and the real rate of interest. For example, in *Lecture 3* earlier we have already discussed in some detail the two main alternative ways of theorizing economic growth. One of these, the 'Keynes-type' theory, was much more plausible than its 'Classics-type' rival. But in neither case was there any difficulty in transitioning from the static equilibrium analysis to the growth context.

In the textbooks, the various explanations that are given as to *why* the level of real GDP cannot be expanded beyond $Y^N$ were often quite

---

[8] Toward the end of the twentieth century, the practice in textbooks came to be to present the model of the equilibrium capital/output ratio in an early chapter before actually going into the details of the static AD/AS model. Presumably, this was meant to illustrate the background against which the events of the static model were thought to be taking place. See, for example, Chapter 4 of N. Gregory Mankiw, *Macroeconomics* (New York: Worth Publishers, 1992).

confusing — certainly as they were explained to the intermediate student. Sometimes, for example, it was hinted that $Y^N$ is the ultimate physical capacity of the economy. As we have already seen, however, beyond the basic levels of subsistence and shelter for the population, neither real GDP nor economic growth are ultimately materialistic concepts at all. And, in fact, economies do tend to grow each year as measured in terms of real 'value-added' (including all such things as services and intellectual output) to a greater or lesser extent. At other times, the argument was alternatively presented as a question of implacable market forces. This is the idea that there is always an optimal structure of relative prices that will not provide any incentive for change beyond the supposed equilibrium level. But, here again, the relevant relative prices, such as the average macroeconomic real wage rate, the real rate of interest, or the real exchange rate, do change. Moreover, in some cases they are functions of the growth rate itself. In the end, none of the explanations offered is able convincingly to explain why (in the mathematical idiom) the macroeconomic equilibrium should always be a 'fixed point'. That is just an assumption.

The idea that $Y^N$ is actually the physical capacity of the economy is immediately belied by the very narrative usually accompanying a diagram such as *Figure 4.4*. Suppose that there is an increase in demand which shifts the aggregate demand schedule (AD) out and to the right. In the short run, the economy is supposed to move along the short-run aggregate supply schedule (SRAS) to a point like 'b' in the diagram. Therefore, (unlike in the microeconomic rental housing scenario) output does increase in the short run. Clearly, $Y^N$ was not the literal physical capacity of the economy after all.

How does the temporary increase in output come about? Once again, there is no really clear-cut explanation of what is supposed to be going on. A popular argument is (along the lines that) as money wages rise during the boom, the workers are 'fooled' into putting in more work effort. They forget that prices are rising also. They mistakenly think that they are better off and therefore work harder.[9] However, they are really worse off as real wages are actually falling. Eventually, or so the argument goes, the workers will catch on to the true situation, and then push for still higher money wages to offset the prices increases. This is shown by successive shifts upward in the SRAS. In the end, the original equilibrium level of real

[9] Mankiw, *Macroeconomics*.

wages will be restored, the boom will fade away, and the economy will be back to where it started. The only lasting result is a higher price level. In reality, this argument does not hold up at all. For one thing, it definitely implies that real wages are actually falling during a boom, not rising, and that the workers are indeed mistaken. However, as already argued in *Lectures 1, 2*, and *3* earlier, there is no empirical evidence for this. If anything, the opposite is true. The causal sequence is more likely the other way around, that real wages *rise* during the boom because the bargaining power of labour increases.

Overall, therefore, the standard textbooks of the second half of the 20th century left us with a strange legacy of inconsistency between the two different modes of economic reasoning — microeconomics *versus* macroeconomics — that have never been resolved.

As already mentioned, the new consensus model of the early 21st century did make claims that it was introducing (or rather re-introducing) some different ways of thinking about the conduct of monetary policy. But, as far as the micro–macro split was concerned, this was definitely not the case. From this point of view, the new consensus was simply a continuation and development of the standard textbook macroeconomic argument. There was a much-hyped notion of the 'micro-foundations of macroeconomics', but this turned out to refer only to the type of mathematical formulation employed in the more advanced versions of the theory. It was not in any way a return to the fundamental lessons of Economics 101. In what follows, we now proceed to develop a three-equation version of the new consensus model that is directly comparable to my own AMM — which takes a very different point of view on these issues.

## 4.3 The 'New Consensus' on Monetary Policy

To call any theoretical tendency a consensus obviously does run the risk of exaggeration. But essentially all that is meant to be conveyed by the expression 'new consensus' is the approach to macroeconomics that was widely accepted in academia, central banks, finance ministries, and research institutes around the beginning of the 21st century, both for theoretical debate and policymaking. It should go without saying that even if a consensus does exist on any topic at a given point in time, this by no means necessarily implies that it is 'true', scientifically accurate, or not subject to rational criticism. It just means that it has majority support within the relevant peer group at a particular time. The point of covering this material, therefore, is simply to get some idea of the thought processes that were going on in mainstream academic and policymaking circles at the time.[10] Whether they were correct or not, these ideas certainly had a definite negative influence on economic outcomes in that era.

The basic framework for policy analysis in the new consensus model can be shown to consist of just three macroeconomic relationships, as follows;

$$y = \varepsilon_0 + (g - t) - \varepsilon_1 r, \quad \varepsilon_1 > 0 \tag{4.1}$$

$$p - p_{-1} = \beta(y_{-1} - y^N), \quad \beta > 1 \tag{4.2}$$

$$r = r^N + \gamma(p - p^*). \quad 0 < \gamma < 1 \tag{4.3}$$

Unlike the model shown in *Figures 4.3* and *4.4*, this specification has been tailored such that it relates the *growth* rate to the *inflation* rate for direct comparison with the AMM. It is not restricted to propositions about the price level and the level of GDP. As in earlier work on this topic, I have used Greek letters to stand for the various intercepts and coefficients in each of the three equations.[11] The remaining variables have the same meanings that were previously assigned to them in *Lecture 3*.[12]

Equation (4.1) does accurately represent the ideas of the new consensus about aggregate demand, but for our purposes it turns out that it can most easily be derived from the closed-economy version of the 'Keynes-type' growth equation as discussed in *Lecture 3*. (From the point of view of the new consensus itself this works because whatever Keynesian elements may remain are easily neutered by the assumptions made about aggregate supply.) According to equation (4.1), aggregate demand growth depends positively on a parameter, $\varepsilon_0$, defined as the 'net autonomous demand of the private sector as a percentage of GDP', and negatively on the real rate of interest. To derive equation (4.1), the Keynes-type growth equation is reinterpreted as purely a demand-side relationship, namely;

---

[10] Barrows and Smithin, *Fundamentals*.

[11] John Smithin, 'Teaching the new consensus model of "modern monetary economics" from a critical perspective: pedagogical issues', in Giuseppe Fontana and Mark Setterfield, eds., *Macroeconomic Theory and Macroeconomic Pedagogy* (London: Palgrave, 2009).

[12] Lower case $y$ stands for the growth rate of real GDP, $p$ for the inflation rate, $r$ for the real rate of interest, $g$ for government expenditure as a percentage of GDP, and $t$ for the average tax rate.

$$y = (x - s) + (g - t). \tag{4.4}$$

where the reader will recall (from *Lecture 3*) that the term, $x$, is given by $x = C_0/Y + I_0/Y$, and that $s$ stands for the marginal propensity to save. The next move is to then specify an 'investment' (or better 'firm spending') function of the form $I/Y = I_0/Y - \varepsilon_1 r$, with $\varepsilon_1 > 0$. Using this in (4.4) yields (4.1). The term $\varepsilon_0$ in (4.1) is therefore given by $\varepsilon_0 = C_0/Y + I/Y - s$.

The next relationship is a short-run supply function as shown in (4.2). This can be thought of as essentially a short-run 'Phillips curve'[13] (SRPC) or, rather, because it relates inflation to output growth rather than to unemployment, a short-run 'accelerationist' aggregate supply equation (SRAS).[14] As explained in earlier work, such as my *Controversies in Monetary Economics*,[15] this terminology originated in the *faux* monetarist/Keynesian debate of the second half of the 20th century and all of these elements carried through quite unchanged into the new consensus. The particular version of the SRAS that is used here specifies that if the rate of GDP growth in the previous period was greater than the supposed natural rate of growth, inflation in the current period will increase. Moreover, that as long as the discrepancy is maintained, the inflation rate will continue to increase in each period. As inflation depends only on past events, the dynamic short-run supply 'curve' actually comes out flat and the model will therefore have at least some Keynes-like properties in the short-run. However, equation (4.2) also makes it quite clear that the flat SRAS will not stay in place in subsequent periods. The Keynesian features always disappear in the long-run.

The third and final element of the new consensus model is the central bank reaction function in (4.3). This is a simplified version of the much-discussed 'Taylor rule' for monetary policy.[16] It states that the central bank will increase the real policy rate of interest if the inflation rate is higher than some arbitrary target level, $p^*$, and *vice versa*. The basic monetary policy is therefore one of *inflation targeting*, which was the default mode

---

[13] A.W. Phillips, 'The relation between unemployment and the rate of change of money wages in the United Kingdom, 1861–1957' (*Economica* 25, 1958).

[14] In this context, an increase in 'supply' evidently means an increase in the rate of growth of output supplied.

[15] John Smithin, *Controversies in Monetary Economics: Revised Edition* (Cheltenham: Edward Elgar, 2003).

[16] Taylor, 'Discretion …'.

for monetary policy on the part of most central banks over the turn of the 21st century. As the actual policy instrument is a nominal interest rate (usually a nominal overnight rate), in practice this means increasing the policy instrument by more than one-for-one whenever there is an increase in observed inflation. This has sometimes been called the 'Taylor principle',[17] by which is meant a sort of calculated over-reaction designed to show that the monetary authorities 'mean business'. This willingness to actually increase real rates of interest when deemed necessary (rather than simply responding to inflation, as I personally favour) played a crucially important role in the political economy of the new consensus.[18] But it was a bad idea. It introduced an entirely unnecessary destabilizing element and was a fatal flaw in the whole scheme.

Substituting (4.3) into (4.1), re-arranging, and imposing the equilibrium condition that the actual economic growth rate converges to the 'natural rate' in the long-run, it is then possible to construct a simple aggregate demand and supply model in inflation-growth space, as follows;

$$p = (1/\varepsilon_1 \gamma)(\varepsilon_0 + g - t) + p^* - (1/\gamma) \, r^N - (1/\varepsilon_1 \gamma)y, \quad \text{AD} \qquad (4.5)$$

$$p = p_{-1} + \beta(y_{-1} - y^N), \qquad\qquad\qquad \text{SRAS} \qquad (4.6)$$

$$y = y^N. \qquad\qquad\qquad\qquad\qquad\qquad \text{LRAS} \qquad (4.7)$$

The model consists of an aggregate demand (AD) relationship between the economic growth rate and the inflation rate, a flat short-run supply function (SRAS), and a vertical long-run supply function (LRAS). The latter is simply the equilibrium condition. The derived demand relationship shows a downward-sloping demand-side schedule in inflation/ growth space, obtained by substituting the monetary policy reaction function into (4.1). An important implication of this is that the negative relation between growth and inflation is due solely to the assumed response of monetary policy. Whenever the rate of inflation is seen to increase, the central bank will deliberately raise interest rates, and thereby reduce aggregate demand *via* the investment function.

---

[17] N. Gregory Mankiw, 'US monetary policy during the 1990s', NBER Working Paper 8471, September 2001.

[18] Smithin, *Rethinking*.

Altogether there are five shift variables for the aggregate demand function. Firstly, there are the three demand parameters. These are, $\varepsilon_0$, which is the autonomous demand of the private sector, and $g$ and $t$, which refer to fiscal policy. Next, there is the inflation target itself, $p^*$. A lower inflation target will reduce demand growth because the central bank will need to raise real interest rates in the attempt to hit the target, and *vice versa*. This means that the target itself is effectively the main indicator of the stance of monetary policy. The remaining shift variable in the constructed demand function is $r^N$, which is the intercept in the central bank reaction function. However, this term has a highly ambiguous status. As our notation suggests, most of the textbooks have seemed to think of this as representing the Wicksellian natural rate of interest itself. And recall that the natural rate supposedly has more to do with the supply-side of the economy than with money or the demand-side. *If* that were true, then $r^N$ could not be changed by monetary policy and would just have to be taken as given. We already know, however, that this idea is far removed from reality. It literally *cannot* be true as there is no such thing as a natural rate of interest in a monetary economy. Even if it did exist, there would still be no way for central banks to know beforehand what the specific number should be put into the model. In practical applications, therefore, the intercept term can never be anything more than an arbitrary number chosen by the central bank. Whether based on a rule of thumb, their own internal econometric modelling exercises (valid or otherwise), or simply political expediency, that number can always be changed. In effect, the intercept term becomes merely another indicator of the stance of monetary policy. A higher 'guesstimate' of $r^N$ implies that there will be a tighter monetary policy, and *vice versa*.

For an example of how demand changes will work out in this framework, the graphical exercise in *Figure 4.5* shows the impact of an increase in government spending as a percentage of GDP. There was clearly nothing at all that was 'new' about the new consensus in this respect. *Figure 4.5* looks quite similar to those that have been in use in the textbook analysis of fiscal policy for decades (ever since the academic reaction against Keynesian ideas began in full force in the late 1970s). And this element of continuity is really not surprising as the basic economic philosophy remained unchanged. The only real difference from the earlier narrative is the interpretation of what is occurring behind the scenes in the monetary policy response to the original stimulus.

In fact, much of what is going on is deliberately caused by the reaction of the monetary policy authorities, rather than being the result of market forces. A demand expansion will cause an initial boom in the economy which is shown in *Figure 4.5* by a move from point 'a' to point 'b'. (Again, note the inconsistency with the idea that $y^N$ represents some kind of physical capacity.) Thereafter, precisely as a result of the boom, the inflation rate will begin to rise, and the flat SRAS will begin to shift upward. According to the (perverse) monetary policy reaction function, the central bank will respond by raising interest rates with each increase in the inflation rate, thereby consciously slowing the economy at each stage. The process continues until the new long-run equilibrium is reached at point 'd', with the growth rate having fallen back to the original level. The economy is back to where it started albeit (in spite of the central bank's best efforts to counter this) with a permanently higher rate of inflation. The central bankers will simply congratulate themselves with the thought that it might have been worse, as far as the rate of inflation is concerned. They have no interest in actually improving the performance of the real economy by fiscal means.

In terms of political economy, the point of the argument set out in *Figure 4.5* is to suggest that there should never have been any attempt to stimulate the economy in the first place. But the argument is disingenuous. The initial boom did come about as a result of the fiscal policy stimulus and the subsequent slowdown or pullback did not have to happen. It was self-imposed by the reaction of monetary policy.

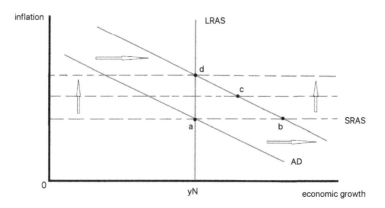

*Figure 4.5*: The Effects of a Demand Expansion According to the 'New Consensus'

A second graphical exercise, in *Figure 4.6*, shows the predictions that would be made by the new consensus model when the inflation target itself is revised downward. This is therefore a straightforward example of an 'inflation-targeting' policy. In the late 20th and early 21st centuries, inflation targeting was widely regarded as one of the most important monetary responsibilities of the central bank. As already mentioned, in the attempt to hit the new target the central bank will need to raise the real policy rate of interest, as *per* the monetary policy reaction function, and the AD schedule moves back and to the left. The immediate effect is to cause a recession, shown at point 'b' in the diagram. This is a blatant piece of social engineering as the recession is entirely policy-induced. It will typically be defended by the slogan of 'long-term gain for short-term pain', or similar.

The idea, to put things bluntly, is to force the public to adjust their economic expectations downward. Only if they can be made to do this, so the argument goes, will the inflation rate begin to fall, and the SRAS begin to shift downward. (We are not supposed to notice, presumably, that the target was arbitrarily imposed in the first place.) Only after the inflation rate has fallen will the central bank be willing to reduce real interest rates. Thereafter, the growth rate is supposed eventually to be able to recover from its low point. Ideally, there will be a series of ever more favourable temporary equilibria such as point 'c'. The process will continue until a new long-run equilibrium is reached at point 'd', with the original growth rate restored and a continuing lower rate of inflation. The selling point of the policy is that in spite of the short-term 'pain', there need be no permanent reduction in the economic growth rate.

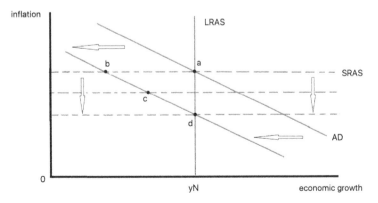

*Figure 4.6*: The Effects of a Lower Inflation Target According to the 'New Consensus'

In practice, things rarely work out this way. The narrative does not ring true. There may well be some small signs of recovery from the very depths of the recession, but it usually turns out that to keep the inflation rate down, the pressure must be kept on. It is highly unlikely that the economy will recover to its previous level of performance under its own steam. Typically, some other form of stimulus will eventually be needed to get the economy back to where it started. The political calculus behind the inflation-targeting narrative is to convince the public that lower inflation *per se* is a desirable policy objective, in spite of the initially depressing impact on jobs. There is an implicit promise that in the long run the negative effects will disappear. However, by the time the long run arrives, these assurances will have long been forgotten. The public will have adjusted to the new normal of lower growth and higher unemployment.

An interesting curiosity about these results is that even in the best case scenario of a return to the original growth rate, the inflation target itself will never actually be achieved. Setting a lower target will eventually succeed in reducing the inflation rate from what it was before. However, unless the intercept term in the monetary policy reaction function is *also* adjusted appropriately (which, by the way, adherents of the new consensus do not think is possible), the target itself will always be elusive. Although it is lower than before, the final equilibrium rate of inflation does not conform to the target $p^*$. The actual equilibrium solution for inflation is;

$$p = p^* + (1/\varepsilon_1)(\varepsilon_0 + g - t - y^N) - (1/\gamma)\, r^N. \qquad (4.8)$$

This is clearly not equal to $p^*$. From the point of view of those who favour inflation-targeting, the discrepancy probably does not matter very much. The main thing is simply to reduce the inflation rate — which is indeed always the outcome. Moreover, the error can be disguised by publishing a target 'range' as the objective for inflation rather than any specific number, and this is what is always done in practice.

If the natural rate of economic growth were genuinely to be believed to be immutable, there would not be much more to say about macroeconomics in the new consensus framework. However, if we were to resurrect the more detailed expression for the natural rate of growth derived in *Lecture 3*, things would be slightly different. The more detailed formula was;

$$y^N = s(1 - t)/O. \qquad (4.9)$$

(It is reproduced here with a very large caveat that this is not, in fact, a tenable explanation of the process of economic growth.) In equation (4.9), $s$ is the average propensity to save, $t$ is the average tax rate, and $O$ is the output/capital ratio. For the purposes of the graphical analysis, this definition of the natural rate of growth allows for at least some shifts in the vertical LRAS schedule. For example, the LRAS will shift outward when either the average propensity to save increases, taxes are reduced, or productivity improves. Therefore, the growth rate of real GDP can, in principle, be permanently increased in such circumstances, although not by any demand-side policy. (It will be recalled that this was the main argument of the supply-siders in the 1970s and 1980s.) In the case of a tax cut, the supply-side effect is supposed to combine with the existing demand effects and reduce the inflationary consequence of the latter. Either of an improvement in productivity, or an increase in the savings propensity, would also allow for an increase in the growth rate, combined with a lower rate of inflation. However, because of the underlying problems with the Classics-type approach to growth, none of these results are reliable. Whatever is of scientific value in them is easily incorporated into the AMM, as shown in what follows.

## 4.4 The Alternative Monetary Model

The purpose of this section is a direct comparison of the above results from the new consensus with my own 'alternative monetary model' (AMM) as set out in previous books and articles.[19] The contention will be that this does a far better job of describing economic reality than the usual mainstream approach, including that of the new consensus. In what follows, each of the various symbols retains the meaning given to them in *Lectures 1* and *3*.[20]

$$y = e_0 + (g - t) + e_1 k, \qquad 0 < e_1 < 1 \qquad \text{economic growth} \quad (4.10)$$

---

[19] For example, Smithin, *Rethinking*; and Smithin, *Essays*.

[20] That is, $y$ = the growth rate of real GDP, $p$ = the inflation rate, $k$ = the (natural logarithm of) the aggregate mark-up factor, $r$ = the real rate of interest, $w$ = the (natural logarithm of) average real wage rate, $a$ = the (natural logarithm of) average labour productivity, $g$ = government expenditure as a percentage of GDP, $t$ = the average tax rate, and $r_0$ = the real policy rate of interest.

$k = a - r - w,$                                               income distribution   (4.11)

$p = p_0 + w - a,$                                                      inflation   (4.12)

$w - t = h_0 + h_1 y_{-1},$   $0 < h_1 < 1$   the current after-tax real wage rate (4.13a)

$w - t = h_0 + h_1 y,$                      the equilibrium after-tax real wage (4.13b)

$r = m_0 + m_1 r_0 - (1 - m_1)p$                       the real interest rate   (4.14)

In equations (4.11), (4.12), and (4.14), the reader will immediately recognize the equilibrium versions of the expressions for income distribution, inflation, and the real interest rate, from *Lecture 3*. The growth equation in (4.10) is analogous to that in (4.1) but contains a different firm spending (investment) function. Firm spending now depends positively on profitability (that is, on $k$, the natural logarithm of the aggregate mark-up factor, $1 + K$), rather than on interest rates alone. Once again, the claim is that this is a more realistic and empirically plausible specification of the underlying relationship than that favoured by the new consensus. The terms $e_0$ and $e_1$ in (4.10) are therefore analogous to $\varepsilon_0$ and $\varepsilon_1$ in (4.1). In equations (4.13a) and (4.13b), two alternative specifications of the after-tax real wage function are given. The first gives the behaviour of the (natural logarithm of) the current after-tax real wage rate in the dynamic (disequilibrium) context. The second is the equilibrium version of the same relationship.

To conduct a simple graphical analysis for comparison with the new consensus, the AMM model may easily be reduced to the following three expressions, which are (i) the *effective demand schedule* (ED), (ii) a *short-run supply schedule* (SRS), and (iii) a *long-run supply schedule* (LRS). The results are as follows;

$p = - [1/e_1(1 - m_1](e_0 + g) + (1 + e_1)/(1 - m_1)t + [1/(1 - m_1)](h_0 + m_0 - a)$
$\quad - [m_1/(1 - m_1)]r_0 + [(1 + e_1 h_1)/e_1(1 - m_1)]y,$    (ED)        (4.15)

$p = (p_0 + t - a + h_0) + h_1 y_{-1},$                        (SRS)        (4.16)

$p = (p_0 + t - a + h_0) + h_1 y.$                              (LRS)        (4.17)

There are several important differences between this construct and the graphical version of the new consensus as described earlier. Firstly, the demand-side relationship is labelled as effective demand (ED) rather than aggregate demand (AD). This is highly significant in the context of a genuinely monetary model. In these *Lectures*, we have consistently interpreted the notion of 'effective demand' to mean that there is enough money available to actually pay for the goods and services required.[21] This is not necessarily the case with the more mainstream concept of aggregate demand. In that type of theory, the demand for goods and services is merely a notional concept. If some of the agents in the model have themselves produced goods and services, which they subjectively perceive to have some sort of value, that is thought to be sufficient to constitute the 'demand' for the output of others regardless of whether or not they have yet actually been able to sell their own output for money.

Secondly, the ED schedule is upward-sloping just as Keynes originally thought it would be (albeit with different variables on the horizontal and vertical axes). It is no longer downward-sloping as it usually appears in the textbooks. It can now clearly be seen that the idea of a downward-sloping AD curve in *P, Y* or *p, y* space, was due only to a mistaken analogy to the microeconomic demand curve. The analogy, however, is inapplicable in an endogenous money environment. We should recall that in the development of the theory behind the new consensus the only way to make the demand-side relationship downward-sloping was for the central bank to pursue a deliberate counter-inflationary policy. This should have given a very large clue about the mistake that was being made.

Finally, and most importantly, the LRS is positively-sloped rather than vertical. In contrast to the arguments from the demand side, this is an area in which macroeconomists *should* have taken their cue from microeconomics. The positive slope for the LRS is crucial. It means that whatever are the effects of policy initiatives and other macroeconomic changes, they carry through to the long-run as well as the short, for better or for worse. There is no automatic return to a previous equilibrium. This idea of a positively-sloped LRS schedule runs directly contrary to the conventional macroeconomic wisdom, but the analogy to the usual

---

[21] This is a slightly different concept of the difference between aggregate demand and effective demand than is sometimes given in the Post-Keynesian literature — as, for example, in Victoria Chick's authoritative *Macroeconomics After Keynes: A Reconsideration of the General Theory* (Cambridge, MA: MIT Press, 1983). She writes, '*effective* demand, in contrast to aggregate demand, is not a schedule — it is the point on the schedule ... which is 'made effective' by the firms' production decisions'. In this treatment, the point that I wish to stress is that to be 'effective' the demand must actually be in terms of money. Therefore I call the whole schedule 'the ED schedule'. But, of course, Chick is quite correct in stating that the only actual realization of money and profits is at the point where the schedules cross.

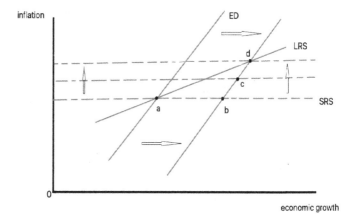

*Figure 4.7*: The Effects of a Demand Expansion in the Alternative Monetary Model (AMM)

*microeconomic* argument, as shown in *Figures 4.1* and *4.3* earlier, is inescapable. It is also indispensable for any balanced discussion of the different possible macroeconomic outcomes.

*Figure 4.7* shows how an increase in effective demand (taking the case of an increase in government spending as a percentage of GDP, for example) will work out in the context of the three-equation AMM. The ED schedule shifts out and to the right. However, in the short-run the inflation rate does not change as it takes time for the wage-push/cost-push mechanism to begin to operate. There will be an economic boom, shown at point 'b', but no immediate inflation. After a while the boom itself will begin to cause an increase in cost pressures. At this stage, the SRS schedule will start to shift upward and the inflation rate will rise. The boom nevertheless continues, as shown by the move to point 'c'. The economy finally settles to a new long-run equilibrium at point 'd', with admittedly a higher inflation rate, but also a higher long-term growth rate. Nor does the inflation rate itself get out of hand. It settles down to a new equilibrium value. It is not 'ever-accelerating'.[22]

---

[22] Smithin, *Controversies, Revised Edition.* This was the type of terminology used in the literature about the 'expectations-augmented Phillips curve' in the 1970s and 1980s. It gave rise to the concept of the NAIRU, which means the 'Non Accelerating Inflation Rate of Unemployment'. Typically, this was thought to be a unique value of the unemployment

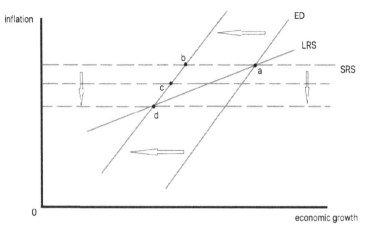

*Figure 4.8*: A Contractionary Monetary Policy in the AMM

The short-run behaviour of the model is therefore consistent with what has usually been suggested in the standard textbooks and by the new consensus. However, there is a big difference in the final analysis. A boom caused by a fiscal stimulus does cause a somewhat higher inflation rate, but will permanently increase the rate of economic growth unless some other deliberate counter action (*e.g.*, by the central bank) is taken to offset it. Keynes himself described the situation in the following way[23];

> The right remedy for the trade cycle is not to be found in abolishing booms and thus keeping us permanently in a state of semi-slump, but in abolishing slumps and keeping us in a state of semi-boom.

The AMM thus restores basically 'Keynes-type' insights about the effects of government spending financed by borrowing, not only for the short-run but also the long-run. This is an important change in emphasis.

The next graphical example in *Figure 4.8* shows the impact of an increase in the real policy rate of interest set by the central bank. This is a 'contractionary' monetary policy and is thus analogous to the case of a lower inflation target in *Figure 4.6* above. Assuming that the high real

---

rate (a sort of elaboration of the idea of the natural rate of unemployment). However, in the AMM *all* of the possible equilibrium values of the rate of unemployment are (in effect) NAIRUs.

[23] Keynes, *General Theory*.

policy rate is consistently maintained, the effect of the increase will be to permanently lower the inflation rate. There is no possibility or promise, however, of the monetary authorities ever being able to eventually lower the real policy rate once again. Also, the price of pursuing such a policy is that the economy will fall back to a permanently lower long-run growth path. An increase in the real policy rate, $r_0$, shifts the AD curve back and to the left, and there will initially be a recession along the SRS at point 'b'. The recession then starts to reduce wage pressures and the inflation rate itself will begin to fall. This, after all, is the whole point of the exercise. (We must remember that the recession is deliberately created for this purpose, however questionable a motive that may be from the moral point of view). The moral concerns become even more urgent in the context of the AMM because, unlike in the more optimistic scenario presented by the new consensus, the fall in inflation does nothing to improve the economic situation. The recession just gets worse. Instead of merely 'short-term pain for long-term gain' there is a much more serious long-run trade-off that has to be considered.[24] The economy moves along the path 'a', 'b', 'c', 'd', and the end result of the exercise is not only a lower rate of inflation but also a permanently lower average growth rate. Perhaps if the problem came to be understood in this way in the political arena, then stringent 'inflation-targeting' policies (or 'austerity' policies in fiscal policy) might not be as high on the agenda in future as they have so frequently been in the recent past.

We next turn to consider a different type of fiscal policy to that depicted in *Figure 4.1*, in this case a change in the average tax rate. Tax changes have a somewhat different impact in the AMM than would have been the case in the new consensus model. In the version of the new consensus set out earlier, for example, the natural rate of growth was supposed to be immutable. Therefore, the effects of tax changes were always symmetrical to those of changes in government expenditure. A tax *cut* would have the same effect as an *increase* in government expenditure. It will cause a temporary boom but in the long-run only serves to increase inflation. An increase in taxes would be considered deflationary. Instead

---

[24] Also from the ethical point of view, and as I have pointed out elsewhere, even in the optimistic short-run scenario we should note that those suffering the 'pain' (the workers) are not the same group as those receiving the 'gain' (the rentiers). Smithin, *Controversies: Revised Edition*.

of increasing prices, as might seem likely from a microeconomic point of view, the theory holds that higher taxes actually reduce prices *via* their macroeconomic impact. Moreover, as any negative supply-side effects are ruled out, the higher taxes are not thought to cause any lasting damage to the economy. They are seen as merely a means of reducing inflation and balancing the budget.

Things are different in the AMM, as illustrated in the diagram in *Figure 4.9*. This deals with the case of an increase in the average tax rate with no comparable increase in government spending. The increase in the tax rate shifts the LRS schedule up and to the left, and the SRS schedule also shifts upward. Simultaneously, the ED schedule shifts back and to the left. Now there are both demand-side and supply-side effects, and they are all negative. The first impact is a recession, at point 'b' in the diagram, and at the same time the inflation rate has increased.

Contrary to both the new consensus and the textbook version of Keynesianism, an increase in taxes is inflationary, not deflationary. It is true that in the next phase there will be something of a recovery from the depths of the recession. However, the inflation rate will keep rising and the economy never returns to the original rate of growth. The economy moves along the path 'a', 'b', 'c', 'd'. The most important conclusion to be drawn from this exercise is that an increase in the average tax rate is one of the possible causes of so-called 'stagflation'. There will be increases in both the unemployment rate and the inflation rate. There is a strong contrast between these results and traditional ideas about 'sound

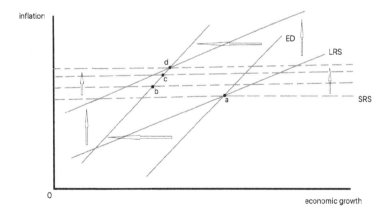

*Figure 4.9*: An Increase in the Average Tax Rate in the AMM

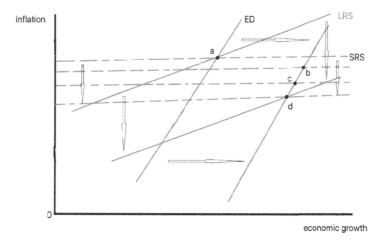

*Figure 4.10*: The Effects of an Improvement in Productivity in the AMM

finance' which suppose that a balanced budget is a prerequisite for both higher growth and lower inflation.

A final exercise to be undertaken in the AMM framework is to consider what happens when there is an improvement in labour productivity that might be caused, for example, by some sort of economy-wide technological innovation as in Schumpeter (recall *Lecture 2*). This is the case illustrated in *Figure 4.10* and the result is the opposite of stagflation. The improvement in productivity, shown by an increase in the term $a$ in equations (4.15), (4.16), and (4.17), shifts both the SRS and LRS schedules downward. The increase in productivity also directly improves profits (as $k = a - r - w$), which will increase firm spending. Therefore, demand growth increases also, and the ED schedule shifts outward. The economy moves along the path 'a', 'b', 'c', 'd', with the end result being both a higher growth rate and a lower inflation rate. Because of the higher growth rate, real wages will also increase. Moreover, because of the lower inflation rate, there is actually also a higher real rate of interest.

Combined with the increase in profitability, this is therefore a 'win–win' situation in terms of income distribution. This is not to say that the resulting distribution of income will be 'optimal' in any sense of that term (a question to be discussed in more detail in *Lecture 7* that follows), but just that all the competing groups are better off than they were in the original situation. Therefore, against the backdrop of endogenous money, this is a rare case in economics on which all the competing groups might agree. Having made these results explicit, it should also be mentioned that a reduction in the average tax rate (in other words, the opposite case to that illustrated in *Figure 4.9*) would have a similar set of effects. This emphasizes the point that whether tax increases are inflationary or deflationary remains one of the key 'unsettled questions' in monetary macroeconomics.[25] Note also that, as promised, this case shows that whatever was of scientific value in the political economy of the 'supply-siders' of forty years ago is easily incorporated into the AMM.

## 4.5  Conclusion

This chapter has presented a straightforward version of the three-equation neo-Wicksellian model of the 'new consensus', and a detailed comparison between that approach and my own AMM. I have long thought that to teach a similar comparative sequence in a university or college setting, thereby showing the precise differences between the competing points of views, would be a far more legitimate pedagogical exercise than the usual one-sided approach of the textbooks — in which typically only one macroeconomic theory is ever presented as the 'truth'.

There is no doubt that the new consensus model was the economic orthodoxy of the early 21st century and was widely accepted at the time. However, it was always naïve and misleading to represent this as simply the latest results of diligent scientific research into economic issues in the manner of textbooks in the natural sciences. The pitfalls of doing so might have been revealed merely by a backward glance at any one of the various mainstream textbooks of 20, 30, or 50 years previously, each of which presented the orthodoxy of their own day with a similar dogmatic confidence. The new consensus was itself nothing new. It is essentially the same approach to monetary theory as that set out by Wicksell more than a century ago and, for that matter, by Thornton in the English language work *The Paper Credit of Great Britain*, nearly one hundred years before

---

[25] John Smithin, 'What is the sign of the balanced-budget multiplier?' in Steven Pressman and John Smithin, eds., *Debates in Monetary Macroeconomics: Tackling Some Unsettled Questions* (New York: Palgrave Macmillan, 2022).

that.[26] They are all nothing more than variants of the failed 'Classics-type' approach to macroeconomic and monetary issues.

However, there has always been another potential rival waiting in the wings, a genuinely *monetary* macroeconomics, the best-known attempt at which historically was the work of Keynes during the Great Depression. Keynes did not win his own particular battle and did not ultimately succeed in converting the economics profession to his viewpoint. Nonetheless, the comparative approach set out in this *Lecture* has hopefully shown how this might now be done.

---

[26] Henry Thornton, *An Inquiry into the Nature and Effects of the Paper Credit of Great Britain*, 1802 (as reprinted by Augustus M. Kelley: Fairfield NJ, 1991).

# Lecture 5

# The International Economy, the Balance of Payments, and Exchange Rates

## 5.1 Introduction

In previous *Lectures* we have discussed the importance, for practical policy discussion, of thinking about the balance of payments and exchange rates, and of the differences between closed-economy and open-economy models. In *Lecture 5*, it is now time for a more detailed technical exposition of the issues.

## 5.2 The Balance of Payments: Basic Concepts

In *Rethinking the Theory of Money, Credit and Macroeconomics,* I provided a stylized numerical example of the balance of payments (BOP) numbers for the domestic economy under fixed exchange rates, for a given accounting period such as a quarter or a year.[1] This exercise is repeated here in *Table 5.1* to help define terms. The overall balance of payments of the domestic economy is defined as the sum across the current and capital accounts. The capital account reflects new international borrowing and lending, and the results of international equity investment. The current account comprises the balance of trade in goods and services and the net interest and dividend payments on past capital transactions (this last item is called foreign investment income, *FII*, which can either

---

[1] Smithin, *Rethinking*; Barrows and Smithin, *Fundamentals*.

be positive or negative). In each case the numbers supplied are the net figures. A positive number implies a net flow of funds into the domestic economy and *vice versa.* In the particular year illustrated in *Table 5.1,* the current account for the domestic economy was positive. This means either that exports were greater than imports or that foreign investment income was high, or both. The capital account was negative which means, roughly speaking, that the citizens of the domestic economy were lending more to foreigners than the other way around. The current account turned out to be greater than the capital account, and therefore the overall balance of payments was in surplus. This was reflected in an increase in central bank or 'official' holdings of foreign exchange reserves of the same amount.

Foreign exchange reserves have increased because to keep the exchange rate fixed the central bank must have had to intervene in the foreign exchange markets at various times during the year, to prevent the domestic currency from appreciating. They would have been selling their own currency and buying foreign exchange, thus building up the foreign exchange reserves. But the reader should note that in the officially published statistics an *increase* in the holdings of foreign exchange reserves will sometimes (very confusingly so, to my way of thinking) be entered with a *negative* sign. The reason for this is that the statisticians are trying to conform to the principles of 'double entry book-keeping' and make the bottom line come out to zero. We are not going to do that here, as we want to see what is actually happening to the holdings of foreign exchange reserves. Are they going up or down?

Letting the symbol $\Delta$ stand for 'change in', we can express the above relationships as;

$$BP = CA + KA, \qquad (5.1)$$

*Table 5.1*: A Numerical Example of the Balance of Payments (BOP) for the Domestic Economy (Billions of Dollars)

| | |
|---|---|
| Current Account (*CA*): | − 61,864 |
| Capital Account (*KA*): | − 47,435 |
| Overall Balance of Payments (*BP*): | + 14,429 |
| Change in Foreign Exchange Reserves (*ΔFE*): | + 14,429 |

and;

$$\Delta FE = BP. \tag{5.2}$$

Therefore, the change in foreign exchange reserves under fixed exchange rates can be written as;

$$\Delta FE = CA + KA. \tag{5.3}$$

Implying that;

$$CA = KA - \Delta FE. \tag{5.4}$$

The above results apply in a fixed exchange rate system. In a pure *floating exchange rate* system (otherwise known as a *flexible exchange rate* system), on the other hand, the domestic authorities should not as a matter of principle be intervening in the foreign exchange markets. If they kept strictly to this rule, overall deficits or surpluses in the balance of payments would not emerge as they are always eliminated by exchange rate changes. There will be no change in official holdings of foreign exchange reserves, and;

$$\Delta FE = BP = 0. \tag{5.5}$$

The case of pure float therefore establishes unambiguously the important general principle embodied in the following expression, which is obtained from equations (5.4) and (5.5);

$$CA = -KA. \tag{5.6}$$

The principle is simply that the current account usually moves in the opposite direction to the capital account. As already seen in equation (5.4), this is also true even outside the case of the pure float, up to a correction for changes in the volume of official financing. Although there have been historical exceptions in certain circumstances, the latter will typically not be large enough to upset the basic relationship. (If both the current account and capital account were positive, for example, there would have to be a really massive inflow of FE reserves to offset this. This would not by any means be a productive use of domestic funds.)

The reason for noting the generally inverse relationship between the current and the capital accounts is that in the past, and even in many quarters still today, economists have typically visualized the direction of causality in the balance of payments as flowing from the former to the latter. The theory has been that an improvement in the 'competitiveness' of the domestic economy leads to a current account surplus. Exports are greater than imports, and the nation as a whole is earning more than it is spending. It would then seem quite natural for the domestic 'capitalists' to try to find outlets to invest these surplus funds abroad, causing capital outflow. On the other hand, a nation 'living beyond its means', with a negative current account and imports greater than exports, would be forced to borrow abroad to make up the difference causing capital inflow. This has been the standard way of looking at the causes of international capital flows for centuries.

However, in the modern financialized world all this seems to have come unstuck and this has caused much heart-searching and/or puzzlement on the part of the experts in international trade and finance. It is much more likely that the chain of causality is the other way around. The capital flows have become so large that capital account developments dominate the current account and the trade performance of the nation emerges as a mere side-effect of, or reaction to, what is happening on the capital account. The implications of this reversal are very far-reaching, and potentially transform our understanding of how the global economy functions.

## 5.3  Macroeconomic National Accounts Relationships in the Open Economy

The balance of payments numbers, as illustrated above, can be linked up with the standard macroeconomic national income and product accounts framework by recalling the definition of gross domestic product (GDP) used in previous chapters. That is;

$$\text{GDP} = Y = C + I + G + (EX - IM), \qquad (5.7)$$

where $C$ stands for consumption spending, $I$ for investment spending, $G$ for government spending, and $(X - IM)$ for net exports. As the figures given in our numerical example were nominal (dollar) sums of money, then in the present context (and strictly speaking) we probably should have written something like $\$Y = \$C + \$I + \$G + \$(EX - IM)$, *etc*. In what follows, however, the $ symbol is omitted for convenience. (In fact, the basic national accounts relationships hold for both nominal and real magnitudes).

At this stage we are now explicitly concerned not only with trade, but also with capital flows, and we should therefore be careful to note that GDP or *gross domestic product* (as the name implies) only relates to the value-added produced within the domestic economy's borders. As already mentioned, for an open economy there is another potential source of income, namely *FII*. It is therefore important to now carefully distinguish between the *gross national product* (GNP) of an open economy and it's GDP ($Y$) as follows;

$$GNP = Y + FII. \tag{5.8}$$

The *FII* numbers can be either positive or negative, depending on whether the domestic economy is a net creditor or a net debtor. Thus, in an open economy the total national income (GNP) can be either greater or less than what is produced domestically (GDP).

Another important point to note is that any measure of income, including GNP itself, must by definition be equal to the sum of consumption spending $C$, savings $S$, and taxes $T$. Whatever the source of income, there are ultimately only three main ways in which it can be disbursed. First, the government will always take away a big chunk of it in taxes. The recipient of the income then has basically only two choices left with whatever is left over, to either spend it ($C$), or save it ($S$). This must be as true in the aggregate as it is for each individual. By definition therefore;

$$GNP = C + S + T. \tag{5.9}$$

Thus, using equations (5.7), (5.8), and (5.9), cancelling the '$C$s' and rearranging, we arrive at the following important algebraic expression;

$$(G - T) + (I - S) = (IM - EX) - FII. \tag{5.10}$$

Equation (5.10) may also usefully be re-stated as;

$$(G - T) + (I - S) = -CA. \tag{5.11}$$

Here $(G - T)$ is the 'primary' government budget deficit, $(I - S)$ stands for the domestic investment/savings balance, and once again $CA$ is the current account of the BOP.

The identity in equation (5.11) became quite well-known at the end of the twentieth century. It was the basis for the so-called 'twin deficits' argument, in the public policy debate in the USA, and caused a lot of controversy at the time.[2] This is the idea that a government budget deficit must somehow inevitably lead to a deficit on the current account of the balance of payments. The term $(G - T)$ stands for the primary government budget deficit and if it is positive, this means that government expenditures are greater than taxation. Therefore, *if* (a very big if ) we can also assume that investment is roughly equal to saving, or $(I = S)$, then mathematically there must also be a positive number on the left-hand side (LHS) of the equation. But, the term on the LHS is the negative of the current account. Therefore, the current account itself must also be in deficit. Hence, it might seem, or at least it could be argued, that a government budget deficit literally causes a current account deficit. No matter how influential this notion was in the twentieth century policy debate, however, there is an obvious flaw in the argument. This is that there is no warrant for the $I = S$ assumption on which it depends. In reality, a government budget deficit can be associated with any of a current account deficit, a current account surplus, or a neutral position on current account, depending only on the sign and magnitude of the term $(I - S)$. A rather more meaningful way of expressing equation (5.11) is therefore;

$$[(G - T) + I] - S = KA - \Delta FE. \qquad (5.12)$$

This now says, reasonably enough at least as far as the basic algebra is concerned, that if domestic saving is not enough to finance both the budget deficit and domestic investment, the funds must either be borrowed from abroad, leading to positive capital inflow $(KA)$, or obtained from sales of foreign exchange reserves $(-\Delta FE)$, with the latter usually relatively small in magnitude. The underlying relationship is sometimes explained by saying that net national *dis-saving* must be financed either by capital inflow or sales of foreign exchange reserves. (This statement is clearly subject to the various caveats about the specific meaning of terms such as 'savings', 'finance', 'investment', *etc.* in the endogenous money environment, as discussed in previous *Lectures*). Note that this way of putting things once again emphasizes the capital account as the active element in balance of payments developments.

---

[2] Barrows and Smithin, *Fundamentals.*

Under flexible exchange rates there will no changes in foreign exchange reserves, and in this case net national dis-saving can only be financed by capital inflow (*KA*);

$$[(G - T) + I] - S = KA. \tag{5.13}$$

The capital flows will therefore necessarily lead to a deficit on the current account, regardless of how productive or otherwise the domestic economy may be. The actual economic mechanism that brings these results about will be changes in the real exchange rate. A large capital inflow, for example, may well increase the real exchange rate, thereby causing domestic exports to become 'uncompetitive'.

## 5.4 Possible Alternative Configurations for International Economic Relations

Earlier, the nominal spot exchange rate, *E,* was defined as the foreign currency price of one unit of domestic currency. For example, if Canada is the domestic economy, this would be $US per $C. Given this definition when *E* falls the domestic currency, the Canadian dollar in this case, is said to *depreciate,* and when *E* rises, the domestic currency is said to *appreciate.* In *Lecture 1* we have already made the crucial distinction between the nominal exchange rate and the much more important real exchange rate, *Q*. This is given by $Q = EP/Pf$, where *Pf* is the foreign price level and *P* is the domestic price level. Although the real exchange rate is by far the more important concept of the two, the policy debate about the relationship between different currencies usually revolves around the issue of whether the nominal rate of exchange between alternative standards of value should be floating or fixed. There seems always to have been an almost total lack of understanding on this point by the supposed experts and policymakers, which has caused countless difficulties in the field of international economic relations, over a period of many centuries.

In the case of floating, or flexible, nominal exchange rates, the exchange rate between any two national currencies is proximately determined by their relative demands and supplies in the international financial markets. In the case of a fixed exchange rate, the relationship between national currencies is kept within narrow limits according to some international agreement or convention. The domestic central bank must stand ready to take whatever action is needed to force the nominal value of their own currency to remain within the pre-set bounds. As already noted, this explains why payments imbalances lead to changes in foreign exchange reserves when exchange rates are fixed. The central bank has to intervene in the foreign exchange markets to buy or sell as large a volume of the currency as seems to be required. In the case of an overvalued currency, they are required to sell. Therefore, if the currency continues to be overvalued, they will eventually run out of FE reserves and there will be a foreign exchange crisis. However, the crisis is entirely self-imposed. There would have been be no crisis if the exchange rate was floating.

As an alternative to the extremes of an irrevocably fixed exchange rate and a pure floating rate regime, there are also advocates of some sort of compromise between the two, such as a 'fixed-but-adjustable' exchange rate. This also might be called a 'managed float', a 'crawling peg', or similar. And there is another point of view which became popular in the late 20th and early 21st centuries (very unfortunately so, in my opinion, because of the dire practical consequences). This is to push the concept of fixed exchange rates to its logical conclusion, thereby questioning whether there is any merit in different political jurisdictions having separate currencies in the first place. This leads to the advocacy of a *currency union* between several different states that nonetheless theoretically retain separate national governments. It is a situation which became a reality in the Euro-zone of the European Union (EU) in the 21st century. The different options that are available are summarized in *Table 5.2.*

However, it is not at all clear that all of the different options really are viable choices. The last two, in spite of their seemingly reassuring names, are actually *unstable* systems, as history seems to have shown quite unambiguously and on several occasions.

As demonstrated elsewhere, for example in my *Essays in the Fundamental Theory of Monetary Economics* and in *Rethinking*, in an economy with a floating exchange rate the effects of most policy and other macroeconomic changes will be qualitatively the same as those in the equivalent closed-economy case.[3] This is a case of full 'monetary sovereignty' for the government of the domestic economy. This expression refers to what I have called (in the preface to this volume) the

---

[3] Smithin, *Rethinking.*

*Table 5.2*: Alternative Configurations for International
Economic Relations

| |
| --- |
| A Flexible (or Floating) Nominal Exchange Rate |
| A 'Fixed-But-Adjustable' Nominal Exchange Rate |
| An Irrevocably Fixed Nominal Exchange Rate or 'Hard Peg' |
| A Common Currency |

'logically unassailable' proposition of the modern monetary theory
(MMT) school, to the effect that the government of an economy with its
own sovereign currency and a floating exchange rate faces no binding
financial constraints. In these circumstances, fears about unsustainable
budget deficits are groundless, and the authorities will have no difficulty
in issuing debt denominated in their own currency. Therefore, they are
able to conduct exactly the same fiscal and monetary policies as they
would be able to do in a closed economy. All that would then be needed
for a complete analysis of the open economy would be simply to add the
results for changes in the real exchange rate and the foreign debt position
to those already worked out for the closed economy case (see, for example,
*Lectures 3* and *4* above). In an economy with a fixed-but-adjustable
exchange rate, the results will also resemble those of the closed economy,
which again allows there to be domestic control over monetary and fiscal
policy. These two considerations completely overturn the old idea, derived
from the Mundell–Fleming model of the 1960s, that monetary policy can
be assigned to a floating exchange rate regime and fiscal policy to fixed
exchange rates.[4] In the light both of theoretical considerations as well as
much of the actual experience of the past 50 years, this notion has proven
to be misleading.

None of this, however, applies to jurisdictions that have an irrevocably fixed exchange rate or to those embedded in a currency union. Nor
does it apply to the individual Provinces or States in a federal system. In
spite of the name, a putative hard peg for the nominal exchange rate
(such as a metallic standard, a credible fixed exchange rate regime, or a
currency board with no loopholes) is actually an unstable system and
inevitably will eventually break down. There are numerous historical

---

[4] Smithin, *Essays*.

examples.[5] There is no effective sovereignty in this case. A hard peg cannot be a viable policy choice for the long-run. The further idea of a currency union is to do away with exchange rates altogether. It is a total abandonment of sovereignty. Remarkably, however, even though the intent is to eliminate exchange rate problems altogether, experience shows that when actually applied the currency union has more-or-less the same instability characteristics as a hard peg (*cf.* the actual historical case of the Euro-zone). Unless the domestic economy is willing to give up control over economic policy entirely, there are only two possible long-run outcomes, either (a) a break-up of the system, which would be the equivalent of an exchange rate crisis in this context, or (b) eventual evolution into a true federal state, with a developed system of fiscal federalism. In the latter case, the different countries literally turn into mere 'Provinces' and no longer have even the semblance of national sovereignty.

## 5.5  The Real Exchange Rate and the Concept of Purchasing Power Parity

The well-known '*purchasing power parity*' (PPP) theory is perhaps the standard view held by most of the economics profession on how nominal exchange rates are determined. It is based simply on the definition of the real exchange rate $Q$, given above, which is as follows;

$$Q = EP/Pf. \tag{5.14}$$

The underlying assumption driving PPP is that this real exchange rate is a given from the point of view of monetary theory. It is supposed ultimately to be determined by the independent 'real' or barter terms of trade, and therefore cannot permanently be changed by anything that is going on in the sphere of money and finance. In previous *Lectures,* we have argued that this is one of the two key issues that need to be decided in monetary macroeconomics, the other being the question of whether or not there is a natural rate of interest. According to a genuinely monetary analysis (in Schumpeter's sense from *Lecture 1*) both assumptions are actually false.

---

[5] Smithin, *Rethinking.*

They are classic examples of a naïve 'naturalist' mode of analysis[6] which fails to take into account important results in social ontology, and neglects altogether the significant differences between the ontology of the social world and that of the natural world.[7] Such notions as 'states of nature', and appeals to supposed analogies to the physical and biological sciences, are besides the point when it comes to discussions of human institutions and social relations, especially of those involved in the construction of composites such as money, contracts, and markets. This applies *a fortiori*, I would argue, to the highly complex and always negotiable realm of international economic relations — with all the nuances of power relations, social positioning, and geopolitical strategy that these inevitably imply. However, the PPP theory of the determinants of the real exchange rate *via* the terms of trade ignores all such criticism.

In a theoretical treatment the underlying idea of PPP can in fact be 'simulated' by invoking the idea of 'absolute PPP', or the 'law of one price'. For mathematical convenience, we assume that the terms of trade are fixed at one-for-one, and therefore that $Q = 1$. (We should be clear, however, that this is merely a simplifying assumption. The results would be exactly the same with other values of $Q$.) If we do make the assumption that $Q = 1$, the PPP theory of the determination of nominal exchange rates conveniently reduces to;

$$E = Pf/P. \tag{5.15}$$

Moreover, for $Q = 1$ the natural logarithm of the equilibrium real exchange rate, for which we will use the symbol $q$ (lower case), is zero;

$$q = lnQ = ln(1) = 0. \tag{5.16}$$

In this situation, the alternative hypothesis to PPP, which would be that the real exchange rate is a monetary variable and hence endogenous to the system, is simply that $q$ is different than zero in equilibrium. For example, this does turn out to be the case for the alternative monetary model (AMM) from *Rethinking*. In that framework, the *real* exchange rate is

---

[6] John Pheby, *Methodology and Economics: A Critical Introduction* (London: Macmillan, 1988).

[7] John Searle, *Making the Social World: The Structure of Human Civilization* (New York: Oxford University Press, 2010).

indeed a strictly *monetary* phenomenon.[8] The two situations being compared are both mathematical equilibria, but one of them (the PPP equilibrium where $q = 0$) is a fixed point, while the other is not. In the world of the AMM, as is surely also the case in reality, changing *social* relations can and do have causal effects on the material world. In short, monetary and financial questions do have a decisive influence on the provision and distribution of real economic goods and services, both locally and on a global scale.

## 5.6  Interest Parity Conditions

There is a forward market for foreign exchange, and we will define the forward exchange rate $(F)$, symmetrically with the spot exchange rate $(E)$, as the foreign currency price of one unit of domestic currency for forward delivery. The economic role of the forward market is to hedge foreign exchange risk. In turn, the existence of the forward market in foreign exchange gives rise to three potential *interest parity* conditions.[9] Letting $i$ stand for the domestic nominal rate of interest, *if* for the foreign nominal rate of interest, $r$ for the domestic real interest rate, $rf$ for the foreign real interest rate, and $E_{+1}$ for the expected nominal spot exchange rate (in the future at time $\tau_{+1}$) the three conditions are as follows;

*Covered Interest Parity* (CIP);

$$if - i = (F - E)/E \qquad \text{(requires perfect capital mobility)} \qquad (5.17)$$

*Uncovered Interest Parity* (UIP);

$$if - i = (E_{+1} - E)/E \qquad \text{(requires perfect asset substitutability)} \qquad (5.18)$$

*Real Interest Parity* (RIP);

$$r = rf \qquad \text{(requires CIP, UIP and PPP)} \qquad (5.19)$$

In the case of covered interest parity (CIP), the basic idea is that given so-called *perfect capital mobility* the rate of return on financial investments in the different international centres should be the same everywhere, when covered by a forward contract. This results from the phenomenon of

---

[8] Smithin, *Rethinking*.

[9] John Smithin, 'Interest parity, purchasing power parity, "risk premia" and Post Keynesian economic analysis' (*Journal of Post Keynesian Economics* 25, 2003).

*arbitrage* whereby investors are willing and able to actively transfer funds from one centre to another in search of unexploited profit opportunities. If $(1 + i)$ is the return on \$1 invested domestically, and $E(1 + if)(1/F)$ is the return on \$1 invested abroad when covered by a forward contract, arbitrage will bring about a situation such that;

$$(1 + i) = E(1 + if)(1/F). \qquad (5.20)$$

Taking natural logarithms, using the approximation, for example, that $ln(1 + i) = i$, and re-arranging, will give[10];

$$if - i = lnF - LnE, \qquad (5.21)$$

which is equivalent to (5.17). The equivalence holds because the expression $lnF - lnE$ (the natural logarithm of '$F$' minus the natural logarithm of '$E$'), is approximately equal to $(F - E)/E$. At this point we should also pause to note that the expressions (5.17) and (5.21) are how the CIP condition is written when the spot exchange rate is defined as the foreign currency price of one unit of domestic currency, as we have done. If the exchange rate were to be defined the other way around, the CIP condition would turn out to be the other way around also.

The reason for expecting overall rates of return in the different financial centres to be equal when covered by a forward contract is because, in that case, the whole transaction can be rendered risk-free by selling the foreign exchange returns forward before the holding period begins. Moreover, if there are no technological or political impediments to the free flow of funds (if there is 'perfect capital mobility'), then there is no reason for arbitrage not to take place. On the other hand, if the investor does not bother to make the forward contract and leaves the investment uncovered, the transaction is not risk-free. In those circumstances, regardless of whether there is perfect capital mobility or not, the investor is always taking a chance. The point is that the forward exchange rate and the expected future spot rate are not the same thing. The forward rate is the rate paid now for the forward delivery of foreign exchange, whereas the expected future spot rate is that which it is expected will actually have to be paid 'on the spot' for foreign exchange in the next period, in (say) three months or one year's time. If there is no forward contract, maybe the

---

[10] When (5.20) is expanded one of the terms will turn out to be small enough to be neglected, leaving $if - i = (F - E)/E$.

investor will indeed end up having a higher return abroad than by leaving the money at home, but maybe not. To take this 'risk' into account, the price paid for forward delivery of foreign exchange will differ from the consensus expectation of the future spot rate, according to;

$$lnF = lnE_{+1} + Z. \tag{5.22}$$

The term $Z$ is the 'currency risk premium', or discount. Perhaps the expression *uncertainty* premium would actually be a better descriptive term. After all, a true Keynesian would insist that there is a difference between genuine uncertainty and probabilistic risk. Nonetheless, for convenience we continue to use the standard terminology. Having introduced the notion of currency risk, we can now see that although under perfect capital mobility CIP always holds, the same argument does not apply to UIP (the case when there is no forward contract). From equations (5.21) and (5.22), we have;

$$if - i = lnE_{+1} - lnE + Z. \tag{5.23}$$

The nominal rate of interest in the domestic economy can therefore differ from interest rates prevailing abroad.

For UIP to hold, investors would literally not have to care about the risk one way or another. They would be totally indifferent to the currency composition of their portfolios. Such a state of mind requires *perfect asset substitutability*, implying that the currencies are thought to be perfect substitutes for each other. In that case, and only in that case, we would have $Z = 0$, and UIP would then hold;

$$if - i = lnE_{+1} - lnE. \tag{5.24}$$

Up to now we have been discussing the case of flexible exchange rates, but we should also note that even in the case of fixed but adjustable exchange rates, the requirement of perfect asset substitutability will still not hold. In this situation exchange rates are not expected to change and, therefore;

$$lnE = lnE_{+1}. \tag{5.25}$$

However, there is always at least the *possibility* of an adjustment and there will still be a risk premium. Nominal interest rates will differ between the jurisdictions according to;

$$if - i = Z. \tag{5.26}$$

Once again the domestic nominal interest rate can differ from the foreign interest rate.

## 5.7 The Cases of a 'Hard Peg' or 'Credible' Fixed Exchange Rate Regime, and of a Currency Union

If there can be no perfect asset substitutability, and hence no UIP, under either a floating exchange rate regime or a regime with a fixed-but-adjustable rate, in what conditions might such a situation exist? The answer that would be given by most economists is that the nominal exchange rate should be permanently fixed. This explains the fascination historically with the idea of an 'irrevocably fixed' exchange rate, also known as either a 'credible' fixed exchange rate, or as a 'hard peg'. Perfect asset substitutability, for assets with similar terms to maturity and microeconomic risk characteristics, would also apply to common currency arrangements. Then there is perfect asset substitutability for the obvious reason that there is only one currency.

In both cases, domestic nominal interest rates will have to conform to those prevailing elsewhere and it would not be possible to conduct an independent monetary policy.

To further explain this proposition in the case of a hard peg, first note that in a (supposedly) irrevocably fixed exchange rate regime the nominal exchange rate is indeed expected to stay the same for ever. That is;

$$E = E_{+1} + E_{+2} + \cdots + E_{+n}. \tag{5.27}$$

Moreover, if it is thought that there is no possibility the exchange rate will ever change, then;

$$Z = 0. \tag{5.28}$$

In these circumstances, therefore;

$$i = if \tag{5.29}$$

I have had to say a 'supposedly' irrevocably fixed exchange rate in the above discussion because, as will be demonstrated shortly, in reality the system will actually be unstable and will eventually break down. At that point the exchange rate will have to change, of course. This is therefore yet another instance in which fashionable theoretical notions such as rational expectations, efficient markets, *etc.*, are shown to be equivocal in the real world. Presumably, therefore, whenever $i = if$ does hold in practice, one can only assume that the traders and market participants are basing their opinions on the theoretical models of finance and economics that they learned in business school, rather than the lessons of history.

The main conclusion to be drawn from the above discussion is that when a hard peg is in place, nominal interest rates in the small open economy must conform to 'world' interest rates. The case of a currency union is analogous. In this case, by definition there is only one 'money', and thus a single union-wide monetary policy and nominal interest rate.[11] As the nominal policy rate is the main monetary policy instrument, this means that the domestic economy will no longer have the power to pursue an independent policy. If monetary policy does 'matter' for economic outcomes, this will clearly have serious consequences, and indeed this outcome is implicit in the very idea of perfect asset substitutability.

## 5.8   Real Interest Rate Parity?

The third and final interest parity condition is 'real interest parity' (RIP)[12] where the real rate of interest in the domestic economy is equal to the foreign or 'world' real interest rate, $r = rf$. This is a much stronger condition and even less likely to prevail than $i = if$. Strangely, however, in much of the academic literature the idea seems rather to be taken for granted. It is treated simply as an extension of the idea of the natural rate of interest to the context of the global economy. The analysts are often content simply to assume that the domestic real interest rate is a given, determined by global market forces and beyond the influence of the domestic policymakers. But the discussion so far has already provided enough material to show that this is not a valid interpretation. There is no natural rate of interest for the

---

[11] Markus Marterbauer and John Smithin, 'Fiscal policy in the small open economy within the framework of monetary union', WIFO Working Paper #137/2000 (Vienna, November 2000).

[12] This, ironically, seems to be a highly appropriate acronym for the likely state of economic activity in the domestic economy, should the condition actually hold.

world as a whole, any more than there is for a closed economy taken individually.

To see why, re-consider the expression for the nominal interest differential in (5.21) above, and substitute in the definitions of both the spot and the expected future real exchange rate. And also use the definitions of the expected domestic and foreign real rates of interest, $r = i - p_{+1}$ and $rf = if - pf_{+1}$, respectively. Thus, we obtain;

$$rf - r = [(Q_{+1} - Q)/Q] + Z \qquad (5.30)$$

In the general case, therefore, and contrary to RIP, domestic real interest rates can and do deviate from foreign real interest rates. There are two main reasons for this, (a) an expected real appreciation or depreciation of the exchange rate, and (b) the risk premium. Moreover, even if the real exchange rate is not expected to change implying that $Q_{+1} - Q = 0$ (a condition that has sometimes been called '*ex-ante* PPP', as opposed to PPP *per se*), it is still true that;

$$rf - r = Z. \qquad (5.31)$$

Thus, with either a floating exchange rate or a fixed-but-adjustable exchange rate, and even in a world of perfect capital mobility, it is always possible for the real rate of interest in the domestic economy to permanently differ from that in the rest of the world. Only if *all* of covered interest parity (CIP), uncovered interest parity (UIP), and purchasing power parity (PPP) were to hold simultaneously would there ever be real interest parity (RIP). If CIP and UIP hold, we know that;

$$Z = 0 \qquad (5.32)$$

But, the next crucial requirement is that PPP, purchasing power parity, must also hold. This is the assumption that would actually be needed before one could legitimately say that;

$$Q_{+1} - Q = 0. \qquad (5.33)$$

Therefore, the only circumstance in which we can achieve RIP, or $r = rf$, is when all three of the other conditions, CIP, UIP, and PPP, are already in place.

## 5.9   A Hard Peg for the Nominal Exchange Rate Leads to an Unstable Regime (as also a Currency Union in the Absence of an Effective System of Fiscal Federalism)

The statement made in the above heading to this section is crucially important to an understanding of the problems of international political economy. Why then have these sorts of regimes ever been popular? The answer seems to be that many theoreticians and policymakers have traditionally confused the proposition that a fixed rate regime causes nominal interest rates to converge with the (much more contentious) idea of what might be called a global natural (real) rate of interest. Having once made this mistake, 'fixed exchange rates' would seem to be just what is required to make the conditions assumed by classical and neoclassical economics come true. They may come to believe that, merely with fixed nominal exchange rates, real interest rates, economic growth rates, and the unemployment rate would all be at their 'natural levels', and that the real exchange rate would be determined by the barter terms of trade. The dream of free markets, free trade, balanced budgets, low inflation, and so on and so forth, would be realized, and 'objective' market forces would prevail. None of this is real — it is not how economies work — but these sorts of strongly held beliefs seem to be the only way to explain the passionate advocacy historically of things like metallic standards, fixed exchange rates, currency boards, currency unions, *etc.* History itself has not been kind to these notions, however. The imposition of policy regimes based on this mindset has very frequently caused severe economic distress, and eventually they seem always to break down in crisis.

As we have already seen, with a credible fixed exchange regime there will be both CIP and UIP and, therefore, *nominal* interest rates will be indeed equal. However, contrary to popular opinion this is not a reliable method of enforcing a natural rate of interest globally. The argument does not work unless the third necessary condition for real interest parity condition, PPP, also holds. In the context of equation (5.31) mentioned earlier, although it will be true that $Z = 0$ because of the hard peg, this still does not make $Q_{+1}$ equal to $Q$. We can discover the precise source of the instability by once again substituting in the definitions of expected real interest rates at home and abroad. This will give;

$$(if - pf_{+1}) - (i - p_{+1}) = [(Q_{+1} - Q)/Q].   (5.36)$$

Re-arranging this expression, and lagging one period, it now becomes obvious that behaviour of the real exchange rate will be unstable. As *i* and *if* are equal, the real exchange rate depends solely on the inflation differential, as seen in equation (5.37). There can be no PPP.

$$[(Q - Q_{-1})/Q_{-1}] = p - pf. \tag{5.37}$$

If, for example, inflation is relatively lower in the rest of the world than in the domestic economy, the real exchange rate will continuously be appreciating. The goods produced in the domestic economy will become chronically uncompetitive. The only way open to the domestic authorities to attempt to enforce $p = pf$ would probably be draconian austerity policies. But these will do nothing but reduce economic growth and increase unemployment in the domestic economy, and cause political unrest. This sequence has occurred, and recurred, time and time again in history, and in *Rethinking* I gave numerous real world examples of such episodes. The list included the many problems in the Euro-zone in the 21st century, the end of the currency board (so-called 'dollarization') in Argentina in 2001, multiple exchange rate crises in the 1990s, the end of the ERM in 1992, the various pseudo foreign exchange crises in the Bretton Woods era (notably, for example, in Britain), and the collapse of the restored gold standard back in the early 1930s.[13] At the end of the day, it does not matter at what rate the nominal exchange rate is 'pegged' as the real exchange rate will keep on changing regardless. A hard peg is in fact an unstable system, and eventually breaks down in an exchange rate crisis. In the case of a common currency, the equivalent of an exchange rate crisis would be the eventual break-up of the system.

## 5.10 Balance of Payments and Exchange Rate Dynamics for Sovereign Monetary Systems

The only reasonable conclusion to be drawn from the above discussion is that in neither of the cases we have just described earlier, a hard peg for the exchange rate or membership in a currency union, are there any viable options for domestic macroeconomic policy-making. By definition, the jurisdictions involved have given up monetary sovereignty entirely.

---

[13] Smithin, *Rethinking*.

In the case of sovereign monetary systems (systems with flexible exchange rates or fixed-but-adjustable exchange rates), the impact of the various policy initiatives, and other macroeconomic changes, will be broadly the same as those discussed in *Lectures 3* and *4*. Such 'Keynes-type' solutions as a *lower* average propensity to save, a primary budget *deficit* as percentage of GDP, and a balance of payments *surplus* as a percentage of GDP would all lead to prosperity. We have already pointed out that this is not saying that it is impossible for growth to occur with a higher savings propensity, a budget surplus, or a balance of payments deficit. It simply means that at least one of the original three conditions must prevail, and also be large enough to outweigh the other two.

All that now remains is to work out the dynamics of the foreign debt position and of the real exchange rate itself. We can focus here solely on the case of a flexible exchange rate system because, as shown elsewhere, the dynamics for the case of a fixed-but-adjustable exchange rate are very similar.[14]

Recall that in a flexible exchange rate system, the capital account of the BOP will be the inverse of the current account (that is, $KA = -CA$). Thus, continuing to use the same notation as that employed above, we may write;

$$KA = -(EX - IM + FII) \qquad (5.38)$$

Letting the symbol $B$ stand for the total real value of domestic bonds outstanding in the hands of foreigners (which are assumed to be denominated in domestic currency and give rise to negative $FII$), this gives;

$$B - B_{-1} = -(EX - IM) + r_{-1}B_{-1}. \qquad (5.39)$$

Next, divide through by real GDP ($Y$), to obtain;

$$B/Y - (B_{-1}/Y_{-1})(Y_{-1}/Y) = -[(EX - IM)/Y] + r_{-1}[(B_{-1}/Y_{-1})(Y_{-1}/Y)]. \qquad (5.40)$$

Defining the foreign debt to GDP ratio, $b$, as $b = B/Y$, and specifying that the trade balance as a percentage of GDP is a negative function of the real exchange rate, namely $(EX - IM)/Y = ex - im = -e_2q$, we arrive at the following difference equation in the foreign debt position;

$$b - b_{-1} = e_2q + (r_{-1} - y)b_{-1}. \qquad e_2 > 0 \qquad (5.41)$$

---

[14] See Smithin, *Essays*; Smithin, *Rethinking*.

The coefficient on (the natural logarithm of) the real exchange rate, $q$, is labelled $e_2$ by analogy to the similar terms, $e_0$ and $e_1$, from *Lecture 4* earlier. As before, lower-case $y$ stands for the growth rate of real GDP.

The exchange rate dynamics themselves may also be inferred by modifying equation (5.30) as follows;

$$[(Q - Q_{-1})/Q_{-1}] = r_{-1} - rf_{-1} + Z_{-1}. \tag{5.42}$$

Supposing that the risk premium $Z$ may be specified as $Z = -z_0 - z_1 b$, this implies;

$$q - q_{-1} = r_{-1} - rf_{-1} - z_0 - z_1 b_{-1}. \tag{5.43}$$

For a debtor country, $Z$ will be a negative number, and will become the more negative the greater is the foreign debt to GDP ratio. The term $z_0$, meanwhile, may be thought of as a measure of 'international liquidity preference'. It is an index of the extent to which investors feel safer in holding foreign currencies rather than the domestic currency. The following is thus a continuous time approximation to the original system;

$$db/dt = e_2 q + (r - y)b, \quad e_2 > 0 \tag{5.44}$$

$$dq/dt = rf - r - z_0 - z_1 b. \quad z_1 > 0 \tag{5.45}$$

Temporarily setting $drf = dr = dz_0 = 0$, this reduces to;

$$\begin{vmatrix} db/dt \\ dq/dt \end{vmatrix} = \begin{vmatrix} e_2 & (r-y) \\ 0 & -z_1 \end{vmatrix} \begin{vmatrix} dq \\ db \end{vmatrix}. \tag{5.46}$$

Global stability for this system (in the mathematical rather than the geopolitical sense) would require that the trace (*Tr B*) of the right-hand side (RHS) matrix '*B*' is negative, and that the determinant (*Det B*) is positive. However;

$$Tr\ B = -e_2 z_1, \quad (<0) \tag{5.47}$$

$$Det\ B = -e_2 z_1. \quad (<0) \tag{5.48}$$

The trace is negative but so also is the determinant. It is not positive, as global stability would require. A negative determinant, in fact, indicates that the equilibrium is actually a so-called 'saddle-point'. The upshot is that the system is neither globally stable, nor completely unstable. What are the implications of this finding? The usual argument is that if some sort of economic mechanism exists to place the economy on the single 'stable arm' of the phase plane, then the system will be able to eventually reach an equilibrium. In this case, for example, the stabilizing factor might be expectations of how the exchange rates themselves are going to adjust. [15] If the system does follow the 'stable arm,' the solution is;

$$
\begin{vmatrix} -e_2 - (r-y) \\ 0 \;+\; z_1 \end{vmatrix} \begin{vmatrix} dq \\ db \end{vmatrix} = \begin{vmatrix} 0 & 0 & 0 \\ 1 & -1 & -1 \end{vmatrix} \begin{vmatrix} dr \\ drf \\ dz_0 \end{vmatrix}
\tag{5.49}
$$

Next we can work out the determinant ($Det\,A$) of the left-hand side (LHS) matrix '$A$'. This will turn out to be;

$$
Det\,A = - e_2 z_1.
\tag{5.50}
$$

With this information we may then solve by Cramer's Rule[16] to obtain the following results;

$$
dq/dr = -(r-y)/e_1 z_1 \;(?), \quad dq/rf = (r-y)/e_1 z_1 \;(?), \quad dq/dz_0 = (r-y)/e_1 z_1 \;(?),
$$
$$
db/dr = 1/z_1 \;(+), \quad db/drf = -1/z_1 \;(-), \quad db/dz_0 = -1/z_1 \;(-).
\tag{5.51}
$$

In this truncated system, the only policy option available to the authorities of the domestic economy is to influence the domestic real rate of interest *via* monetary policy. In context this remains a valuable policy tool, precisely because the domestic authorities need not be influenced or

---

[15] John Paschakis and John Smithin, 'Exchange risk and the supply side effects of real interest rate changes' (*Journal of Macroeconomics* 20, 1998); Eric Kam and John Smithin, 'Monetary policy and demand management for the small open economy in contemporary conditions with (perfectly) mobile capital' (*Journal of Post Keynesian Economics* 26, 2004).
[16] Alpha C. Chiang and Kevin Wainwright, *Fundamental Methods of Mathematical Economics,* Fourth Edition (New York: McGraw-Hill, 2005).

constrained by whatever is happening in the rest of the world. The above results show that a lower domestic real rate of interest improves the foreign debt position by reducing capital inflow and improving the current account. In turn, this will improve the economic growth rate, reduce unemployment, and increase real wages. Interestingly enough, the effect of a lower domestic real interest rate on the real exchange rate is ambiguous. It will all depend on the starting value of the term $(r - y)$, which is the domestic real rate of interest less the growth rate. Thus, there are some circumstances in which a policy of lower real interest rates may improve the economy by so much as to actually cause an eventual appreciation of the real exchange rate.

## 5.11  Different Orientations in International Political Economy

At this stage, it might be useful to summarize the options available for international political economy in a four-quadrant diagram such as I have previously deployed in earlier works.[17] The diagram distinguishes, on the one hand, between socialism and 'enterprise' (as in Weber's 'method of enterprise', which, as discussed, is a better term for a commercial society than the amorphous 'capitalism') as alternative economic systems. On the other hand, globalism *versus* nationalism in politics. This will yield the different options listed in *Table 5.3*.

The terms in the NW, NE, and SW quadrants of the diagram are no doubt self-explanatory. Each of them, for different reasons, carries a lot of intellectual and historical baggage and the analysis of the preceding pages has highlighted several of the reasons why this is so. There is a question mark, however, for the label of the SE quadrant. This is unfortunate, because it seems to be the only option left for the promotion of an 'open society' in the domestic economy, to use Popper's term for it.[18] But what to call this type of policy stance? It will surely have to be something along the lines of 'monetary mercantilism,

---

[17] See, for example, Smithin, *Money, Enterprise and Income Distribution*; and Smithin, *Rethinking*.

[18] Karl Popper, *The Open Society and Its Enemies*, 1945 (as reprinted by Princeton University Press, Princeton, NJ: 2013). Also known as '*The Open Society by One of its Enemies*'. On this point, see the remarks by Alan Ryan in the introduction to the volume cited.

*Table 5.3*: Different Orientations in Political Economy

|  | Globalist | Nationalist |
|---|---|---|
| Socialism | International socialism | National socialism |
| Enterprise | Globalization | ? |

'economic nationalism', or similar. In *Rethinking*, I even suggested at one point that it should be called a policy of 'capitalism in one country', a pun on Stalin's notorious 'socialism in one country'.[19] 'Capitalism in one country', presumably anathema to Stalin, is meant to refer to the prospects for a non-socialist domestic economy having the ability to control its own economic destiny by putting in place the appropriately expansionary policies.

As I see it, the expression '*monetary* mercantilism' (emphasis added), which I have also used previously, can be taken to mean much the same kind of thing. This term is not meant to refer to protectionism as such but, rather, in the specific context of the open economy, again to a general policy of stimulating effective demand by various financial and monetary techniques (and thereby trying to bring about full employment, economic growth, and general prosperity). As just explained, such policies might indeed also be understood as having a similar impact on the balance of payments and the foreign debt position to those of conventional protectionism (*cf.* also *Lecture 3*), but that is not their primary purpose. The primary purpose is expansion as such. The terminology is far from ideal, mainly because of the negative connotations of the term 'mercantilist' to almost all professional economists and apparently, it now seems from recent political debates, to all shades of political opinion. Some such convenient expression, however, clearly *is* needed to denote the space between international socialism, on the one hand, and 'free trade', 'globalism', 'the power of market forces' (and so forth) on the other.

Keynes, interestingly, did seem to concur with this argument at one stage in his career. For example, Chapter 23 of the *General Theory* is titled 'Notes on Mercantilism, the Usury Laws, Stamped Money and Theories of Under-Consumption'. According to Keynes[20];

---

[19] Joseph Stalin, *Foundations of Leninism: Lectures Delivered at the Sverdlov University*, 1924 (As reprinted by Foreign Languages Press, Peking: 1975).
[20] Keynes, *General Theory*.

For some 200 years both economic theorists and practical men did not doubt that there is a peculiar advantage to a country in a favourable balance of trade, and grave danger in an unfavourable balance, particularly *if it results in an efflux of the precious metals* (emphasis added). But for the past 100 years there has been a remarkable divergence of opinion. The majority of statesmen and practical men in most countries, and nearly half of them even in Great Britain, the home of the opposite view, have remained faithful to the ancient doctrine; whereas almost all economic theorists have held that anxiety concerning such matters is absolutely groundless, except on a very short view, since the mechanism of foreign trade is self-adjusting[21] and attempts to interfere with it are not only futile but greatly impoverish those who practice them because they forfeit the advantages of the international division of labour. It will be convenient, in accordance with tradition, to designate the older opinion as *Mercantilism* and the newer as *Free Trade* (original emphasis), though these terms, since each of them has both a narrower and broader signification, must be interpreted with reference to the context.

And later he goes on to say;

Let me first state in my own terms what now seems to me to be the element of scientific truth in mercantilist doctrine[22] ... Given the social and political environment and the national characteristics which determine the propensity to consume, the well-being of a progressive state essentially depends, for the reasons we have already explained, on the sufficiency of ... inducements ... [to invest]. They may be found either in home investment or foreign investment (including in the latter the accumulation of the precious metals), which, between them, make up aggregate investment. In conditions in which the quantity of investment is

---

[21] In empirical practice this seems to be the very thing that the 'mechanism of foreign trade' is *not*.

[22] Keynes goes on to say, 'It should be understood that the advantages claimed are avowedly national advantages and are unlikely to benefit the world as a whole'. In my view this is wrong. In world of floating exchange rates and sovereign national currencies, if all jurisdictions simultaneously pursue expansionary policies the result will be trade balance *via* exchange rate adjustment, and a global increase in growth. See what follows.

determined by the profit motive alone,[23] opportunities for home investment will be governed, in the long-run, by the domestic rate of interest;
whilst the volume of foreign investment is necessarily determined by the
size of the favourable balance of trade. Thus, in a society in which there
is no question of direct investment under the aegis of public authority,
the economic objects, with which it is reasonable for the government to
be preoccupied, are the domestic rate of interest and the balance of foreign trade.

As mentioned, it has always seemed to me this is a quite different argument from protectionism as such (the active advocacy of tariffs or non-
tariff barriers to trade). As for the latter, it does seem reasonable to argue,
as economists have done for centuries, that conventional protectionist
measures are unlikely to achieve the results claimed for them. Most likely
they would have negative macroeconomic effects similar to those of
higher taxes as discussed in *Lecture 3*.

Later in his career, Keynes seemed to back off from these opinions, and
he played a major role in the negotiations leading up to the founding of the
ill-fated Bretton Woods system that dominated the immediate post WW2 years.
At one point, he even defended the Bretton Woods agreement, in a speech to
the British House of Lords in 1944, with the following words[24];

We are determined that, in future, the external value of sterling shall
conform to its internal value as set by our own domestic policies, and
not the other way round. Secondly, we intend to retain control over our
domestic rate of interest so that we can keep it as low as suits our own
purposes, without interference from the ebb and flow of capital move-
ments or flights of hot money. Thirdly, whilst we intend to prevent inflation at home we will not accept deflation at the dictate of influences
from the outside. In other words, we abjure the instruments of bank rate
and credit contraction operating through the increase of unemployment
as a means of forcing our domestic economy in line with external factors. Have those responsible for the monetary proposals been sufficiently careful to preserve these principles from the possibility of

[23] Note the direct analogy here to the formulation in my AMM as it has been set out in these
*Lectures*.
[24] As quoted by John Smithin and Bernard Wolf, 'What would be a "Keynesian" approach
to currency and exchange rate issues?' (*Review of Political Economy* 5, 1993).

interference? *I hope your Lordships will trust me not to have turned my back on all I have fought for.* To establish those three principles I have just stated has been my main task for the last 20 years ... Am I so faithless ... that at the very moment of triumph of these ideas ... I go off to help forge new chains to hold us fast in the old dungeon? I trust, my Lords, that you will not believe it ... It is above all as providing an international framework for the new ideas ... that these proposals are not least to be welcomed. (emphasis added)

But it is obvious that Keynes did have considerable doubts. I am not sure that 'trust me' is ever the best policy advice, regardless of where it comes from. The only saving grace of the Bretton Woods regime was that in principle at least, it was a regime of fixed but *adjustable* exchange rates. In practice, adjustments were only made with great fanfare amid political controversy. They invariably devolved into an old-fashioned exchange rate crisis of the traditional type. Bretton Woods was not Keynes's finest hour. He was on much firmer theoretical ground when writing the *General Theory* than he was to be a decade later under the pressure of events.

## 5.12   Conclusion

The framework set out in this chapter has been able to illustrate in more detail the various growth scenarios for an open economy. The key to 'capitalism in one country' is the existence of a separate monetary and financial system with either a floating exchange rate regime, or a fixed-but-adjustable regime in which adjustments can be made as required without political or other difficulties. This framework is also capable of explaining the problems experienced by jurisdictions that are not in a comparable state of affairs, such as those trapped in the hopeless situations of either an irrevocably fixed exchange rate, or in a currency union with no adequate system of fiscal federalism.

It is not correct to describe the 'monetary mercantilist' approach as similar to the much derided 'beggar-thy-neighbor' policies of the 1930s. It is true that if only one country pursues the type of policy suggested here, and the others do not, then this will be to the first mover's sole advantage. They may eventually gain a hegemonic position and build up a commercial or political empire, as has certainly occurred historically. However, our analysis also strongly suggests that the principles of monetary economics, correctly understood, mean that the world economy is not a zero-sum game. If each nation, always given the necessary socio-political pre-conditions in them all, were to pursue the same type of policy simultaneously, the result would be higher overall world growth and eventual balance across both the current and capital accounts of the balance of payments *via* exchange rate adjustment. There seems to be nothing, therefore, to preclude the economic analyst offering similar policy advice to each jurisdiction separately. It is up to the decision-makers in each case to decide whether or not to accept the advice, and thereby whether they end up as creditors, debtors, or in balance.[25]

---

[25] Eric Kam and John Smithin, 'Unequal partners: The role of international financial flows and the exchange rate regime' (*Journal of Economic Asymmetries* 5, 2008).

# Lecture 6

# Interest Rates, Inflation, and Economic Instability

## 6.1 Introduction

I think it is fair to say that the previous *Lectures* in this series have already provided enough material for a comprehensive explanation of both economic growth and the ups and downs of the business cycle. The various possible co-movements of the inflation rate with the rate of growth of real GDP have also been discussed. Still more detail on the interrelationships of growth, the cycle, and inflation was provided in *Rethinking*.

However, any discussion of business cycle fluctuations, popularly known as episodes of 'boom' and 'bust', must inevitably raise the question of whether or not the enterprise (or capitalist) economy is somehow inherently unstable.[1] And if so what, if anything, can be done about it? This is obviously an idea that goes all the way back to Karl Marx. As already stated in *Lecture 2*, and to repeat my own words from that chapter, in Marx's opinion 'there will be an ever-worsening series of crises, and the eventual demise of the system is inherent in its own logic'. Naturally enough, whenever dramatic economic and financial crises do occur, as in the historical and more recent examples discussed in previous *Lectures*, this sort of argument will seem to be reinforced.

---

[1] Smithin, *Rethinking*; and Smithin, *Essays*.

In a perceptive review of *Rethinking*, Philip Armstrong has characterized my own approach to the issues in the following way[2];

> Before applying the model to explain complex macroeconomic phenomena, Smithin considers the question of whether a monetary production economy should be viewed as *inherently* unstable (original emphasis). At this point Smithin's work comes into confrontation with Hyman Minsky's financial fragility hypothesis (Minsky, 1986). Smith[in] depicts Minsky's approach as akin to that of the Austrian school in the sense that both regard excessive credit expansion as the root of macroeconomic instability. However, Smithin notes that Minsky and the Austrian school (the latter represented by Salin, 2014) disagree on the causes of the excessive issuance of credit: for Minsky, it is the result of the private sector's aggressive pursuit of profit and unjustified appetite for risk; from the Austrian perspective it is rooted in expansionary monetary and fiscal policy on the part of the state.
>
> Whereas Minsky and the Austrians would favour 'turning off the [credit] tap', Smithin argues, in common with Keynes, that credit creation is the lifeblood of the economy and the tap must therefore be kept open. Smithin believes that stability can be achieved by adopting the correct approach to monetary policy. He places his faith in a real interest rate rule as the best way to avoid instability. Smithin's advocacy of a real interest rate policy rule is what distinguishes his approach from other non-mainstream models (which otherwise generally share the first four features of his AMM).[3]

This quote from Armstrong, therefore, does introduce in a concise manner a number of the key issues that need to be addressed. As such, it can usefully serve as the starting point for the rest of the discussion in this *Lecture*.

## 6.2 Credit, Economic and Financial Instability, and Crisis

Hyman Minsky had the reputation of being a 'Post Keynesian' economist, and therefore of being broadly sympathetic to Keynesian ideas, whereas

---

[2] Philip Armstrong, 'Review of *Rethinking the Theory of Money, Credit and Macroeconomics by John Smithin*' (*Review of Political Economy* 31, 2018).
[3] The initials AMM stand for 'alternative monetary model'.

the proponents of Austrian business cycle theory such as Hayek and von Mises were explicitly anti-Keynesian. Nonetheless, in his original PhD thesis Minsky acknowledged the strong influence of Hayek and others on the early development of his thought.[4] Of course, as the quote from Armstrong indicates, the Austrians themselves did not think that the enterprise economy as such was inherently unstable. On the contrary, they believed that if left to itself the market economy would always be self-stabilizing, or self-organizing. They did think, however, that excessive credit creation by the monetary authorities, or by the government generally, could very easily destabilize it. They were worried about instability, but according to their ideas this would be the fault of the government, not the private sector. The system itself is not inherently unstable.

And, in fact, Minsky himself readily concedes at least the possibility that there might be a stable configuration of the financial system. In a passage setting out the basic thesis of his 'financial instability hypothesis' (FIH),[5] he writes;

> ... [the] first theorem of the financial instability hypothesis is that the economy [does] ha[ve] financing regimes in which it is stable.

In principle, therefore, there is at least some set of conceivable arrangements in which crisis and instability may be avoided. In practice, however, so Minsky goes on to argue, and *particularly* whenever the system seems to have been succeeding in delivering prosperity for a time, this has a tendency to unravel. The positive experience of the boom itself triggers further excessive credit creation (this time from the private sector) who have been lulled into a sense of false security;

> ... the second theorem ... is that over periods of prolonged prosperity, the economy transits from financial relations that make for a static system to financial relations that make for an unstable system.

A main difference from the Austrian argument is that the culprits are thought not to be the various government agencies but, rather, private sector

---

[4] Jan Toporowski, 'Minsky's induced investment and business cycles' (*Cambridge Journal of Economics* 32, 2008).

[5] Hyman Minsky, 'The financial instability hypothesis', Working Paper No.74, Levy Economics Institute, 1992.

financial actors in their greed in the pursuit of profit. It is significant that the system is supposed to be prone to this state of affairs most particularly after a period of prosperity when otherwise the economy seems to have been performing well. This is somewhat different to the traditional Marxian notion of the falling rate of profit, but nonetheless the argument once again seems to be along the lines that the underlying logic of the system will bring about its own downfall. The sequences of boom and bust or, to describe them in Minsky's own words, 'inflations and debt deflations which have the potential to spin out of control',[6] are thought to occur because of the very nature of the banking and financial system. A disturbing feature of the narrative from the Keynesian point of view is that this must also tend to bring into question the long-term viability of the traditional Keynesian methods for rescuing the economy from the slump. These certainly do entail credit creation and reflation. Supposing that the government has responded responsibly in a crisis, and that broadly Keynesian policies have succeeded for a time, what then? Once prosperity has been restored, all this then would seem to do is set the stage for another crisis at some point in the future. This is why there is something of a convergence with the avowedly anti-Keynesian, but similarly pessimistic, Austrian analysis, even though the latter starts from a different set of underlying premises.

In the above quotation, Armstrong states that this is the point at which my own system, meaning by this the AMM and so on (as discussed in previous *Lectures*), comes into confrontation with that of Minsky. However, I don't think that the expression 'confrontation' is quite the right way to put it. It is quite true that the argument of previous *Lectures* has been that a Keynes-type solution will always be available, at least given the background of an appropriate monetary policy. Nonetheless, in my view, the task at hand is more accurately described as that of being able to explain precisely the conditions under which the outright instability described by Minsky becomes a reality. And, when such conditions occur, what to do about them. Certainly, the phenomena of periodic severe financial and economic crises are themselves real, as the present generation has now learned on several occasions within our own lifetimes.

For a complete explanation of the boom and bust phenomenon, we need to be clear, I would argue, about two specific points. These are, firstly, what exactly is the causal mechanism that sets off the boom in the first place? What converts the putatively stable regime into an unstable

---

[6] Minsky, 'The financial ...'.

one? Secondly, what is the precise turning point that eventually provokes the crisis, the 'Minsky moment' as some writers have taken to calling it?[7] Can this reliably be identified?

In an endogenous money environment, what needs to be explained in particular is what prevents the credit enhanced boom, inflationary or otherwise, from just going on and on forever. If it were true that there is a fixed supply of base money, it can be easily seen how there might be a limit to the 'money multiplier'. As already explained, however, this does not apply in an accommodative banking environment. Why, therefore, is it not possible simply to keep creating credit indefinitely? This may well cause inflation (but also perhaps *not*, as we have seen in *Lecture 4*, for example) but it is not inevitable that the inflation rate should be 'ever-accelerating'. And regardless of the inflationary or other possible side-effects, what actually is the mechanism which finally is supposed to prevent the central bank, or anyone else, from simply continuing to create credit?

In *Lecture 2* earlier we already quoted a passage from Hayek on this very topic, one to which I have frequently drawn attention in previous work.[8] Hayek was clear that in his system the starting point of the boom was when the policy rate of interest of the central bank was set lower than the supposed natural rate of interest, as in Wicksell.[9] For the turning point, however, the model relied heavily on the existence of a gold standard or similar (unlike in Wicksell's pure credit economy) that was supposed to back up the monetary system and restrain the amount of credit creation that is possible. At one point, in fact, Hayek was pressed about this problem by an otherwise friendly interviewer. On his principles, he was asked, how he could possibly explain the long boom of the late 1940s, 1950s, and 1960s after WW2? At the time this was perceived, correctly in my view, as a vindication of Keynesian rather than Hayekian ideas. This experience seemed to be a very obvious weak point in the argument. Hayek's reply included the partial quote cited in *Lecture 2*, and it will now be useful to write out the whole passage again in full[10];

[7] John Cassidy, 'The Minsky moment', *The New Yorker* (February 04, 2008).

[8] Smithin, *Essays*; Smithin, *Money, Enterprise, and Income Distribution*.

[9] John Smithin and Eric Kam, 'Hicks on Hayek, Keynes, and Wicksell', in Hassan Bougrine and Louis-Philippe Rochon, eds., *Economic Growth and Macroeconomic Stabilization Policies in Post-Keynesian Economics: Essays in Honour of Marc Lavoie and Mario Seccareccia: Book Two* (Cheltenham: Edward Elgar, 2020).

[10] Hayek, *Hayek on Hayek*.

The particular form I gave it was connected with the mechanism of the gold which allowed credit expansion up to a point and then made a certain reversal possible. *I always knew that in principle there was no definite limit for the period to which you could stimulate expansion by rapidly accelerating inflation.* But I just took it for granted that there was a built-in stop in the form of a gold standard, and in that I was a little mistaken in my diagnosis of the postwar development. I knew the boom would break down, but I didn't give it as long as it lasted. That you could maintain an inflationary boom for something like 20 years, I did not anticipate.

While on the one hand, immediately after the war I never believed, as most of my friends did, in an impending depression, I anticipated an inflationary boom. My expectation was that the inflationary boom would last five or six years, as the historical ones had done, forgetting that then the termination was due to the gold standard. If you had no gold standard — if you could continue inflating for much longer — it was very difficult to predict how long it would last. Of course, it has lasted very much longer than I expected. The end result was the same. (emphasis added)

This seems to me to be a quite remarkable statement, particularly in the admission that the author had forgotten about the role the gold standard was supposed to play in choking off the effects of any expansion. From the point of view of the monetary economics of his day, this would clearly have been the central issue in any objective analysis of the situation. How could an expert in the field simply forget such a thing? The italicized phrase above also shows that the author seems to have been well aware that, in principle, in the case of endogenous money there is no absolute limit to an expansion. Note, also, that no real explanation is given as to why 'the end result must be the same' when the stop of the gold standard is no longer relevant. As discussed in *Lecture 4* earlier, in more recent neo-Wicksellian models with endogenous money it has been usual to argue that outcomes hinge on supposed discrepancies between the natural rate of interest and the policy rate of interest, that cannot be maintained. Presumably, Hayek had something like this in mind? But, in a genuine monetary analysis there is no natural rate of interest. It does not exist in reality, and the 'real' economy must simply adjust to whatever is the level of the real rate of interest established in the banking and financial sector. All of this has been sufficiently explained in previous *Lectures*, and the upshot is that under endogenous money there is no automatic check on expansion as there would be in a gold standard. Any practical checks that the theorist *supposes* to be in place must therefore be based on behavioural or political assumptions, or by invoking some other non-monetary constraint (including the traditional assumption of a natural rate itself). The same logic must apply, equally so, to the various narratives that have been constructed in the spirit of Minsky. (For example, to take just one argument frequently seen in the literature, that there is some desired debt/asset ratio on the part of the various actors that will provoke a pull-back/retrenchment when violated.)

To return to Hayek's own analysis, another objection is to the rather casual use of the idea of an 'inflationary boom', suggesting that every improvement in economic fortune must come at the price of an unacceptably higher rate of inflation. It is simply not true, as the discussion of the AMM in previous *Lectures* has already shown, that every boom will be accompanied by a rate of inflation that gets out of hand. Indeed, in the specific case of the postwar boom as discussed by Hayek, the very high rates of inflation did not appear until the 1970s, and then not in the context of a boom at all but rather that of 'stagflation', high inflation accompanied by high unemployment. This was around 40 years or so after the first discussion of Keynesian ideas in the 1930s and therefore was certainly not a vindication of the predictions of Hayek, nor of those friends mentioned in the above quote. The main point to be established, I think, is that neither in my AMM, nor more importantly in the real world, does the logic of the vertical long-run Phillips curve apply. All combinations of inflation and economic growth are possible, and all have indeed actually occurred in history. On this issue, I would like to quote my own words from an encyclopedia entry on the topic of inflation from some years ago[11];

> Inflation is a complex social process, and it seems unlikely on the face of it that there is any one explanation of the phenomenon that is valid for all times and all places. Empirically, all possible combinations of growth and inflation have been observed in reality, high growth with high inflation (an inflationary boom), low growth with low inflation (a depression), low

---

[11] John Smithin, 'Inflation', in John King, ed., *The Elgar Companion to Post Keynesian Economics*, second edition (Cheltenham: Edward Elgar, 2012).

growth with high inflation (stagflation), and, more benignly, non-inflationary growth.

The argument I was making is that any theory of inflation, and for that matter any theory of economic growth or the business cycle worth its salt, has to be able to handle all of these cases equally well, not just one of them.

In case of a supposed inflationary boom, therefore, we continue to be faced with the twin problems of just what it is that sets off boom in the first place and, then, what explains the turning point or crisis. The next section will look into these issues in more detail and make the argument that the most important issue is not the distinction between the mythical natural rate and the policy rate, but rather the genuine difference that exists between real and nominal rates of interest. It is necessary to pay close attention to this distinction, and combine it with the fact that in an endogenous money environment the causes of changes in the inflation rate are many and varied.

In terms of the big picture for political economy, the main significance of the overall argument is that, as already stressed in the quote from Armstrong above, the existing explanations for the boom and bust cycle, seemingly from all sides, focus on the idea that 'excessive' credit and money creation (in some sense), and from whatever source public or private, is at the root of the problem. Further that the excesses can be cured by 'turning off the tap' as Armstrong puts it, either by regulation, tight fiscal policy, high interest rates, or some other method. The problem with this kind of argument is always that, in suggesting various methods to choke off the prior boom *via* restrictions on credit, we lose sight of the vital point that some substantial amount of credit and money creation is still going to be required even for the normal functioning of the system. In particular, this is a necessity for the realization of money profits which in turn are a prerequisite if there are ever going to be real profits, strong economic growth, full employment, and high real wages. Going 'cold turkey', to switch the analogy from hydraulics to that of a medical addiction, is not an option. In yet another medical allusion, Joseph Schumpeter apparently once wrote disparagingly of the various recovery policies put in place in the 1930s as 'capitalism in an oxygen tent'.[12] However, the patient will die if the air supply is cut off altogether. Keynes, on the other

---

[12]As quoted by Robert Solow, 'Heavy thinker' (*New Republic*, May 21, 2007).

hand, *did* seem to see the fundamental difficulty. In *Lecture 4* earlier, we have already quoted his statement about the need to keep the economy in a state of 'semi boom' rather than 'semi slump'.[13] This, it seems to me, is the basic difference between an essentially Keynesian approach to economic difficulties and the other suggested remedies at both ends of the political spectrum. The alternatives would tend to keep the economy permanently in a slow growth, high unemployment, low wage mode. This is not going to be a situation that is politically sustainable regardless of who is administering it.

## 6.3  The Demand for and Supply of Endogenous Money, Revisited

To explore the various questions about the stability of the system in more technical detail, first recall the following simple model of the supply of and demand for endogenous money from *Lecture 3*. The endogenous supply of money was expressed as multiple of the lagged nominal wage bill, and the 'voluntary' demand for money as a fraction of nominal GDP;

$$Ms = \phi W_{-1}N_{-1}, \qquad \phi > 1 \tag{6.1}$$

$$Md = \psi PY. \qquad 0 < \psi < 1 \tag{6.2}$$

The symbol $M$ stands for the total of the broad money supply in period $\tau$, consisting primarily of commercial bank deposits of one kind or another, and $W_{-1}N_{-1}$ is the aggregate nominal wage bill of the previous period. As already explained in *Lectures 2* and *3,* for the industrial system to be viable, in the sense of being able to generate positive monetary profits in the aggregate, the coefficient $\phi$ must actually be greater than one. The coefficient thus represents all other types of borrowing over and above that needed to finance the aggregate wage bill. Recall also that there is implicitly a one-period production lag in the model, whereby the expression $Y = AN_{-1}$ maps lagged labour input into the current level of GDP. The equilibrium condition in the money market is therefore that the voluntary demand for money in the current period, the willingness of agents to hold

---

[13] Keynes, *General Theory.*

commercial bank deposits created in the previous period through the current period, should be equal to the money supply currently in existence;

$$Md = Ms. \tag{6.3}$$

From equations (6.1), (6.2), and (6.3), it can therefore be seen that the value of the aggregate price level, $P$, must satisfy, in the sense of being consistent with;

$$P = (\phi/\psi)(W_{-1}/A). \tag{6.4}$$

The expression for $P$ thus includes the ratio of the two terms $\phi$ and $\psi$, from the supply side and demand side of the money market, respectively. In the earlier treatment in *Lecture 3,* the natural logarithm of the ratio $(\phi/\psi)$ was defined *as $p_0 = \ln\phi - \ln\psi$* and the term $p_0$ was interpreted as an inverse measure of liquidity preference specifically in the sense of Keynes's general notions of 'bullishness' and 'bearishness' from the *Treatise on Money.* Next, dividing equation (6.4) through by the lagged price level, $P_{-1}$, and taking natural logarithms, we can also see that the inflation rate (lowercase $p$) must itself satisfy;

$$p = p_0 + w_{-1} - a. \tag{6.5}$$

For the present purpose, of investigating the question of inflationary and deflationary instability, we now propose a somewhat more complicated specification for the behaviour of the ratio $(\phi/\psi)$ than was used in *Lecture 3.* This is as follows;

$$\phi/\psi = [(\phi_0/\psi_0)]e^{-\lambda(r_{+1} - r)}. \quad 0 < \lambda < 1 \tag{6.6}$$

What this adds to the mix is another version of Keynes's theory of liquidity preference, namely, that of the 'speculative demand for money' from the *General Theory.* In the case of endogenous money, and as already mentioned, there must also be a speculative *supply* of money arising from bank loans for all other purposes than the wage bill. (These sums certainly do include all borrowing done for financial speculation as such, but also borrowing for things like autonomous consumption spending, capital spending, *etc.*, each of which has a significant forward-looking aspect.) When they are making economic decisions in period $\tau$, the various economic agents, and the central bank itself, are presumed to share short-term expectations of economic variables one period forward in $\tau_{+1}$, based on information generally available to all.[14]

It is important also to realize that the two relevant monetary ratios, $\phi$ and $\psi$, are themselves real variables, that is, dollar values divided by price indices. Therefore the speculation that is going on must be supposed to be about real asset prices and real interest rates. This is actually a somewhat different argument to that of Keynes who, in common with most economic writers of his day, seemed to be interested only in nominal interest rates and nominal asset prices. Taking natural logarithms once again, we obtain;

$$ln\phi - ln\psi = (ln\phi_0 - ln\psi_0) - \lambda(r_{+1} - r), \qquad (6.7)$$

The $p_0$ term from *Lecture 3* can now be re-defined as $p_0 = (ln\phi_0 - ln\psi_0)$, and equation (6.7) can thus be re-written as;

$$ln\phi - ln\psi = p_0 - \lambda(r_{+1} - r). \qquad (6.8)$$

There are now two slightly different notions of liquidity preference represented in equation (6.8). The $p_0$ term can still be thought of as representing the purely 'psychological' element of liquidity preference, so to speak, such as is implied by the expressions bullishness and bearishness from Keynes's *Treatise*. The $\lambda$ term, meanwhile, is essentially the interest elasticity of the genuinely speculative demand for money. Going back to equation (6.4), and again taking natural logarithms and substituting into (6.8), it is therefore possible to derive a somewhat different expression for inflation than that in (6.5), as follows;

$$p = p_0 - \lambda(r_{+1} - r) + w_{-1} - a. \qquad (6.9)$$

This expression provides another, slightly different, account of the various possible influences on inflation. It involves all the same factors as in (6.5), but now also includes expected changes in the real rate of interest *via* the impact of the interest elasticity parameter $\lambda$.

---

[14] The important distinction made by Keynes between long-term and short-term expectations was discussed earlier, in *Lecture 3*.

## 6.4 A Real Interest Rate Rule for Monetary Policy?

To focus now on the question of inflationary or deflationary instability as such, notice that if the economy has indeed been able somehow to get into a real equilibrium (with respect to the growth rate, real wages, *etc.*), the inflation equation becomes simply;

$$p = p_0 - \lambda(r_{+1} - r) + w - a, \tag{6.10}$$

where $w$ is the equilibrium real wage rate. I do not mean to suggest by this that in the real world inflationary and real economic instability are unconnected, and there will be more discussion of this important issue in what follows. The point of the exercise at this stage is merely to focus solely on the mathematics of the inflation dynamics.

We are now therefore in a position to be able to complete the discussion of inflation stability or instability *per se* by adding the following two equations drawn from the AMM, and already introduced in previous *Lectures*;

$$i = m_0 + m_1 i_0. \qquad 0 < m_1 < 1 \tag{6.11}$$

$$r = i - p. \tag{6.12}$$

Here, equation (6.11) is the monetary policy transmissions mechanism expressed in nominal terms, as explained in *Lectures 1* and *3*. The symbol $i$ is the nominal market rate of interest on money, $i_0$ is the nominal policy rate of interest set by the central bank, $m_1$ is the pass-through coefficient, and $m_0$ is the average commercial bank mark-up between deposit rates and lending rates. In equation (6.12), $p$ is taken to stand for the currently observed inflation rate, and $r$ is the inflation-adjusted real interest rate. As we have already seen in *Lecture 1*, for example, equations (6.11) and (6.12) together yield a version of the 'forced saving' or 'Mundell–Tobin' effect[15] of the following form;

$$r = m_0 + m_1 r_0 - (1 - m_1)p. \tag{6.13}$$

---

[15] Eric Kam, 'A note on time preference and the Tobin effect' (*Economics Letters* 89, 2005).

In principle, therefore, there is a negative relation between the inflation rate and the real rate of interest on money (as also discussed in previous *Lectures*).

With the above materials in place, it is thus possible to discover the actual source of inflationary or deflationary instability. There will be instability whenever the central bank adopts a peg, or target, for the nominal policy rate of interest, rather than a target for the real policy rate. It does not matter whether the nominal interest rate is set at a 'high' or 'low' level. Moreover, whatever the nominal target may be, the instability can go in either direction. In my opinion, these are findings that are ultimately of the utmost *practical* importance. Historically, setting the nominal rate of interest, in one way or another, is exactly the way in which monetary policy usually has been conducted. This dates from the earliest history of central banking (with its frequent discussions about setting the 'bank rate' or the 'discount rate'), right down to the present day. These circumstances therefore do go a very long way toward explaining much of the actual instability, both inflationary and deflationary, that has been observed in history.

For a clear-cut example, consider the likely consequences of a 'zero interest rate policy' (ZIRP). This is a proposal which has, in fact, been put forward on several occasions by the contemporary school of modern monetary theory (MMT). As already explained, the underlying premise of MMT is that a sovereign government, with its own currency and a floating exchange rate, faces no purely financial constraints — and this is a premise fully shared with the AMM. The ZIRP itself, however, is not so much part of the core structure of that particular argument but, rather, a policy recommendation that happens to be favoured by several prominent members of the school. The idea is simply that the nominal policy rate of interest of the central bank should be set or left at zero;

$$i_0 = 0. \tag{6.14}$$

I choose this example of a ZIRP, not only because of the presumptions about fiscal policy and taxation that the current approach shares with MMT, but also because, as stated earlier in this book, I have also been a long-time advocate of 'low' policy rates of interest and of 'rules' rather than 'discretion' in monetary policy.[16] It seems to be important, therefore,

---

[16] Smithin, *Controversies.*

to be clear exactly what expressions like 'low' or 'zero', when referring to policy rates of interest, should actually be taken to mean. Indeed, I have recently made the case that zero *real* policy rate (ZRPR) would be a 'near-optimal' monetary policy.[17] This would be along the lines of;

$$i_0 - p = r_0 = 0. \tag{6.15}$$

Evidently, the crucial difference between (6.14) and (6.15) is whether it is a real or a nominal interest rate that is set at zero. (Nothing, however, in the argument to follow, actually hinges on the choice of the particular numerical target of zero. The same reasoning about real *versus* nominal interest rates will apply whatever the specific numerical value of the target.)

Continuing with the case of a ZIRP in nominal terms, next apply equation (6.14) to equations (6.10) and (6.13). This results in the following dynamic expression for inflation;

$$p = p_0 + w - a + \lambda(p_{+1} - p). \tag{6.16}$$

Lagging by one period and re-arranging then yields the following difference equation in the rate of inflation;

$$p = [(1 + \lambda)/\lambda]p_{-1} - (1/\lambda)(p_0 + w - a). \tag{6.17}$$

This is clearly unstable as the coefficient $[(1 + \lambda)/\lambda]$ is greater than one. Therefore, whenever participants in financial markets are operating along the lines of Keynes's 'speculative' theory of the demand for money and the real rate of interest is allowed to change because the nominal policy rate of the central bank is not adjusted appropriately, the rate of inflation cannot be stabilized.

I had originally made this argument in two papers published in 2016, which were intended as a commentary on an exchange between two prominent members of the MMT school, namely Eric Tymoigne and L. Randall Wray, and their 'critics' as represented by Thomas

---

[17] John Smithin, 'Interest rates, income distribution, and the monetary policy transmissions mechanism under endogenous money: What have we learned thirty years on from horizontalists and verticalists?' (*European Journal of Economics and Economic Policies*: *Intervention* 17, 2020).

Palley.[18] Moreover, the relevance of this result for the evaluation of a ZIRP in the given context has not been disputed. At the same time, however, I also made the familiar assertion from my own writings that an alternative real interest rate rule would suffice to promote both inflation stability and general economic stability. This is an argument that I have consistently been making, both formally and informally, for the past 25 years and more.[19] It was not perhaps strictly pertinent to the exchange between Tymoigne/Wray and Palley, as neither camp advocates a real interest rate rule, but nonetheless seemed to be in place as an aside to the main discussion. Somewhat to my surprise this last statement did attract some attention and debate. For example, Martin Watts, another prominent member of the MMT school,[20] has made a number of useful contributions, intended as a defence of ZIRP,[21] which discuss various technical mathematical issues around the specification and solution of difference equations (and also point out some algebraic slips, sign errors, missed typos, *etc.*, on my part, for which I am most grateful).

For instance, Watts has noticed that in the specific circumstances under discussion in the above passage the simplest possible version of a real rate rule, that is, a rule of the form $i_0 - p = r_0$ exactly as in (6.15) will also fail to achieve the goal of inflation stability. Watts's contention does turn out to be formally (that is, mathematically) correct in this particular case. Nonetheless, in terms of the underlying political economy I don't think that this materially affects the general case for adopting a real rate rule of some sort, rather than simply a nominal peg. In the first place, it obviously does not overturn the argument *against* a nominal peg.

---

[18] John Smithin, 'Endogenous money, fiscal policy, interest rates, and the exchange rate regime: a comment on Palley, Tymoigne, and Wray' (*Review of Political Economy* 28, 2016); John Smithin; 'Endogenous money, fiscal policy, interest rates and the exchange rate regime: correction' (*Review of Political Economy* 28, 2016).

[19] Smithin, *Controversies.*

[20] William Mitchell, L. Randall Wray, and Martin Watts, *Macroeconomics* (London: Red Globe Press, 2019).

[21] Martin Watts, 'Fiscal policy and the Post Keynesians' (paper presented at the AHE annual conference, Glasgow, Scotland, July 2016; 'The merits of economic modelling: an application to interest rate policy' (manuscript, University of Newcastle, NSW, Australia, 2018); 'The methodology for assessing interest policy rules: Some comments' (*European Journal of Economics and Economic Policies: Intervention* 18, 2021).

Secondly, and as will be shown in what follows, the formal problem is itself easily remedied by the adoption of a real rate rule only slightly more sophisticated than the very simplest version but which nonetheless has the desired effect of stabilizing the real policy rate at the target level (zero or otherwise), and thereby also stabilizing the inflation rate. It has never been suggested, by the way, that a real rate rule is ever going to be able to achieve any particular target for the inflation rate, much less actual price stability, or zero inflation. To do that is well beyond the scope of monetary policy alone. (It would require also a contribution from fiscal policy and, as already explained in previous *Lectures*, may well have serious adverse consequences for the real economy.) Thirdly, going beyond the particular mathematical specifications and arguments used here and elsewhere in the literature, it can be argued that, in general the mere commitment on the part of the monetary authorities to a real rate rule of some kind (as opposed to simply setting the nominal policy rate) will inevitably cause market participants to change the way in which their economic expectations are formed. What I mean by this is simply that the financial actors will not be able to speculate if there is nothing to speculate about.

Nevertheless, to see both sides of the mathematical argument and its formal solution (and for the sake of completeness) first note that if we let the term $r_0$ stand for the target itself and the target is zero, the simplest version of the real rate rule will be as in (6.15). Then, using equation (6.15) in equations (6.13) and (6.10), the following difference equation in the expected rate of inflation will emerge;

$$p_{+1} = \{[1 + \lambda(1 - m_1)]/\lambda(1 - m_1)\}p - [1/\lambda(1 - m_1)(p_0 + w - a)]. \quad (6.18)$$

Again lagging by one period, the difference equation in the actual rate of inflation rate turns out to be as follows;

$$p = \{[(1 + \lambda(1 - m_1)]/\lambda(1 - m_1)\}p_{-1} - [1/\lambda(1 - m_1)(p_0 + w - a)]. \quad (6.19)$$

As Watts has argued, this dynamic process has precisely the same issues as that examined in equation (6.17) above. It is unstable.

However, only a slight modification to the real rate rule quickly eliminates the difficulty. The specific rule which works in the present case is;

$$i_0 - p = r_0 + [(1 - m_1)/m_1]p, \quad (6.20)$$

which reduces to;

$$i_0 - p = r_0 + (1/m_1)p. \qquad (6.21)$$

This would apply for any specified target value of $r_0$, but here we are particularly interested in the case where the target is zero,

$$r_0 = 0. \qquad (6.22)$$

Therefore, using equations (6.21), (6.22) and (6.13) in equation (6.10), it can readily be shown that;

$$\lambda(r_{+1} - r) = \lambda[m_0 + (1 - m_1)p_{+1} - (1 - m_1)p_{+1} - m_0 - (1 - m_1)p + (1 - m_1)p] = 0. \qquad (6.23)$$

The second term on the right-hand side (RHS) of equations (6.9) and (6.10) thus disappears, and the inflation rate converges to;

$$p = p_0 + w - a. \qquad (6.24)$$

In my view, this result is generalizable to all other specifications of both the inflation equation itself and the particular real rate rule, whatever it turns out to be, that might be relevant in each different case. (Another simple example will be taken up and discussed in the next section of this chapter.) Clearly, however, no such solution will be available when there is only a nominal interest rate target.

Equation (6.24) is nothing other than the original inflation equation used in previous *Lectures*. Cost and productivity changes are still taken into account, as are the original parameters of the money demand and supply functions. However, these parameters now once again reflect only the general notion of liquidity preference, in the sense of Keynes's bullishness *versus* bearishness from the *Treatise*, rather than the later idea of the speculative demand for money. Changes in the general attitude of bullishness or bearishness still do affect real interest rates in the market-place, just as Keynes himself suggested. But, the potentially even more damaging type of financial speculation, as outlined in the theory of the speculative demand for money in the *GT*, is no longer present. This has been eliminated by the real rate rule itself, and this is the most important contribution that such a rule can make. The various effects of 'changes in the real policy rate', worked out in the context of the macroeconomic theory in *Lectures 3, 4,* and *5* above, can now be interpreted as referring directly to changes in the target.

## 6.5  Rules *versus* Discretion in Monetary Policy: the Case of the AMM

In another relevant contribution, Watts and a co-author, George Pantelopoulos,[22] have recently defended the overall case for 'rules rather than discretion' in monetary policy. They are in agreement with the basic argument made in this set of *Lectures* that (in their words) 'interest rate setting should be subject to rules … rather than remaining discretionary', and also, as a corollary, 'that agile fiscal policy should be the main policy instrument'. Among the issues, however, that they think are still subject to debate are some of those we have been discussing in the present *Lecture*, such as whether the policy rate or a market rate should be targeted, and whether the target should be expressed in real or nominal terms. My own view, of course, is firmly that the policy rate should be targeted and that the target should be expressed in real terms.

The authors have also criticized what they call 'incomplete' models of the inflationary process, by which I take it they mean exercises of the sort undertaken above, with relatively few equations, or just a single equation as, in equation (6.10). Their point seems to be that not only is a single mathematical exercise in itself insufficient to decide the key questions of political economy (which is unobjectionable), but further that even when one, or more, such exercises add to the case against the policy they themselves favour, the results should somehow be discounted if they are not part of a complete and fully specified macroeconomic model. In the absence of any positive case made for the alternative policy recommendation, the latter argument does not seem to me to be methodologically sound. The various technical/mathematical questions raised earlier by Watts himself have already been answered, which therefore just leaves the general methodological point about incompleteness to be discussed. That

---

[22] Martin Watts and George Pantelopoulos, 'Should the implementation of monetary policy be subject to rules?' (in Steven Pressman and John Smithin, eds., *Debates In Monetary Macroeconomics: Tackling Some Unsettled Questions*, New York: Palgrave Macmillan, 2022).

argument seems to me simply to ignore the wider context of the various 'partial' exercises in the literature under discussion. These do include a number of fully specified macro models, such as my AMM as already set out in these *Lectures*, as well as contributions by a number of other authors.

To further explain the counter-argument it will thus be useful in this section to now revisit the issue of the necessity of a real rather than nominal interest rule in the context of the AMM itself. This will provide both a further example of how a real rate rule is conducive to inflation stability (and, in this case, also general economic stability), as well as an indication of how a fairly simple real rate rule might be implemented in practice.

In what follows the various dynamic equations of the AMM as set out in *Lectures 3* and *4* are repeated, where $y$ as usual stands for the real economic growth rate, $p$ stands for the inflation rate, $k$ stands for the (natural logarithm of) the aggregate mark-up factor, $w$ for the (natural logarithm of) the average real wage rate, $r$ for the real rate of interest, and $r_0$ for the target for the real policy rate. The AMM itself, of course, also includes a large number of other exogenous variables and/or parameters describing such things as the stance of fiscal policy, the current level of productivity and technical progress, and psychological states such as animal spirits or liquidity preference. It is certainly a complete macro model in that sense. In order to focus on the dynamics, however, all the exogenous variables are now set at zero.

| | | | |
|---|---|---|---|
| $y = e_1 k,$ | $0 < e_1 < 1$ | effective demand | (6.25) |
| $k = -r - w_{-1},$ | | income distribution | (6.26) |
| $p = w_{-1},$ | | inflation | (6.27) |
| $w = h_1 y,$ | $0 < h_1 < 1$ | real wages | (6.28) |
| $r = m_1 r_0 - (1 - m_1)p$ | $0 < m_1 < 1$ | real rate of interest | (6.29) |

For comparison with our earlier discussion, we should note that instability due to Keynes's specific notion of the 'speculative demand' for money is not actually present in the AMM. However, there are indeed other sources of instability (including that due to other versions of liquidity preference) that would cause similar problems if not taken into account by the monetary authorities. (The AMM, moreover, does seem to do a good job in simulations of real world economic events in which instability has actually occurred, and might have been prevented by a real rate rule.)[23]

Substituting equations (6.24), (6.25), (6.28), and (6.29) into (6.26) and re-arranging, the following difference equation in the rate of inflation will emerge;

$$p = [e_1h_1(1 - m_1)/(1 + e_1h_1)]p_{-1} - [e_1h_1/(1 + e_1h_1)]r_0 \qquad (6.30)$$

This is convergent as the co-efficient $[e_1h_1(1 - m_1)/(1 + e_1h_1)]$ is a positive fraction, $0 < [e_1h_1(1 - m_1)/(1 + e_1h_1)] < 1$. The equilibrium rate of inflation will therefore be;

$$p = -[e_1h_1/(1 - m_1)]r_0. \qquad (6.31)$$

As we already know, an increase in the target for the real policy rate of interest (which is precisely a 'tight money' policy) will permanently reduce the equilibrium inflation rate.

There is also a parallel first-order difference to equation (6.30) in the real economic growth rate which takes the form

$$y = -e_1h_1m_1y_{-1} - e_1m_1r_0. \qquad (6.32)$$

Equation (6.32) will be 'convergent with oscillations' as the coefficient $-[e_1h_1m_1]$ is a negative fraction, $-1 < -[e_1h_1m_1] < 0$. In this case, there clearly *is* a very close relationship between inflationary, or deflationary, instability and real economic stability or instability. A real interest rate rule of the general form $i_0 = r_0 + p$ delivers both inflation stability and real economic stability.

It does not, however, guarantee either economic prosperity as such or low inflation as such, which are also functions of many other economic variables. The equilibrium growth rate itself, in the truncated system, is given by equation (6.24). As we can see, a lower target value of the real policy rate of interest will lead to higher rate of economic growth and *vice versa*.

$$y = -[e_1m_1/(1 + e_1h_1m_1)]r_0. \qquad (6.24)$$

There will also be three more similarly convergent first-order difference equations for the other endogenous variables, the profit mark-up $k$, the average real wage rate $w$, and the market real rate of interest $r$.

---

[23] Collis, *Three Essays*.

Therefore, in the context of the AMM, and with a straightforward real interest rate rule of the form $i_0 = r_0 - p$, although cyclical behaviour in the economy will continue, and there will be various permutations of the co-movements of the different economic variables, ultimately the dynamic processes are convergent. Therefore, there can be an intelligible and predictable account of the effects of changes in the fiscal policy variables and other economic changes, which will be along the lines of the analysis in *Lectures 3* and *4*.

Once again, in terms of the practical policy discussion, it seems that a real rate rule of some kind is the best general template for central bank operating procedure for a rule-based policy, subject always to modification along the lines discussed in previous sections when proven necessary or desirable. On the other hand, a monetary policy that involves simply pegging, or fixing, the nominal policy rate is highly unlikely to succeed in providing a stable backdrop against which to achieve economic success, or to implement activist fiscal policy.

## 6.6  The Potential, in Practice, for Outright Instability in the Economy

One very clear-cut conclusion, I think, that can be drawn from the above discussion, is that if the monetary authorities are indeed willing to stabilize the real policy rate of interest at a low level, or even at zero, there can be an effective and permanent expansionary policy in which the inflation rate does *not* get out of control. This is quite contrary to the views so often expressed by writers such as Hayek, and many others, over the entire history of classical, neoclassical, and mainstream economics.

In real life (perhaps needless to say) this does not mean that there will never be any more economic difficulties, no more business cycle fluctuations, no economic shocks. Nothing good, or bad, lasts forever. Even when things are going reasonably well, there are always going to be various setbacks and obstructions from time to time. Plenty of candidates for role of the 'efficient cause' of the business cycle have been identified in previous *Lectures*. These include, very prominently, policy mistakes — certainly high on the list in many actual historical situations — changes in business confidence, changes in the financial markets arising from the remaining sources of liquidity preference, changes in the political environment, and so on.

Nonetheless, overall there are three key analytical points that can be made. Firstly, that there is no real difficulty in explaining how such things as a 20 year boom with only moderate inflation can occur or, for that matter (at the other extreme), a long-lasting and seeming intractable depression such as that which faced Keynes in the 1930s. Nor in explaining any other combinations of growth and inflation that may occur. Secondly, given the stabilizing monetary policy described in these *Lectures*, there is actually no inherent or immanent mechanism within the economic or financial sphere, no inexorable market force, that inevitably brings the boom (or slump) to an end. Although there will always be cyclical behaviour, ups and downs of the business cycle, *etc.*, the 'equilibrium' growth rate is itself a *moving* equilibrium. It can permanently change, for better or worse, unless something is done about it, in short a policy initiative of one kind or another. Thirdly, even if, in spite of a stabilizing monetary policy in the form of a real interest rate rule, things do get off track, our previous analysis has already pointed out the several policy options and various routes by which the situation may be rectified.

It is now clear that the various narratives about financial instability, such as Minsky's FIH, are most likely to come into play when the monetary authorities are *not* attempting to stabilize real interest rates. As already stressed, the two key points in developing such a narrative are to discover (a) what actually sets off an unstable boom (for example) in the first place, converting a stable financing regime into an unstable one, and (b) what exactly is the turning point that causes the crisis? The idea of a fixed or 'sticky' nominal policy rate of interest, combined with the underlying theory of inflation set out in these pages, turns out to be sufficient to explain them both. Historically, and down to the present day, that is exactly the way in which central banks have usually conducted monetary policy — focusing solely on setting the nominal policy rate.

In the unstable case, suppose that something occurs to touch off an inflation in the economy, but that the monetary authorities pay no attention to this. They keep the nominal policy rate constant. With nominal interest rates constant, the real rate of interest will fall, and this is what provides the incentive for the transition from the stable to the unstable regime. There will be both a boom and an inflation, but the boom will not be of the steady character that Keynes was looking for. The inflation rate will be unstable, as shown multiple times in the mathematical development of the argument above. Moreover, recall that for simplicity in the mathematical exposition the real economy itself was assumed to be in equilibrium. In the real world, and also in the AMM (as we have just seen), that will obviously not be the case. When the inflation rate is unstable, so also will be the rate of economic growth. The boom will seem to be continuously gathering pace, and the inflation rate will indeed be accelerating.

This argument explains the transition from the stable financial regime to the unstable situation, but we also need to explain the crisis that is supposed to inevitably follow. As already explained, in the endogenous money environment there is really nothing in the purely mathematical logic of the situation to invariably/inevitably cause an abrupt turnaround. However wild a ride it may be, in principle there is nothing to stop the creation of credit and therefore of money going on forever. If so, why not simply 'let the good times roll'? In the field of political economy this seems always to have been an impossibly difficult question to answer. Sir John Hicks, for example, has written that the old classical economists[24];

> ... were *afraid* of that question, for they did not know the answer to it. Yet they felt in their bones that the suggestion in it was wrong. (emphasis added)

Moreover Hicks, like many another economist before and after, also thought that the 'Classics';

> ... were quite right in refusing to look that way, though they did not quite know just *why* they were refusing. (emphasis added)

But Hicks does not explain the *why* of it either. As so often in economics, the generalized 'fears' seem to be based on nothing more than a false analogy to physics — along the lines of 'what goes up must come down'. The meme about economists not knowing exactly why these things happen therefore continues to apply after all these years. They do not know the answer because the possibility of stabilizing the real policy rate, rather than just fixing the nominal rate, has not occurred to them.

How then to explain the eventual onset of the crisis in the unstable case with a fixed nominal interest rate? Some recent mathematical modelling has tried to resolve the issue by the simple device of using nonlinear specifications of the underlying mathematical functions. But this also seems to be based on nothing more than misleading analogies to the physical sciences. No purely mechanical, or mathematical, resolution of

---

[24] John Hicks, *Critical Essays in Monetary Theory* (Oxford: Clarendon Press, 1967).

the problem is able to address the underlying issues of economic sociology and political economy that must be at the root of any genuinely economic explanation.[25] The answer is not so much a question of economic 'laws' or 'market forces' but rather both psychological and explicitly political reactions to the unfolding of events.

As we have seen, if the monetary authorities fail to adjust the nominal interest rate appropriately after an initial inflationary shock, this will set off a boom by reducing real interest rates against the backdrop of a fixed nominal rate. But the opposite, a deflationary shock, can always occur at any point in the future. For example, as we saw in *Lecture 3*, the $p_0$ term, which is the inverse measure of liquidity preference is also one of the main determinants of inflation or deflation. If, therefore, after the boom/inflation has been underway for some time there is a sudden shift toward an attitude of 'bearishness' in the financial markets, and the monetary authorities still do not react, this would be enough to account for the turning point which turns the boom into a recession/depression. Inflation will now be falling, and the real rate of interest rising. Such an increase in liquidity preference is precisely a psychological reaction. It does not have to happen, and may not have done so under different circumstances, or if the economic actors concerned had more faith in the policymakers' ability to control the situation. When such a reaction does occur, it can very easily be part and parcel of the deflationary process, just as Keynes said it would. However, this can hardly be modelled mathematically except as an exogenous change or shift.

In many actual historical episodes of crisis, the boom has often been brought to a premature end *not* by any inevitable market forces but by the deliberate, and arguably politically motivated, policy actions of the central bank. In this case, they no longer leave the nominal policy rate unchanged, but actually raise it to a new higher level enough to reverse the original fall in real interest rates, making them even higher than they were to begin with. Cutting through the obfuscations of conventional economic theory, the reason this sort of thing occurs is that although there may be nothing in the logic/mathematics of the situation to prevent the boom going on forever, there may very well be political objections. Specifically, objections to the changes in income distribution that the boom may bring about. Even though production is booming, there may be, for example, quite 'rational' economic objections from the wealth-holders, or rentiers, who find that the real value of their monetary holdings is falling.

[25] Barrows and Smithin, *Fundamentals*; Smithin, *Rethinking*.

A typical response to the situation, therefore, might be a campaign in the financial press, and by orthodox economists generally, to return to a 'tight money' policy. Indeed, if this was just a question of stabilizing the real rate by raising the nominal policy rate just enough to offset the rate of inflation, and no more, it would do no harm. (That is exactly the policy suggested *via* a ZRPR rule). In actual historical practice, however, the nominal rate has often increased by much more than is necessary, thereby raising the real rate. Also, if/when inflation rates do begin to fall, the nominal rate then tends to be left at the higher level for too long, exacerbating the problem. In this sort of situation the problem is not only a question of the psychology of investors in the stock market. The policymakers are themselves ultimately responsible for causing the crisis. In the late 20th and early 21st centuries, for example, many policymakers and academics subscribed to the so-called 'Taylor principle'[26] which made explicit the view that nominal interest rates should always be raised by *more* than one-for-one with the rate of inflation, and kept at a high level as long as necessary. This misguided idea seems greatly to have contributed to the economic dislocation of the period. If such a reaction is programmed into the system, any boom is always very likely to turn around with a sharp crash, and then deteriorate into a slump. This is, in fact, a concise description of a process that I once called the 'revenge of the rentiers',[27] which in turn was a reference back to Keynes's original, if somewhat hyperbolic, 'euthanasia of the rentier'.[28]

In a doctoral dissertation of 2018, already cited several times in previous *Lectures*,[29] Reid Collis conducted an empirical investigation of some notable booms, downturns, and crises episodes in North America, both in Canada and the USA, using a method which entailed a careful identification of precisely which of the various possible causes of either an upturn or a downturn was operative, and in which temporal sequence. The results strongly support the conclusion that a real interest rate rule would have been a stabilizing influence in all cases, and that a focus on nominal interest rates only is destabilizing. Among the events studied were the 'Great Depression' of the 1930s, the economic expansion financed by deficit

---

[26] Mankiw, 'US monetary policy …'.

[27] John Smithin, *Macroeconomic Policy and the Future of Capitalism: The Revenge of the Rentiers and the Threat to Prosperity* (London: Routledge, 1996).

[28] Keynes, *General Theory*.

[29] Collis, *Three Essays*.

spending in WW2, 'stagflation' in the 1970s, and the global financial crisis (GFC) of the early 21st century. In all of these episodes counterfactual simulation exercises show that a real interest rate rule for monetary policy would have been an important stabilizing factor.

## 6.7 Conclusion

What lessons are there to be drawn for macroeconomic policy from the fact that these situations of drastic financial and economic instability do have the potential to occur, and have in fact occurred at various times in history? The most obvious response would be simply to pursue those sorts of macroeconomic policies that lead to stable and sustainable outcomes. If so, the Keynesian remedy of keeping the economy permanently is a state of 'semi-boom' is surely well within reach. There was no need for the classical economists, nor for any of the other generations of economists in the centuries since, to have 'refused to look' in that direction. It should have been their duty to do so. The implementation of some kind of real interest rate rule, such as the ZRPR, would not in itself eliminate either business cycle fluctuations, or the possibility of the economy becoming stuck in an underemployment equilibrium due to bad policy choices or otherwise. It would, however, prevent the sort of catastrophic downward spirals that we have been discussing here, and also provide the stable backdrop against which the necessary recovery polices can be put in place when a bad situation does occur.

What has usually happened in real world crisis situations, however, is almost never a careful re-consideration of monetary and macroeconomic theory. Much more frequently the responses are derived from some pre-existing political agenda, based on the dubious political principle of 'never let a crisis go to waste'. From the left, the situation will be taken simply as confirmation of Marx's prediction of ever-worsening crisis and, if taken to its logical conclusion, the need to overthrow the system entirely. At a very minimum there are going to be calls for less credit creation, increased regulation, increased taxation, a slow-down in economic growth, less 'consumerism', and so forth. From the right, on the other hand, there might alternatively be calls for a return to 'laissez-faire', to budget austerity, or for a tight monetary policy to reduce inflation — and therefore also for less credit creation. Neither of these approaches is at all helpful. The various policy suggestions that have already been made in this *Lecture* (and in those preceding it) would be a better response than either of these alternatives. Ultimately, both the political left and the political right badly misunderstand the crucial role of the credit and money creation in the generation of profit, and therefore the conditions that are necessary to preserve the viability of the system. They are unaware of the importance of a real interest rate rule to correctly regulate the flow of credit to the economy.

# Lecture 7

# Interest Rates and Income Distribution

## 7.1 Introduction

In *Lecture 6*, it was suggested that a zero real policy rate of interest (ZRPR), or for that matter any other real interest rate rule, in a regime with a flexible exchange rate or a fixed-but-adjustable exchange rate,[1] would be conducive to inflation stability, financial stability, and general economic stability. Low real rates of interest will also promote higher economic growth, full employment, and higher real wages.

In *Lecture 7*, the further case will be made that a ZRPR is also a near-optimal setting of the real policy rate of interest from the point of view of income distribution. It will achieve as close an approximation as is possible to a fair distribution of income, in a particular sense. The concept of fairness invoked here is similar to, but not identical with, that attributed by Marc Lavoie and Mario Seccareccia to Luigi Pasinetti. On their definition, Pasinetti's 'fair' rate of interest would have[2];

> ... the nominal rate of interest ... equal to the rate of growth of labour productivity plus the rate of inflation.

---

[1] As pointed out in *Lecture 5* earlier, this caveat is crucial. The various policy options are not available to a jurisdiction with an irrevocably fixed exchange rate or embedded in a currency union.

[2] Marc Lavoie and Mario Seccareccia, 'Income distribution, rentiers, and their role in the capitalist economy' (*International Journal of Political Economy* 45, 2016).

A ZRPR is therefore less generous to the so-called rentier interests than was Pasinetti, but far more so than Keynes, in the *General Theory*, who advocated the 'euthanasia of the rentier'. The term *rentier* was originally used in 17th and 18th century France to denote the recipients of agricultural *'rentes'*. Since the early twentieth century, however, mainly under the influence of Keynes himself, it has come to mean almost exclusively the recipients of interest income. For example, the title of a book that I published in 1996 was *Macroeconomic Policy, and the Future of Capitalism: The Revenge of the Rentiers and the Threat to Prosperity.*[3] This was written in the aftermath of a period of historically high real rates of interest on money.

Strictly speaking, I would argue that the genuine economy-wide optimum for a fair distribution of income (in my sense, not that of Pasinetti) would be that the 'market' real rate of interest on money should itself be zero. However, this may not be achievable in practice for a variety of reasons, including the influence of Keynesian liquidity preference, and as discussed in previous *Lectures*. Nevertheless, both theoretically and empirically the real market rate of interest and the real policy rate are closely related *via* the transmission mechanism of monetary policy. This circumstance, therefore, is the basis for the argument that the ZRPR would at least be a near-optimum. It will achieve the closest approximation to the optimum that is possible in any given set of circumstances.

As with the discussion of inflation stability in the previous chapter, it will be useful to compare the consequences of a ZRPR for income distribution with the alternative proposal of a ZIRP (zero interest rate policy) as advocated by the modern monetary theory (MMT) school. This is the idea that the nominal policy rate of the central bank should be set at zero. It will be shown that a ZIRP, in and of itself, is unable to achieve the putatively fair distribution of income. This is therefore another reason for preferring a ZRPR to a ZIRP.

## 7.2  The Functional Distribution of Income

The reader will recall that a basic equation for the functional distribution of income is;

$$k = a - r - w, \tag{7.1}$$

---

[3] Smithin, *Macroeconomic Policy*.

where $k$ stands for the natural logarithm of the average economy-wide entrepreneurial mark-up factor, $a$ is the natural logarithm of average economy-wide labour productivity, $r$ is the average economy-wide real rate of interest across all terms to maturity, and $w$ is the natural logarithm of the economy-wide average real wage rate.

A next obvious question that arises is how we might put some 'actual numbers' from a 'real economy' into this expression? To see how this might be done, we can re-use the hypothetical national income and product accounts data from *Lecture 1* earlier. In that example, real GDP (assumed to be correctly measured as a flow of funds for a given economy for a certain year), was 100,000 million constant dollars. Further, the number of persons counted as being employed was 10 million. Also, we were told that the labour share in the distribution of income was 55%. Thus, we had;

$$Y = \text{real GDP} = 100{,}000 \text{ million constant dollars.} \quad (7.2)$$

$$N = \text{employment} = 10 \text{ million persons.} \quad (7.3)$$

The average productivity of the workforce was;

$$A = \text{average labour productivity} = Y/N = 10{,}000. \quad (7.4)$$

And the average real wage rate *per* employed person was;

$$W/P = \text{average real wage} = 5{,}500 \text{ constant dollars.} \quad (7.5)$$

The next step would be to work out some measure of the average real rate of interest in the economy as a whole. This, however, is not such an easy task as it might sound. In our simple illustrative theoretical models in previous *Lectures*, with a one-period production lag, the interest rate concept employed was straightforward. It was simply the one-period rate of interest itself. But now, the task is to make some sort of estimate of rentier incomes in the economy as a whole and at all terms to maturity. Reed Collis addressed this problem in his recent York University doctoral thesis, and provided a detailed discussion of the various alternative methods by which such calculations may be attempted.[4] After a careful evaluation of the merits of, and the differences between, the alternative methods, Collis argues that one of the most promising seems to be to use data for total

[4] Collis, *Three Essays.*

property income (that is, including all of bonds, equities, real property, *etc.*) which is then compared to total wealth, to thereby arrive at an estimate of the overall percentage rate of return to 'wealth'. In Collis's view, this provides the most realistic estimate of the balance of forces at work as between wealth-owners, entrepreneurs, and labour in real world political-economic systems. For present purposes therefore, and to cut a long story short, let us provisionally accept this argument and suppose that the necessary calculations work out to a value of (say) $r = 0.15$. As far as I can tell, this is actually a relatively high value compared to the real world estimates of writers such as Collis himself or, for example, to those of Thomas Piketty in the latter's well-known *Capital in the 21st Century.*[5] It is not suggested therefore that this particular number is 'realistic', or would be at all useful in specifying transversality conditions in macroeconomic models. The only consideration is that a relatively high number such as this will be convenient to use in the illustrative numerical arithmetical calculation of income distribution (using logarithms) that will follow. To proceed, therefore, and also taking natural logarithms of equations (7.4) and (7.5), we now have;

$$a = lnA = 9.2 \qquad (7.6)$$

$$w = ln(W/P) = 8.6 \qquad (7.7)$$

$$r = 0.15. \qquad (7.8)$$

Given these assumed levels of real wages and real interest rates, the natural logarithm of the average/aggregate entrepreneurial mark-up factor will work out to $k = 0.45$, as follows[6];

$$k = a - r - w = 9.2 - 0.15 - 8.6 = 0.45. \qquad (7.9)$$

An alternative way of writing equation (7.1) would be to put the term $a$ on the left-hand side (LHS) and move the other terms over to the RHS. The expression that results from this move then explains how the natural logarithm of average labour productivity is split between entrepreneurial profit, interest, and wages;

$$a = k + r + w. \qquad (7.10)$$

---

[5] Tomas Piketty, *Capital in the Twenty-First Century* (Cambridge, MA: Harvard University Press, 2014).
[6] The reader will recall that $(1+K)$, upper-case, is the mark-up factor and that $k = ln(1+K)$.

Next, we can 'normalize' by dividing through by $a$ itself. This gives;

$$1 = k/a + r/a + w/a. \tag{7.11}$$

Thus, the ratios in equation (7.11) are the various income measures relative to the natural logarithm of average labour productivity. They represent one metric among others of how the total of output in existence at any point in time is distributed between the different classes of income recipients. In *Rethinking the Theory of Money, Credit, and Macroeconomics* (in the absence of any other alternative that I could find) I coined the term 'logarithmic shares', or (*ln*)shares, to stand for these three ratios. The most important thing about them, however, is not the label but the fact that together they always sum to unity. Using the assumed numbers from equations (7.9) in (7.11), the result is that income is distributed as follows;

$$1 = \quad 0.5 \quad + \quad 0.02 \quad + \quad 0.93. \tag{7.12}$$

firm (*ln*)share   rentier (*ln*)share   wage (*ln*)share

At least at first sight, perhaps this new concept of (*ln*)shares may not seem to shed much light on the practical 'struggle for income distribution' as experienced by the participants in the struggle themselves. For example, the (*ln*)share of labour in equation (7.12) turns out to be 0.93, whereas we already know that the actual labour share in GDP is 55%. Because of the mathematical properties of logarithms, small changes in the (*ln*)shares always translate into large changes in the actual percentage shares, and *vice versa*. Nonetheless, as we will soon see, this way of putting things does turn out to be very useful in defining what is actually meant by the various normative concepts such as 'exploitation' and 'usury' that typically arise in the discussion of the functional distribution of income.

## 7.3 Numerical Illustrations of the Concepts of Exploitation and Usury

Consider, for example, the familiar Marxian notion of *exploitation*, as already discussed in previous *Lectures*. In the present context, and using our current notation, we can now see that exploitation in this Marxian sense will occur whenever;

$$k + r > 0. \qquad (7.13)$$

On the other hand, if $k + r = 0$, there would be no exploitation, and;

$$a = w. \qquad (7.14)$$

This would therefore be a case where the whole value of the output accrues to those who are (or rather, were supposed by Marx to be) the actual producers.

Similarly, given the initial assumptions about fairness made above, we are also able to define the concept of *usury*, which was a staple of the historical literature on money and banking. The word 'use' is an archaic synonym for interest, and the notion of usury would come into play whenever the rate of interest charged on loans on money was deemed to be excessive in some sense. Historically, so-called usury laws were passed in several jurisdictions limiting the amount of interest that could be charged for any financial transaction. In order for this sort of concept to be operational, there evidently has to be some method of determining what is, and what is not, deemed to be excessive. In terms of our current notation, the case can be made that there will be usury whenever the real rate interest, $r$, is greater than zero. That is, if;

$$r > 0. \qquad (7.15)$$

On the other hand, if;

$$r = 0, \qquad (7.16)$$

then there would be no usury. In this case, the argument can be made that there is a putatively fair distribution of income as between producers and non-producers. We would have;

$$a = k + w. \qquad (7.17)$$

Now the total income available is divided solely between the entrepreneurs and the workers, although specifics of the share-out have yet to be decided. Contrary to Marxism, however, the economic function of entrepreneurship continues to be recognized as well as that of labour. Both groups are entitled to *some* share of current income. The entrepreneurs are not excluded entirely as they would be under Marxism. The rentiers, however, do not participate. The possession of money in itself does not entitle rentiers to any increase in their real money holdings without some contribution to current productive activity. There cannot be further accumulation unless the wealth-holder is willing to take on some sort of additional 'risk'. On the other hand, because the real rate of interest is also non-negative, the rentiers *are* able to preserve the real value of any previously accumulated monetary and financial holdings. This may well raise further questions about the original sources of their income and the legitimacy of those sources. If the original income sources were indeed either wages or entrepreneurial profit, the ethical argument would be watertight. However, to the extent that the past income was, in fact, acquired by either usury or financial speculation, this would clearly raise difficult issues of political economy for any transitional regime.

## 7.4  Is the Optimal Real Rate of Interest on Money Zero?

Given the above discussion, then perhaps the answer to this question is yes? In this next stage of the argument, we will revert to the assumption that all of the rentier income is 'risk-free'. Thus, if $r = 0$, and with $a = 9.2$ and $w = 8.6$ as before, we will have;

$$k = a - r - w = 9.2 - 0.0 - 8.6 = 0.60. \qquad (7.18)$$

Comparing (7.18) with (7.9), it can be seen that when the real rate of interest falls from 0.15 to 0.00, the average entrepreneurial mark-up increases to 0.60 from 0.45. The natural logarithm of the average real wage rate remains unchanged. As just stated, this new distribution of income is 'fair' in the restricted sense that both the entrepreneurs and workers have participated in current production, while the rentiers have not. It is also fair in the sense that the existing real values of the rentier's financial holdings have not been reduced — assuming that these were earned by past productive activity.

There may still be further conflict between the entrepreneurs and workers over the precise size of the mark-up. In the particular case we are considering here, all of the benefit has gone to the entrepreneurs, but in the real world this may very well be contested. However, I would say that this next level of conflict is 'fair game'. It will be decided by such things as collective bargaining and labour legislation, for example, and by a host of other policy initiatives. (Indeed, many of the various policy initiatives suggested in these *Lectures* have had the explicit objective of increasing both the level of employment *and* the average after-tax real wage rate.) Whatever the final resolution, however, and unlike in Marxism, the *k* term itself is never reduced to *k* = 0. If this were to occur, it would render the whole system unviable. Then there would be no incentive for the entrepreneurs to initiate production at all.

Based on the above argument about fairness, it now therefore seems that a zero real market rate of interest is optimal. It is true, however, that starting with a brief statement in *Controversies in Monetary Economics* more than 25 years ago, and then subsequently in many other places, I have usually argued central banks should pursue a monetary policy that sets a target for the real policy rate of interest at a 'low but still positive' level.[7] Given the transmissions mechanism of monetary policy, and under normal circumstances, this would also feed through to a relatively 'low' but 'still positive' real market rate of interest on money, rather than zero. The basis for the argument was, firstly, that lower real interest rates, even if not reduced to zero, do promote economic growth. Secondly, as shown in *Lecture 6* earlier, any real target for the real policy rate of interest, even if greater than zero, would at least stabilize the inflation rate. These sorts of statements, in short, were always meant to be taken in the spirit of pragmatic policy advice, and I have not usually given any precise quantitative target for the real policy rate of interest. The ethical arguments just introduced, however, bring a further and more precise dimension to the notion of optimality. To the extent that the current wealth holdings of rentiers have arisen from past receipts of either wages or profits, they are legitimate. Therefore, subject to the caveats already made, fairness entails that current wealth-owners are entitled to preserve the real value of any past gains due to their own efforts, which means a market real interest rate of (at least) zero. On the other hand, as there is no argument from the point of view of fairness for rentiers to share in the proceeds of current income generated by the work effort and entrepreneurial activity of others, the real rate of interest should also not be allowed to rise above zero. In the terminology introduced here, usury should not be allowed. The effective real rate of interest on money should therefore be $r = 0$.

In the present context, strictly speaking, the rule should probably apply specifically to the risk-free real deposit rate at the commercial banks. However, the definition of *r* in equation (7.1), and throughout this

---

[7] Smithin, *Controversies*.

book, also includes the commercial bank mark-up between deposit and lending rates. This actually represents the return to the activity of bank lending rather than interest or 'use' as such, and in reality it is a special case of entrepreneurial profit. Nonetheless, in the illustrative calculations to follow, which are based on previous work, this distinction is neglected. In practice, this makes only a minor difference to the value of the hypothetical aggregate mark-up for non-financial business firms.

In the case being considered here, to achieve a zero real *market* rate of interest, including the commercial bank mark-up, requires that the target for the real *policy* rate be;

$$r_0 = [(1 - m_1)/m_1)]p - (m_0/m_1), \tag{7.19}$$

and, as already shown in equation (7.14), if a market rate of $r = 0$ is attained, this means the natural logarithm of the average entrepreneurial mark-up factor, across all firms, will be increased to $k = 0.6$. Then, given this new value of $k$, we can once again re-arrange the distributive equation and normalize to obtain the following results for the (*ln*)shares;

$$1 = \quad 0.07 \quad + 0.00 + \quad 0.93. \tag{7.20}$$

firm (*ln*)share          wage (*ln*)share

Unlike in equation (7.12), we can see that there is now no rentier share. It too has fallen to zero. The other (*ln*)shares have either been increased, in the case of the entrepreneurs, or have remained the same in the case of labour.

At this point, it is interesting to note that there is a definite family resemblance between the above argument and the rules of so-called 'Islamic banking'.[8] This is usually understood to be a code of conduct for bankers who wish to comply with certain religious requirements in their business dealings. In this sort of discourse, there is also a basic or underlying presumption that charging interest for loans of money is somehow unethical, as opposed to the receipt of income earned from entrepreneurial profits and wages. Rules are therefore set down for business and financial dealings which, in one way or another, are able to avoid interest charges entirely. (Similar ideas have also been present historically in many other

[8] G. Arnold, *The Financial Times Guide to Banking* (London: FT Publishing, 2014).

religious traditions besides that of Islam. The latter is simply a convenient modern example because that tradition has a large number of adherents worldwide at the present time, and is much discussed in the contemporary news media, including the financial and business media. Another example, but with less contemporary relevance, would be that of medieval Catholicism in the scholastic period).

The objective of avoiding interest charges altogether is not exactly fulfilled in the current argument because it is not always possible to avoid a nominal interest charge. If the real interest rate is to be set to zero, the nominal interest rate must always be equal to the inflation rate. Therefore, the nominal interest rate will have to be positive whenever the inflation rate itself is positive. The main difference from the overtly religious arguments is thus once again whether it is a nominal or real interest rate that is set to zero. Nonetheless, with a zero real rate there would still be no *real* income received by the rentiers, regardless of the inflation rate. The final result therefore would seem to be well within the spirit, if not the letter, of the law of the several religious proscriptions.[9] And it is important to again stress that with a zero real, rather than nominal, rate of interest the rentiers are not being dispossessed altogether. They are not actually being 'euthanized' as Keynes had predicted they would be (or perhaps thought that they should be?). The rentiers are still able to preserve in full the real value of any financial holdings acquired from previous labour effort or entrepreneurial effort.

## 7.5  Is the Optimal *Nominal* Policy Rate of Interest Zero?

In *Lecture 6* earlier, one of the negative consequences of setting the nominal policy rate of interest at zero was discussed at length. It was found that a nominal interest rate peg of any kind, not just zero, will lead to inflationary (or deflationary) instability. It can now be seen that there is yet another important problem with a ZIRP. A zero nominal interest rate will not be neutral in its effect on income distribution, not even as regards those sources of income that are regarded as legitimate according to the concept of fairness employed here. A ZIRP is therefore unable to achieve a fair distribution of income in the sense in which we have been using that term.

---

[9] Smithin, *Rethinking*.

Consider first an inflationary case and suppose that at the current point in time the inflation rate happens to be 14%, or $p = 0.14$. The inflation-adjusted real interest rate is given by the following expression:

$$r = m_0 + m_1 r_0 - (1 - m_1)p. \tag{7.21}$$

And, by assumption the central bank is following a ZIRP and $i_0 = 0$. Therefore equation (7.17) will further reduce to;

$$r = m_0 - p. \tag{7.22}$$

The effective real rate of interest on money, in this particular case, is equal to the commercial bank mark-up between lending rates and deposit rates of commercial banks *minus* the inflation rate. With $p = 0.14$, and if the commercial bank mark-up is given by (say) $m_0 = 0.02$, we have;

$$r = 0.02 - 0.14 = -0.12. \tag{7.23}$$

The market real rate of interest is thus negative at –12%. Given $a = 9.2$ and $w = 8.6$, as before, the natural logarithm of the average/aggregate entrepreneurial mark-up factor is increased to the value of $k = 0.72$ as follows;

$$k = a - r - w = 9.2 + 0.12 - 0.86 = 0.72. \tag{7.24}$$

And, using the information from (7.23) and (7.24) in (7.11), the relative (*ln*)shares will work out to;

$$1 = \quad 0.08 \quad - \quad 0.01 \quad + \quad 0.93. \tag{7.25}$$

firm (*ln*)share     rentier (*ln*)share     wage (*ln*)share

In terms of the functional distribution of income, the workers are still holding their own, but the rentier (*ln*)share has now turned negative. What is happening, to borrow a typical expression often used in mainstream or neoclassical economics, is that 'resources are being transferred' *from* the holders of financial capital *to* business firms. In effect, the business firms or entrepreneurs are 'profiteers' from inflation, just as described by Keynes in a relevant passage from the *Tract on Monetary Reform*[10] when

---

[10] John Maynard Keynes, *A Tract on Monetary Reform* (London: Macmillan, 1923).

discussing the effects of inflation during WW1 and its aftermath. And, what is worse from the point of view of the rentiers, we should recall from *Lecture 6* that the system is unstable. From the wealth-holder's perspective, the situation will continue to deteriorate as time goes by. The inflationary case therefore does eventually lead to Keynes's 'euthanasia of the rentier'. As against Keynes, however, at least from the point of view about fairness outlined above, I don't think that this outcome can be held to represent an ethically defensible position.

Next, consider the alternative (deflationary) case. Suppose now that the price level is currently falling at a rate of 16% per annum ($p = -0.16$). In this situation, even though the nominal interest rate remains zero, the real market rate of interest on money will now be positive. It increases to the relatively high level of $r = 0.18$. The average entrepreneurial mark-up therefore falls to $k = 0.42$, as follows;

$$k = 9.2 - 0.18 - 8.6 = 0.42. \qquad (7.26)$$

The (*ln*)shares will therefore turn out be;

$$1 = \quad 0.05 \quad + \quad 0.02 \quad + \quad 0.93. \qquad (7.27)$$

firm (*ln*)share    rentier (*ln*)share    wage (*ln*)share

In this case, resources are being transferred *to* the holders of financial capital *from* business firms. Rather than the 'euthanasia of the rentiers', this is an opposite example of a process I have called the 'revenge of the rentiers'.[11] Again, the system is unstable and the situation is only going to get worse and worse, but this time from the point of view of Main Street. The boot is on the other foot. It is business that will eventually be euthanized, and with it the entire economy. In this particular example, if the rate of deflation continues to increase, and eventually proceeds to an order of magnitude above 60% or so, the average business mark-up turns negative. Firms in the aggregate, and on average, will then all be making losses. With a 68% rate of deflation, for example, we will have;

$$k = 9.2 - 0.70 - 8.6 = -0.10. \qquad (7.28)$$

---

[11] Smithin, *Macroeconomic Policy.*

I would say that this is the very essence of the process of deflation and depression or recession. This is exactly what happened in the severe episodes of deflation and depression that were seen in the 1930s, and again on several occasions in our own times.

Taking the inflationary and deflationary cases together, the conclusion must be that a ZIRP is not the optimal setting of the monetary policy instrument, neither from the point of view of stability (as seen in *Lecture 6*), nor of income distribution. Far from it. If the nominal policy rate is set at zero, or for that matter at any other nominal value, 'anything can happen'. We can get either a 'South Sea Bubble' (as in the 1720s) or a 'Great Depression' (which was the case in the 1930s), or anything in between.

## 7.6  The 'Near Optimality' of a ZRPR

Conversely, we have suggested that the ZRPR (a zero real policy rate) is at least a 'near-optimal' monetary policy. Perhaps the use of the word 'near' is a little over-optimistic, but it is difficult to come up with a better alternative. What can be shown is that this policy will achieve the closest possible approximation to the optimum that is attainable in practice. To see the argument, suppose that the central bank does decide to set a real target for the policy rate, but not a target of zero. Rather they follow my own previous pragmatic advice about a low, but still positive, real rate of interest. They might, for example, set a target for the real policy rate of something like 1.5%. That is;

$$r_0 = 0.015. \tag{7.29}$$

In this case, the actual real rate of interest on money in the market-place would be given by;

$$r = m_0 + m_1 0.015 - (1 - m_1)p. \tag{7.30}$$

Hopefully, this would also turn out to be a low real rate of interest, but we cannot be quite sure. The overall levels of real market rates also depend on the parameters $m_0$ and $m_1$, and on the inflation rate $p$ (and thereby on liquidity preference, *etc.*). Although a rule such as that in equation (7.25) can be defended on pragmatic grounds, as I have done in the past, it cannot really be optimal in any of the senses in which economists typically use the term. Optimality *per se* requires a risk free real market rate of interest of zero.

How would the situation differ from the above if, instead of settling for the rule in equation (7.25), the central bank goes still further and actually implemented the ZRPR? In this case, the general level of the real market rate of interest, $r$, would turn out to be;

$$r = m_0 - (1 - m_1)p. \tag{7.31}$$

Once again, the market rate would not itself be zero except by accident. It might well turn out to be positive in most cases, but could even be negative on occasion, depending always on the values of $m_0$, $m_1$, and $p$. Perhaps it would still be fairly 'low' in general terms. However, the important point to note in comparing equations (7.26) and (7.27) is that in equation (7.27) the positive term $m_1 0.015$ (in general $m_1 x$) from (7.26) is missing. Therefore, in any given set of circumstances, and for a positive starting value of $r$, the real rate of interest on money is always closer to the distributionally neutral value of zero than it is in equation (7.26). This is the basis for the suggestion that the ZRPR is the closest approximation to the optimum solution attainable in practice. (Moreover, as zero is also obviously a *real* target, the ZRPR will perform just as well on the grounds of inflation stability as would any other real rate rule.)

## 7.7 Implications for Economic Policy and Comparative Economic Systems

In principle, the optimal real rate of interest on money holdings for a 'fair' distribution of income is zero, meaning zero rentier income in real terms (but not the actual 'euthanasia' of the rentier). If it were attainable, it would also eliminate financial speculation in the financial markets based on expectations of real interest rate changes. We have also made the point that even if a zero real rate on money cannot be achieved in practice, a zero real policy rate (ZRPR) set by the central bank does represent a goal that is a close approximation to the distributional optimum. It would also minimize financial speculation, if not eliminate it entirely. With this sort of monetary policy in place, the way would then be open for expansionary policies on the fiscal side that would reduce unemployment, increase growth, and thereby increase the average real wage rate. (Naturally, all these statements remain subject to the caveat that for any policy, monetary, fiscal, or otherwise, to 'work' there must be a floating exchange rate regime, or else the nominal exchange rate should be 'fixed-but-adjustable'.)

Keynes's original fiscal policy recommendations from the *General Theory* specifically mentioned that a policy of so-called 'loan expenditure' by the government would be desirable to achieve these goals.[12] According to Keynes;

> ... loan expenditure ... [is defined as] ... a convenient expression for the net borrowing of the public authorities on all accounts whether on capital account or to meet a budgetary deficit ...

Logically, therefore, such a policy might include either direct increases in the ratio of government spending to GDP, or cuts in the average tax rate. In my view, however, it would not involve the typical 'tax and spend' policies which have become all too familiar to us in the past 70 years or so, and have quite wrongly been identified with Keynesian economics ever since the introduction of the mistaken notion of the 'balanced budget multiplier' in one of the early editions of Samuelson's influential textbook.[13] Samuelson argued that the balanced budget multiplier was positive. In fact, the analysis of the AMM carried out in previous *Lectures* reveals that the balanced budget multiplier is negative, and also that a higher average tax rate tends to cause *inflation* rather than deflation. If, therefore, a tax and spend type of policy is put in place instead of the original Keynesian idea of deficit spending, this will lead to stagflation, a combination of both higher unemployment and higher inflation. This is the worst of all possible worlds, and the precise opposite of the outcome desired by Keynes. As a result of Samuelson's error, I would argue that there has been a popular misidentification of 'Keynesian economics' with high taxes from the very earliest days. This has been entirely unnecessary in my opinion, and over the years has led to numerous serious misunderstandings in both macroeconomic theory and policy.

If there is an increase in the rate of economic growth brought about by either of the genuinely Keynesian methods, higher spending or lower taxes, the outcome for distribution of income is to increase the average real wage rate. At the same time, however, at least according to the

---

[12] Keynes, *General Theory*.

[13] Samuelson, *Economics*; Smithin, *Rethinking*; John Smithin, 'What is the sign of the balanced-budget multiplier?' in Steven Pressman and John Smithin, eds., *Debates in Monetary Macroeconomics: Tackling Some Unsettled Questions* (New York: Palgrave Macmillan, 2022).

version of the AMM so far expounded in these *Lectures*, the mark-up earned by entrepreneurial business will likely be falling in the aggregate and on average. But as already stated, however, and according to the idea of 'fairness' adopted here this sort of change in income distribution, if it does occur, is probably fair game. Both the workers and entrepreneurs have indeed contributed to the production of current output, and both are entitled to some share in the proceeds. However, unlike in neoclassical economics, there is no 'marginal principle', or any such thing to dictate precisely what the share of each group should be. To that extent, the division of the proceeds is always going to be 'up for grabs', to be determined by collective bargaining, *etc.*

A falling mark-up is not quite the same thing as Marx's 'falling rate of profit', but it is obviously a similar sort of idea. In the first flush of the Keynesian revolution, therefore, many decades ago, it was probably this sort of consideration that led left-wing writers such as Michael Kalecki to express concerns about the possible reaction of business leaders to any continued economic prosperity brought about by successful Keynesian policy. Kalecki even went so far as to argue that the industrialists would ultimately have to take steps *via* the political process to bring the expansion to an end[14];

> ... if attempts are made to apply this method ... [*i.e.*, Keynes's idea of loan expenditure on the part of the government] ... in order to maintain the high level of employment ... a strong opposition of 'business leaders' is likely to be encountered ... lasting full employment is not at all to their liking. The workers would 'get out of hand' ... In this situation a powerful block between big business and the rentier interests is likely to be formed, and they would probably find more than one economist to declare that the situation was manifestly unsound.

The argument is that growth increases the demand for labour in the private sector and thus drives up wages. Therefore, if productivity does not change, an increase in the growth rate, and thereby in real wages, may very well tend to reduce the average or aggregate mark-up earned by entrepreneurial business.

---

[14] Michael Kalecki, 'Political aspects of full employment', in *Selected Essays on the Dynamics of a Capitalist Economy 1933–70* (Cambridge: Cambridge University Press, 1971).

However, in trying to decide whether this affects the political viability of Keynesian policies, and as I have argued elsewhere, I think that the real question to be asked and answered about this is whether or not the various individual entrepreneurial entities should really care about a falling mark-up in the aggregate.[15] Decision-making about whether to expand a business is carried out at the level of the individual enterprise. The premise of 'Keynesian economics' is the presence of overall demand constraints and, thus, the existence of downward-sloping demand curves at the firm level (as opposed to the aggregate level) for at least a large subset of the individual oligopolistic firms. Whenever the demand constraints are relaxed there will always be incentives to expand production. Therefore, even in the case of a demand expansion with an unchanging level of labour productivity, the mark-up will not fall to zero.[16] Existing businesses will grow, more start-ups will be able to participate, and the several firms and entrepreneurs will all still be 'making money', both individually and collectively. Keynes himself, in making 'Concluding Notes on the Social Philosophy Towards Which the *General Theory* Might Lead' seems to have addressed this very point.[17] He was clear that there are;

> ... valuable human activities which require the motive of money-making and the environment of private wealth ownership for their full fruition. ... But it is not necessary for the stimulation of these activities ... that the game should be played for such high stakes as at present. Much lower stakes will serve the purpose equally well, as soon as the players have become accustomed to them.

Even Keynes had the typical disdain of the comfortably situated upper-middle class intellectual for the mere 'money-making' activities on which the rest of society depends. Nonetheless, he was surely right in principle.

Additionally, an important advantage of thinking about income distribution in terms of a three-way split between profit, wages, and interest, as we have done throughout this book (rather than just a two-way split) is to

---

[15] Smithin, *Rethinking*.

[16] Smithin, *Rethinking*; John Smithin, 'A re-habilitation of the theory of effective demand from Chapter 3 of Keynes's *General Theory* (1936)' (*International Journal of Political Economy* 42, 2013).

[17] Keynes, *General Theory*.

make clear the typically different motivations of the entrepreneurial and financial interests, which are sometimes expressed as 'Main Street' *versus* 'Wall Street' (or 'Bay Street', or 'the City'). The title of another work by Geoffrey Ingham, published four decades after that of Kalecki, was *Capitalism Divided? The City and Industry in British Social Development* and this title neatly encapsulates the underlying argument.[18] A three-way split raises the possibility of various different combinations and alliances between business, finance, and labour, rather than just capital *versus* labour. (And also, for that matter, different alliances within and between the various factions in those groups.)[19] In any event, if the rentier position is settled as suggested (ruling out the particular 'block' suggested by Kalecki), there still remains the class struggle between entrepreneurs and workers. This boils down to conflict over the intercept term in the wage function. In Collis's PhD thesis, for example, as previously cited, it is shown that an empirically plausible version of the wage function might be as follows[20];

$$w - t = h_0 + h_1 y_{-1} - h_2 q, \qquad h_1 > 0, \ h_2 > 0 \qquad (7.32)$$

where $t$ is the average tax rate, and $q$ is the natural logarithm of the real exchange rate. As in the similar formulation in the AMM, the intercept term ($h_0$) can be plausibly interpreted as a measure of the 'socio-political power of labour'. Using formulae such as that in (7.28), Collis was then able to derive various empirical time series to show the changes that have occurred in this power index in both Canada and the USA over long periods of time.

Put in terms of both equation (7.32) and the AMM, therefore, what Kalecki seems to have been suggesting, in the passage cited above, was that if the employers can somehow collectively or politically take action to push down the intercept term (for example, *via* the sponsorship of restrictive labour legislation or some form of economy-wide lockout), it would be possible to increase the aggregate mark-up *via* this route. This would be a rather open form of class warfare, but, as the AMM also makes clear, it will wreck the economy. In the real world, there will be political

---

[18] Geoffrey Ingham, *Capitalism Divided? The City and Industry in British Social Development* (London: Macmillan, 1984).

[19] Some of the possible alignments and realignments were discussed right at the start of this book, in *Lecture 1*, in the context of contemporary macroeconomic policy issues.

[20] Collis, *Three Essays.*

unrest, war even,[21] and ultimately even the firms themselves will be by no means secure. Against the background of at least some understanding of Keynesian economics, it is not clear that this is a viable long-term strategy. Provided there is sufficient effective demand (actually one of the main points Keynes was trying to make in the *General Theory*), it would presumably make more sense for the firms to acquiesce in the higher wages and then innovate/compete at the individual firm level to try to preserve their relative position in that way. If this were to happen on an economy-wide scale, there could be increases in both wages and profits.

On the other hand, in the opposite situation to that theorized by Kalecki, the overall average real wage rate could alternatively be increased by an increase in the $h_0$ term (an increase in the power of labour due to changes in the socio-political environment, *etc.*) *without* there being sufficient effective demand. In a somewhat more modern situation than assumed by Kalecki, suppose, for example, that employees in the public sector generally, such as the educational system, the bureaucracy, the healthcare system, *etc.*, are able to achieve real wages gains for themselves that do not translate into similar gains for their compatriots in the private sector. These are the groups who never have to worry too much about 'market forces' in the determination of their pay scales. These purely sectional gains will nonetheless imply an increase in the aggregate $h_0$ term, and therefore in the aggregate or average real wage rate itself. The problem is that in the assumed circumstances, with insufficient demand, there would also be slower or negative economic growth, and a rise in total unemployment. In short, some workers (typically in the public sector) would benefit from the increase in the average real wage rate, but others (typically in the private sector) would not. This is surely quite a familiar scenario in the contemporary world. As mentioned, therefore, we cannot rule out the possibility of other political coalitions and alliances between the competing groups, and other fault lines within those groups. The common thread, obviously, that runs through all these discussions and scenarios, positive or negative, is the importance of there always being sufficient effective demand. When there is sufficient effective demand, there is scope for most of the social groups to get at least some share of the benefits, but not otherwise.

---

[21] It is interesting to note that Kalecki's 1943 article, cited above, was actually published during WW2.

There is also another consideration that is likely to be important in practice. The simplifying assumption that was made in our discussion of the AMM, namely, that the natural logarithm of average labour productivity is a constant, was only for ease of exposition in setting out the basic theoretical framework. In fact, however, and as also shown by Reed Collis in his thesis work, a plausible empirical version of the equation explaining productivity is more likely to be something along the lines of[22];

$$a = \alpha_0 + \alpha_1 y + \alpha_2 a_{-1}, \qquad \alpha_1 > 0,\ 0 < \alpha_2 < 1 \qquad (7.33)$$

There is an autoregressive element in the productivity function, represented by the $\alpha_2$ coefficient. However, it also seems to be the case that productivity *increases* during a period of faster growth, in what is apparently some sort of 'learning by doing' scenario (represented by $\alpha_1$). If so, the final outcomes for income distribution are going to depend on the sign of the term $(h_1 - \alpha_1)$ in the general equilibrium solution to the model. (Recall that $h_1$ is the sensitivity of the average real wage rate to the economic growth rate.) If $h_1 > \alpha_1$ (that is, if real wages increase faster than productivity), this reinforces the conclusions reached in the above discussion. If, on the other hand, $\alpha_1 > h_1$, this will turn out to be a win–win situation. Economic growth does tend to increase real wages. At the same time, however, the growth process itself increases productivity and still more so. Therefore, both the average after-tax real wage rate and the entrepreneurial mark-up increase. The result is essentially an 'economics of abundance', as some writers have called it, rather than the traditional economics of scarcity.[23] Both in Collis's thesis, and also in earlier work by myself and Sonmez Atesoglu, there is evidence that in some jurisdictions in the world economy the conditions for $\alpha_1 > h_1$ do obtain.[24] Much depends on the innovation systems, regulatory regimes, the legal status of property rights, detailed tax codes, *etc.*, that prevail in each country.

---

[22] Collis, *Three Essays*.

[23] Marc Lavoie, *Foundations of Post-Keynesian Economic Analysis* (Aldershot: Edward Elgar, 1992).

[24] H. Sonmez Atesoglu and John Smithin, 'Real wages, productivity, and economic growth in the G7', 1960–2002 (*Review of Political Economy* 18, 2006).

## 7.8  Conclusion

A zero real policy rate of interest (ZRPR) is a 'near-optimal' setting of the real policy rate of interest from the point of view of income distribution. It will achieve as close an approximation as is possible to a fair distribution of income as between rentiers, entrepreneurs, and workers, as well as preserving the real value of existing financial wealth. Expansionary economic policies such as those suggested by traditional Keynesian economics, will increase real wages, and in favourable circumstances also the aggregate or average mark-up achieved by business firms.

As mentioned in the previous section, these results highlight the basic question of the economics of abundance *versus* the traditional economics of scarcity. Several times throughout these *Lectures,* I have noted that there seems always to have been a tendency, on the parts not only of the supposed defenders of capitalism (the supporters of austerity, free-trade, globalism, sound money, *etc.*) but also of capitalism's detractors on the left of politics (socialists, Marxists, radical environmentalists, and so forth) to embrace the latter. All too frequently, the recommendations of both groups work out to the detriment of the working class and the middle class. An economics of abundance would be a different matter entirely.

The question of income distribution is evidently a key issue in the political economy of monetary macroeconomics. However, to come to any satisfactory conclusion on these matters will require a considerably more nuanced discussion of the issues than is present in either academic or popular discussion at the present time.

# Lecture 8

# Numerical Methods and Time Series Econometrics in Monetary Macroeconomics

## 8.1 Introduction

This final *Lecture* will illustrate the use of numerical methods (that is, computer simulation techniques) and time series econometrics as research tools in monetary macroeconomics. The macroeconomic model to be used is once again the 'alternative monetary model' (AMM) that has been discussed throughout this book — as described in detail in *Rethinking the Theory of Money, Credit, and Macroeconomics* and in my earlier book *Essays in the Fundamental Theory of Monetary Economics and Macroeconomics*.[1] The computer platform that will be used is the commercially available software package *EViews Version 11*. *Lecture 8* first shows how it is possible to simulate a simple version of the AMM using *EViews*, and will then move on to a discussion of the techniques of time series econometrics.

## 8.2 Comments on EViews Syntax and Notation

There first needs to be some comment on the syntax and notation used by the program. For example, *EViews* does not distinguish between lower and upper case letters, so that the expression $k = a - r - w$ (which the

---

[1] Smithin, *Rethinking*; Smithin, *Essays.*

reader will recognize as a basic equation from the AMM) is the same thing as $K = A - R - W$ as far as *EViews* is concerned. It is possible to use an alpha-numerical notation such as $e0$ (*e* 'zero') or $e1$ (*e* 'one') to denote either exogenous variables or parameters, as is also done in the AMM. However, it is advisable *not* to use an underscore notation for this purpose, and certainly not for the endogenous variables. This is because the output for the endogenous variables in each of the alternative scenarios will itself use an underscore notation. For example, in the case of one of the key endogenous variables in the AMM, namely lower case $y$ (which stands for the rate of growth of real GDP) we would get $y\_0$ or $Y\_0$ for the *Baseline* $y\_1$ or $Y\_1$ for *Scenario 1*, and $y\_2$ or $Y\_2$ for *Scenario 2*, and so on. In dynamic models, such as we have here, the notation $y(-1)$ or $Y(-1)$ means that there is a one-period lag of the variable concerned. Finally, the symbol (\*) means 'multiply'.

## 8.3 The Model

At this point, we can now write out a simple closed-economy version of the AMM, in *EViews* syntax, as follows;

$$y = e0 + g - t + e1*k \tag{8.1}$$

$$k = a - r(-1) - w(-1) \tag{8.2}$$

$$p = p0 + w - a \tag{8.3}$$

$$w = h0 + t + h1*y \tag{8.4}$$

$$r = m0 + m1*r0 - (1 - m1)*p \tag{8.5}$$

A recapitulation of the definitions of each variable is provided in *Tables 8.1, 8.2,* and *8.3. Table 8.1* first lists the endogenous variables. *Table 8.2* then describes the exogenous variables, divided into three categories. These are policy variables, real costs and productivity, and

*Table 8.1*: Endogenous Variables

| |
|---|
| $y$ = the growth rate of real GDP, |
| $k$ = the (natural logarithm of) the entrepreneurial profit mark-up, |
| $w$ = the (natural logarithm of) the average real wage rate, |
| $p$ = the inflation rate, |
| $r$ = the average real rate of interest across all terms to maturity. |

*Table 8.2*: Exogenous Variables

---

*Policy;*

$g$ = government spending as a percentage of GDP,

$t$ = the average tax rate,

$r0$ = the real policy rate of interest.

*Real Costs and Productivity;*

$a$ = the (natural logarithm of) labour productivity,

$h0$ = the intercept in the wage function,

$m0$ = the commercial bank mark-up.

*Market Psychology;*

$e0$ = the net autonomous expenditure of the private sector (including Keynes's 'animal spirits'),

$p0$ = an inverse measure of Keynes's 'bearishness' (a version of liquidity preference).

---

*Table 8.3*: Parameters

---

$e1$ = the sensitivity of firm spending to expected profitability — as measured by the natural logarithm of the entrepreneurial mark-up factor,

$h1$ = the sensitivity of (the natural logarithm of) average after-tax real wages to lagged real GDP growth,

$m1$ = the pass-through coefficient in the monetary policy transmissions mechanism.

---

indicators of market psychology. Finally, *Table 8.3* lists the model's given parameters.

As an economist would see it, the structural model contains five endogenous variables, eight exogenous variables, and three parameters. However, the *EViews* program also treats parameters as 'exogenous variables'. According to the program, therefore, there are five equations to solve for the five endogenous variables $y$, $p$, $k$, $w$, and $r$, and there are eleven exogenous variables, $a$, $e0$, $e1$, $g$, $h0$, $h1$, $p0$, $m0$, $m1$, $r0$, and $t$.

# 8.4 Getting Started with the Computer Software

In this section, we will describe how to navigate through the various *EViews* 'Windows' and 'Pop-Ups' in order to input our equations and data.

I was much helped myself in 'getting started' with the software by consulting the works of Kim Jung-Hoon and Samuel Yao Effah.[2] Both authors were students of Marc Lavoie who, in turn, was one of the co-authors, with Wynne Godley, of the pathbreaking book *Monetary Economics: An Integrated Approach*[3] in 2007. This was a work which used these simulation techniques to very good effect. Previously, I had used the *EViews* software for my own instruction and for teaching purposes, mainly for the teaching of time series econometrics. It is readily adaptable to the method of simulation. In earlier years, for example in my doctoral dissertation of 40 years ago entitled *The Financing of Unemployment Insurance*, I had used another software package for the research known as the Toronto Econometric Modelling System (TEMS).[4] This was obviously developed for use at a far less advanced level of computer technology, but was also adaptable to simulation techniques.

In any event, after sitting down in front of the computer screen and seeing the *EViews* icon appear, the first instruction is to;

• open EViews >

The *E-Views Window* appears.

• in the *Main Toolbar* select >    **File/New/Workfile**

The Pop-Up *Workfile Create* appears. The default *Frequency* is *Annual*.

• enter >    Start date: **2051**    End date: **2075**    WF: **SIMULATION**

But, you should leave the box [Page:    ] blank.

• click >    **OK**

The *Workfile Window* then appears (the title **SIMULATION** will be the name that has been given to the *Workfile*), and there will be two items [~] *c* and [~]*resid* already in place. These two series, however, would only be

---

[2] Jung-Hoon Kim, 'Guide to simulation with EViews 4.1' (mimeo, University of Ottawa, 2005); Samuel Yao Effah, *Household Portfolio Selection in the Real Estate Market* (PhD thesis in Economics, University of Ottawa, 2012).

[3] Wynne Godley and Marc Lavoie, *Monetary Economics: An Integrated Approach to Credit, Money, Income, Production and Wealth* (London: Palgrave Macmillan, 2007).

[4] John Smithin, *The Incidence and Economic Effects of the Financing of Unemployment Insurance* (PhD thesis in Economics, McMaster University, 1982).

relevant to the later econometric exercises. They will play no further role in a deterministic simulation, which is our initial objective here.

- in the *Workfile Window Toolbar* select > **Object/NewObject/Model**

- enter > name for object: **AMM**

- click > **OK**

The *New Object Window* appears (**AMM** is the name for the *Object*).

- align and re-size > For example, you could put the *Workfile Window* on the left and the *Model Window* on the right, within the *E-Views Window*.

- select > **Text**

The cursor will blink in the top left-hand corner of the *Model Window*.

- enter > $y=e0+g-t+e1*k$
  $k=a-r(-1)-w(-1)$
  $p= p0+w-a$
  $w=t+h0+h1*y$
  $r=m0+m1*r0-(1-m1)*p$

This is the model itself, with all the endogenous variables now appearing on the left-hand side (LHS). There must be as many equations as there are endogenous variables.

- in the *Model Window* select > **Equations**

A Pop-Up appears: *Save modifications and compile?*

- click > **Yes**

The equations appear in functional form. If there are any problems, recompile.

- in the *Model Window* select > **Variables**

This step identifies the endogenous and exogenous variables (including parameters). The endogenous variables are **y**, **p**, **k**, **w**, **r**, and the exogenous variables (including parameters) are **a**, **e0**, **e1**, **g**, **h0**, **h1**, **m0**, **m1**, **p0**, **r0**, **t**.

## 8.5  Inputting Numbers (Trial Values)

In this section, we describe how to input the starting or trial numbers for the exogenous variables (including the parameters).

- in the *Workfile Window* select >     **Genr**

The Pop-Up for *Enter Equation* appears.

- enter >     **year=@trend**

The variable **year** will be needed for the later simulation exercises.

- click >     **OK**

- in the *Workfile Window* select >     **Genr**

The pop-up for *Enter Equation* again appears.

- enter >     **w = 7.5**
                 **r = 0.04**

These are two arbitrary values for the lagged endogenous variables, **w(–1)** and **r(–1)**.

- click >     **OK**

- in the *Workfile Window* select >     **Genr**

The Pop-Up for *Enter Equation* appears;

- enter >     **a = 9.2**

This is the starting value we have chosen for the natural logarithm of labour productivity. The reader will recall that is the same value that was already used in some of the numerical illustrations in previous *Lectures*.

- click >     **OK**

- repeat >   the above steps for ***Genr*** command to input the remaining numbers for the exogenous variables, these are as follows;

    **e0 = 0.01**
    **e1 = 0.403**
    **g  = 0.24**
    **h0 = 8.675**

> **h1** = **0.216**
> **m0** = **0.05**
> **m1** = **0.728**
> **p0** = **0.25**
> **r0** = **0.025**
> **t** = **0.29**

The task of data input is now complete.

# 8.6 Solving for the Initial Steady-State (the Baseline)

In this section, we will be solving for the set of initial steady-state values (this set of values is called the *Baseline* in *EViews*), and representing the solutions in graphs.

- in the *Model Window* select >     **Solve**

The *Model Solution* Pop-Up appears. The defaults are *Deterministic* and *Dynamic*.

- click >     **OK**

The output for endogenous variables will appear in the *Workfile Window* as [~]y_0, [~]p_0, [~]k_0, [~]w_0 and [~]r_0.

- in the *Workfile Window* select >     [~]y_0

The *Series Window* for **Y_0** appears. Recall that this is the same as **y_0** in *EViews*. The solution for the steady-state growth rate is **y_0 = 0.027145**. Next, we can represent the process of convergence to the solutions, and the solutions themselves, in graphical form.

- select >     **View/Graph**

The *Graph Options* Pop-Up appears. The default is *Line & Symbol*.

- click >     **OK**

Now a graph appears in the *Series Window* for **Y_0**, as in *Figure 8.1*. This shows the process of convergence to the steady-state. The solution for the steady-state growth rate of real GDP in the *Baseline* is seen to be around 2.7%.

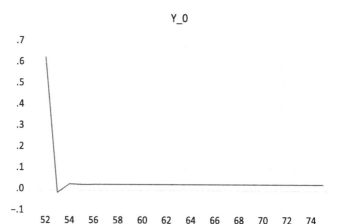

*Figure 8.1*: The Steady-State Real Rate of Economic Growth in the Baseline

Next, in the *Series Y_0 Window;*

- click >     **Name**

This will allow you to name the graph in order to save it.

- click >     **OK**

- click >     **[X]** in the *Series Window* for **Y_0**, to close.

- repeat >    the above steps for **p_0, k_0, w_0**, and **r_0**, to find the following steady-state results, and generate graphs for each of the remaining endogenous variables.

$$p\_0 = 0.020863$$
$$k\_0 = 0.166612$$
$$w\_0 = 8.970863$$
$$r\_0 = 0.062525$$

We will illustrate with just one more of the graphs, that for the real rate of interest as in *Figure 8.2*. It can be seen that the solution for the steady-state real rate of interest is around $r = 6.3\%$. Note that this is considerably above what was described as the optimal real rate of interest in *Lecture 7*, which was zero. We can conclude that the economy would be more prosperous, and there would be a fairer distribution of income (in the specific sense in which 'fairness' was defined in *Lecture 7*), if the real interest rate was lower.

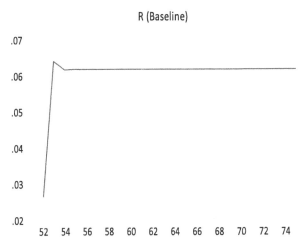

*Figure 8.2*: The Steady-State Real Rate of Interest in the Baseline

## 8.7 Changes in the Exogenous Variables

Our next task is to simulate the impact of changes in particular exogenous variables, for example the policy variables, whichever of them we are interested in. Firstly, we will enter solutions for the steady-state values of all the endogenous variables just derived in the previous section. This is to set up the starting point for the new set of simulations.

- in the *Workfile Window* select >     **Genr**

The Pop-Up for *Enter Equation* appears;

- enter >     **y = 0.027145**

- click >     **OK**

- repeat >     the above steps for **Genr** command as follows;

    **p = 0.020863**
    **k = 0.166612**
    **w = 8.970863**
    **r = 0.062525**

Now all the starting steady-state values of exogenous variables have been entered.

## 8.8  Scenario Analysis

In this section, the task is to set up *EViews* for what is called *Scenario Analysis*, to observe the effects of changes in the several exogenous variables.

- in the *Model Window* select >   **Scenarios**

The *Scenario Specification* Pop-Up appears. It is already set at *Scenario 1*.

- select >   **Overrides**

- enter >   **genr   g=0.24\*(year<15)+0.29\*(year>=15)**

The purpose of this entry is simply to record what *Scenario 1* is. The experiment we are considering is an increase in government spending as a percentage of GDP from 0.24 to 0.29, starting in year 15 and continuing each year thereafter. In the economics jargon, this would be referred to as a 'Keynesian' policy, 'fiscal stimulus', or similar. In the next step, we proceed to actually make the changes.

- click >   **OK**

- in the *Workfile Window* select >   **Genr**

The Pop-Up for *Enter Equation* appears.

- enter >   **g=0.24\*(year<15)+0.29\*(year>=15)**

This makes the change happen in the fifteenth year of the twenty-five year period (2051–2075) (that is, the year 2066).

- click >   **OK**

- In the *Model Window* select >   **Solve**

The *Model Solution* Pop-Up then appears with *Scenario I* active.

- click >   **OK**

The output for endogenous variables now appears in the *Workfile Window* as **[~]y_1, [~]p_1, [~]k_1, [~]w_1, and [~]r_1**. The results are as follows;

$$y\_1 = 0.074165$$
$$p\_1 = 0.031020$$

$$k\_1 = 0.159218$$
$$w\_1 = 8.981020$$
$$r\_1 = 0.059763$$

- in the *Workfile Window* select >      [~]y_1

The *Series Y_1 Window* appears, and the next step will be to represent this particular solution for economic growth in a graph.

- select >      **View/Graph**

The *Graph Options* Pop-Up appears. The default is *Line & Symbol*.

- click >      **OK**

Now a graph (*Figure 8.3*) will appear in the *Series Window* for **Y_1**. This indicates the effect of a permanent change in **g** (government spending as percentage of GDP) from 0.24 to 0.29. The effect of an increase of 5 percentage points is to cause almost as large an increase in the growth rate to around 7.4%. Therefore the 'growth multiplier', if we can put it that way, is slightly less than one.[5] The point is that in the context of the

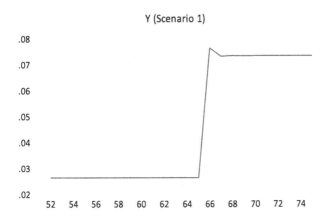

*Figure 8.3*: An Increase in the Ratio of Government Spending on Goods and Services to GDP Increases the Economic Growth Rate

---

[5] The original idea of the 'multiplier' in the *General Theory* was to predict by how much the *level* of GDP would increase for a given increase in the *level* of spending. If *mpc* stands for the marginal propensity to consume, then the simplest version of the government expenditure would be $\Delta Y / \Delta G = [1/(1 - mpc)]$. If, for example, we have *mpc* = 0.8, the multiplier would be 5. This is to say that an increase in government spending of $1 million

AMM, and contrary to the conventional wisdom of many orthodox econo-mists, academics, policy-makers and members of the financial press, fiscal stimulus actually 'works'.

Next, in the *Series Window* for **Y_1**;

- click >    **Name**

Again, this will allow you to name the graph in order to save it.

- click >    **OK**

- repeat >    the above steps for **p_1**, **k_1**, **w_1**, and **r_1**.

We will show just one more of these graphs in *Figure 8.4*, and again chose that relating to **R_1** the solution for the real rate of interest. The most important point to note from *Figure 8.4*, I think, is that the conven-tional wisdom about the effect of a fiscal stimulus on interest rates is completely overturned. The usual argument made in these circumstances is to the effect that an increase in government spending will increase the

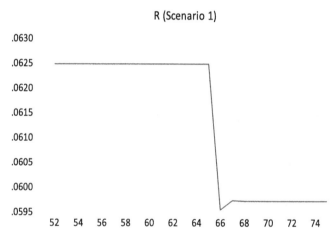

*Figure 8.4*: An Increase in the Ratio of Government Spending to
Real GDP Actually Reduces the Real Rate of Interest

---

would lead to an increase in GDP of $5million. In the simulations here the notion of the multiplier is translated into the growth context and is of a much smaller degree of magni-tude. Nonetheless, it is still positive.

real rate of interest, and hence 'crowd out' at least some private sector investment. This, in turn, will tend to offset the positive effect of the stimulus.[6] This outcome, however, so often canvassed in the textbooks, rarely if ever seems to happen in reality. At the time of writing, for example, there are, and have been, very large government budget deficits in several jurisdictions for some years. Yet, interest rates remain low. How might this be explained? The logic of the AMM helps us to understand why this is the case.

The answer, in fact, seems to be simply that it *is* indeed true that an increase in government spending will tend to cause at least some increase in inflation, even if this is by no means as dramatic in actual practice as some of the older models, with their built-in 'natural rates' of growth or unemployment, would have implied. (There are no natural rates of any kind in the AMM.) At the same time, there is also a *negative* relation between the inflation rate and the real rate of interest, the so-called 'forced saving effect' as discussed in *Lectures 3* and *4* earlier. Therefore, precisely *because* the inflation rate does rise when government spending increases, the real rate of interest will actually fall, not rise. This is what is going on in *Figure 8.4*.

## 8.9  A Second Scenario

To be able to conduct another different simulation (that is, make a change in a different exogenous variable) it will first be necessary to re-set the original exogenous variable that we were considering, **g**, back to its starting value.

- in the *Workfile Window* select >      **Genr**

The Pop-Up for *Enter Equation* appears.

- enter >      **g = 0.24**

- click >      **OK**

- in the *Model Window* select >      **Scenarios**

The *Scenario Specification* Pop-Up appears.

- select >      **New Scenario**

---

[6] Gregory Mankiw, William Scarth, and Jean-Paul Lam, *Macroeconomics, Sixth Canadian Edition* (New York: Worth Publishers, 2020).

Now *Scenario 2* is active.

- select >      **Overrides**
- enter >      **genr   p0=0.25\*(year<15)+0.00\*(year>=15)**

This records what *Scenario 2* is. The scenario is going to be a fall in the **p0** term from 0.25 to nothing (to 0.00). This represents an increase in liquidity preference or 'bearishness' to once again use the familiar terms coined by Keynes. In short, participants in the financial markets are becoming nervous, and there will be a sell-off of financial assets. This will turn out also to have negative effects on the real economy.

- click >      **OK**
- in the *Workfile Window* select >      **Genr**

The Pop-Up for *Enter Equation* appears;

- enter >      **p0=0.25\*(year<15)+0.00\*(year>=15)**

This makes the change in the year 2066.

- click >      **OK**
- in the *Model Window* select >      **Solve**

The *Model Solution* Pop-Up appears, with Scenario 2 active.

- click >      **OK**

The output for the endogenous variables then appears in the *Workfile Window* as [~]**y_2**, [~]**p_2**, [~]**k_2**, [~]**w_2**, and [~]**r_2**.

- in the *Workfile Window*  select >      [~] **y_2**

The *Series Y_2 Window* appears.

- select >      **View/Graph**

The *Graph Options* pop-up appears, the default is *Line & Symbol*.

- click >      **OK**

Now a graph (*Figure 8.5*) appears in the *Series Y_2 Window*. This indicates the effect of the change in **p0**. A sell-off in the financial markets will cause a fall in the economic growth rate to **y = 0.001374**. The financial crisis spills over into an economic crisis. There is an immediate recession,

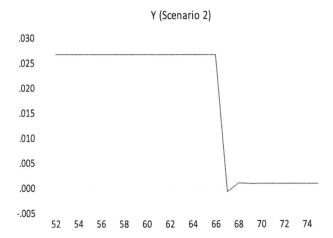

*Figure 8.5*: An Increase in Bearishness and a Financial Crisis Leads to an
Economic Crisis and Continuing Slow Growth and Unemployment

and even after the recession is over, the long-run growth rate falls to barely more than zero. There will be widespread, continuing, and long-lasting unemployment.

Next, we will name the graph and save it for future reference.

- click > **Name**

This allows you to name the graph in order to save it.

- click > **OK**

Finally, in the *Series Window* for **Y_2**,

- click > **[X]** in the *Series Y_2 Window* to close.

- repeat > the above steps for **p_2, k_2, r_2, w_2** to obtain the following;

    p_2 = – 0.234703
    k_2 =   0.102664
    r_2 =   0.132039
    w_2 =   8.965297

As before, we will round off the discussion by looking at just one of the relevant graphs, once again choosing that showing the effect of the change on interest rates. *Figure 8.6* indicates the effect on the real rate of

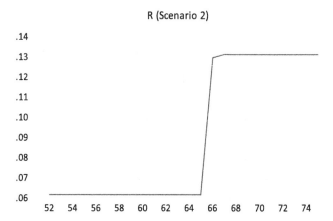

*Figure 8.6*: An Increase in Liquidity Preference (Bearishness)
Leads to an Increase in the Real Rate of Interest

interest of an increase in liquidity preference (the same reduction in **p0**) in year 15. We can see that the increase in liquidity preference will cause the rate of interest to rise. This is exactly as Keynes suggested in the *General Theory* all those years ago. Specifically, in this case there is an increase in the real rate of interest. Just as Keynes was quite correct in his predictions about the impact of an increase in 'loan expenditure' on economic growth, as shown in *Figure 8.3*, so also was he right in suggesting that an important determinant of the rate of interest is liquidity preference. The modern computer simulations continue to lend credence to the theoretical speculations of nine decades ago.

Perhaps it is true that Keynes's own theoretical framework in the *General Theory* was somehow inadequate to fully demonstrate these (and other) points to either the economics profession or the general public of the time. I also think that he was remiss in failing to make clear the important distinction between real and nominal rates of interest, and the significance of endogenous money. Nonetheless, in the end, the AMM, which takes both of these points fully on board, certainly does seem to be able to confirm Keynes's basic insights in almost every respect. In the particular case we are examining here, the increase in the real rate of interest is substantial, to **r_2 = 0.132039** (13%). It is accompanied by deflation, a growth rate not much above zero, falling real wages, and continuing unemployment.

It would clearly be possible to now go on to do many other simulations for each of the exogenous variables, in either direction and for any time period. For the purposes of the present exposition, however, just working through the *Baseline* and *Scenarios 1* and *2* has been sufficient to illustrate the method.

## 8.10  Time Series Econometrics?

The next obvious question to now ask is 'where did all these numbers come from' for the simulation exercises carried out above? The instinct of the mainstream or neoclassical economist in response would no doubt be to refer to one version or another of statistical probability theory, or econometrics. However, a really serious difficulty arises at this point, because the truth of the matter is that the theorems of statistical probability theory, which have been worked out mainly for the physical sciences, do not apply in the social world. There is a major difference between probabilistic risk and fundamental uncertainty.

Here is what I said about the matter in *Rethinking* (along with a number of other criticisms of the methodology of mainstream economics) in a section of the first chapter entitled (I suppose provocatively) 'Is Anything Worth Salvaging From the Wreckage?'[7]

> We need to pause at this point to ask just what is left of the program of the mainstream school … I suppose that a truly honest intellectual answer would have to be 'not very much'. But this can be a tough sell, in particular to people who have already invested a lot of time and energy in learning the various techniques (including myself) … also, more importantly, to … [the] … current cohort[s] of PhD students and young Assistant Professors on whom the future will depend. I think that the wording … above has made enough caveats to cover any potential objections. The criticism was of econometrics as the *main* empirical method, the *virtual* identification of economic theory with differential calculus, and so on. It is not suggested that these techniques will disappear entirely, or that it was a waste of time learning them … For example, I … [have suggested that] … a greater use of numerical methods … (computer simulation techniques) … [is] … one option for the pursuit of fruitful research projects. If so, then one possible source of trial or starting values for the parameters would clearly be exercises in time series econometrics. The emphasis here, however, should be very much on the words 'trial' and 'exercises'. If so, the procedure would not [ultimately]

---

[7] Smithin, *Rethinking*.

violate any stricture against the use of statistical probability theory as the *main* empirical method. Rather, the time series econometrics would be an information-gathering exercise *only*, as part of the first stage of an 'abductive' (or 'retroductive') mode of investigation ...[8]. Any attempt at an *explanation* ... of a specific sequence of events would belong to the second stage which ... [could] ... legitimately include (non-stochastic) computer simulation methods. Nonetheless, these preliminary econometric exercises would still allow young researchers to deploy more-or-less the full range of their technical skills ... acquired in graduate school. (original emphasis)

The point that I was trying to make here is that as the ontology of the social world, including the ontology of money and economics, is different from that of the physical or natural world, then so also should be the epistemology whereby the researcher attempts to gain knowledge of, and provide explanations for, the course of events in that world. Traditionally, however, economic methodology made very little effort to differentiate itself from mainstream debates in the philosophy of science. The discussions and theories of such writers as Popper, Kuhn, Lakatos, Laudan *et al.*, about falsification, paradigm shifts, research programs, and so on, in the physical sciences, have been held to apply without any substantial modification to social science.[9] On the other hand, critics of this approach have called for an 'ontological turn' in economic methodology, and far less reliance on methods of statistical induction, based on the assumption of constant event conjunctions of the form 'whenever event $x$ then event $y$'.[10] What I was trying to suggest in the above quote was to take seriously the various methodological criticisms that have been made, but also to retain whatever is useful from the established toolkit as at least a starting point for the analysis. Specifically, as an information gathering exercise in the first stage of a much more detailed multi-stage empirical investigation. The techniques should not be treated as ends in themselves, nor as being able to provide evidence for constant event conjunctions.

In the attempt, therefore, to find some trial values for the parameters for use in our simulation exercises, we might perhaps usefully begin with

---

[8] On the issue of 'abduction' or 'retroduction' see Tony Lawson, *Economics and Reality* (London: Routledge, 1997).

[9] Pheby, *Methodology and Economics.*

[10] Lawson, *Economics and Reality.*

the following four structural equations from the AMM, which have already been discussed in previous *Lectures*.

$y = e_0 + (g - t) + e_1 k,$ economic growth $\hspace{2cm}$ (8.1)

$p = p_0 + w - a,$ $\hspace{1.2cm}$ inflation $\hspace{3.2cm}$ (8.2)

$i = m_0 + m_1 i_0,$ $\hspace{1cm}$ the monetary policy transmissions mechanism (8.3)

$w - t = h_0 + h_1 y.$ $\hspace{0.8cm}$ after-tax real wages $\hspace{2.5cm}$ (8.4)

A first pass at being able to put some numbers into the simulation models would then be to run some 'regressions' (as these techniques are called), of the following form;

$$yadj = e_0 + e_1 k + error, \hspace{2cm} (8.5)$$

$$padj = p_0 + p_1 x + error, \hspace{2cm} (8.6)$$

$$i = m_0 + m_1 i_0 + error, \hspace{2cm} (8.7)$$

$$wadj = h_0 + h_1 y + error. \hspace{2cm} (8.8)$$

Here $yadj = (y - g - t)$, $padj = (p - w + a)$, $wadj = w - t$, and $x$ stands for any variable, other than the ones previously specified, that might be thought to have an influence on inflation.

However, there is another potential problem, which comes up right away, and is due to the basic nature of time series data. This is the likelihood that many or most time series may be *non-stationary* — for the obvious reason they are themselves likely to exhibit a time trend. Another awkward issue is that some of the equations in (8.5) through (8.8) are actually what is known as 'mixed' equations, in which rates of growth are regressed on the levels of some other variables (or *vice versa*). This also poses problems for the econometrics because, as a practical matter, a linear regression of the level of one variable on the rate of growth of another typically will not work.[11] The intercept terms have a tendency to 'blow up'. They become very large. For these and other reasons, therefore, the estimates provided simply by using the familiar techniques of 'ordinary least squares' (OLS) regression will not be 'consistent' That is, they will not be useful. But there is no reason, of course, why these mixed

---

[11] Clive Grainger, *Empirical Modelling in Economics: Specification and Evaluation* (Cambridge: Cambridge University Press, 1999).

relationships should not actually be present either in theory or in the real world. Indeed, throughout this book we have insisted that they *are* important. This is therefore another potential difficulty with time series econometrics.

I should explain to the reader that all of this jargon, such as the use of acronyms like 'OLS' and so forth, is inseparable from any discussion of econometrics. It goes with the territory. Fortunately though, in practice, the underlying ideas are by no means as complicated as the textbooks sometimes make them out to be. In the next section therefore, there will be a discussion of how to work around these statistical and/or econometric issues. There will also turn out to be a substantial upside to this, as the exercise will even be able to suggest a technique whereby we can generate suitable proxies for the various psychological states of market participants and indices of socio-economic power. This a very large silver lining to the statistical clouds.

## 8.11  Mixed Equations and Non-Stationarity

One method for dealing with the various issues that arise from the use of time series data is to take 'first differences'[12] of the regression equations in (8.5) through (8.8), which will yield the following;

$$\Delta yadj = e_{00} + e_1\Delta k + error \tag{8.9}$$

$$\Delta padj = p_{00} + p_1\Delta x + error \tag{8.10}$$

$$\Delta i = m_{00} + m_1\Delta i_0 + error \tag{8.11}$$

$$\Delta wadj = h_{00} + h_1\Delta y + error \tag{8.12}$$

The advantage of this procedure is that it will ultimately be able to provide consistent estimates of the parameters $e1, p1, m1$, and $h1$. Evidently, these are the same as those in the original formulations. A disadvantage, on the other hand, is that although we will now also have consistent estimates of the new intercept terms, namely $e00$, $p00$, $m00$, and $h00$, the values obtained for these terms will have little or no economic or statistical meaning. In themselves they provide no useful information. Fortunately, however, and this is where the silver lining comes in, we can next 'work

---

[12] That is, (*e.g.*) $\Delta yadj = yadj - yadj_{-1}$.

backwards' from the results in equations (8.9) through (8.12) to retrieve estimates of the original endogenous variables, $e0$, $p0$, $m0$, and $h0$ themselves.

Given the numbers for the regression coefficients provided by the statistical estimates in (8.9) through (8.12), we can then use them in the following calculations, using (8.5) through (8.8), to get back to an actual time series of each of the original exogenous variables. There will be a unique estimate of the value of each exogenous variable in each time period. If $\tau$ is a time index, the necessary calculations will be as follows;

$$e_0(\tau) = y(\tau) + [t(\tau) - g(\tau)] - e_1 k(\tau), \tag{8.13}$$

$$p_0(\tau) = p(\tau) - w(\tau) + a(\tau) - p_1 x(\tau), \tag{8.14}$$

$$m_0(\tau) = i(\tau) - m_1 i_0(\tau), \tag{8.15}$$

$$h_0(\tau) = [w(\tau) - t(\tau)] - h_1 y(\tau). \tag{8.16}$$

This will yield the complete time series behaviour of each of the exogenous variables represented by the intercepts. We can then take these values to represent either the changing psychological states of participants in the marketplace or indices of the various measures of socio-economic power.

## 8.12 Examples Using Historical Canadian Data

In this section, we will illustrate the techniques described above with a couple of examples using Canadian data for the period 1951–1975. The data are taken from the second edition of the *Historical Statistics of Canada*, published in 1982.[13] (The reader will note that this time period is exactly a century before the arbitrary set of 'future' dates that were used in the simulation exercises above.)

I must admit that this choice of dates was somewhat whimsical. The author was born in the year 1951 and first came to Canada in 1975. This, therefore, is the period during which the Dominion had to struggle along by itself without my assistance. More to the point, 1975 is also the last year covered in the *Historical Statistics*, a book which I happened to have on my shelves as I was writing this chapter. After all, the point of the

---

[13] F. H. Leacy, M.C. Urquhart and K.A.H. Buckley, eds., *Historical Statistics of Canada*, second edition (Ottawa: Statistics Canada, 1982).

exercise is merely to illustrate the various techniques, so any set of numbers will do. In the 'real world' the *EViews* software package allows multiple options for downloading relevant data from online sources and other media.

For the first example we will run a first-difference regression purporting to explain inflation during the period, as follows;

$$\Delta padj = p_{00} + p1\,\Delta(r - r_{-1}) + p2\Delta padj_{-1} + error \qquad (8.17)$$

The specification suggests that there is an auto-regressive component to inflation, and it also includes a version of the theory of the speculative demand for (and supply of) money described in *Lecture 6*. Participants in the money market in period $\tau{-}1$ are assumed to make the relevant decisions about whether to hold money or become indebted based on their expectations of what is going to happen in period $\tau$. The results are;

$$padj = -\,0.002748 - 0.749439\,\Delta(r - r_{-1}) + 0.582068\Delta padj_{-1} \qquad (8.18)$$
$$(-0.003) \qquad (0.216) \qquad\qquad (0.208)$$

As an empirical exercise *per se* it would be fair to say that the results of this regression are mixed. On the one hand, the coefficients are indeed of the expected signs and are statistically significant at conventional confidence levels. (The standard errors are the numbers reported in brackets, just below the coefficients themselves.) On the other hand, the explanatory value of the equation turns out to be fairly low. According to the 'adjusted $R^2$' statistic (not reported here), only around 34% of the total change in $\Delta padj$ is actually explained by the chosen regressors. Above all, the sample size is too small at only 25 observations. In any actual empirical work, therefore, the researcher would clearly want to do a lot more work than we have been able to do here, in this practice exercise, to come up with a more satisfactory specification.

For purposes of the present discussion, however, the sketchiness of the results is not really much of a disadvantage. Even *if* these results were to stand, there is still an important practical conclusion to be drawn, namely, that as far as we have gotten with our research, much of the explanation for the changes in inflation in the period under consideration must be attributed to changes in the $p_0$ parameter itself. It must also be stressed, once again, that at this point we are not engaging in hypothesis testing or anything of that kind. The use of time series econometrics in these circumstances is merely an information gathering exercise in the first stage of an abductive empirical exercise. The object is only to arrive at a set of starting or trial values for the parameters that could be used in simulation exercises. The actual empirical investigation, to follow, would consist in finding out how well the eventual non-stochastic simulation exercises are able to explain or reproduce the outcomes of decisive historical episodes. This will inevitably involve a lengthy process of trial and error to arrive at reasonable values for the parameters and exogenous variables in the specific period of interest, up to and including changes in the original model specification itself. For a successful exemplar of how to apply these techniques in practice (in the case of both Canada and the USA for several key historical episodes), the reader can consult the work of Reed Collis in the PhD thesis *Three Essays on Monetary Macroeconomics*, which has frequently been cited in earlier *Lectures*.[14]

With these caveats, we next proceed to derive the historical time series for $p_0$ as follows:

$$p_0(\tau) = p(\tau) - w(\tau) + a(\tau) + 0.749439[r(\tau) - r(\tau_{-1})] \quad (8.19)$$
$$+ 0.582068p(\tau_{-1})$$

The graph of the resulting series is then reproduced in *Figure 8.7*.

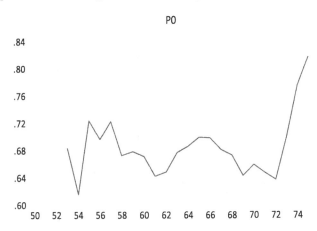

*Figure 8.7*: Changes in an Inverse Measure of Liquidity Preference on Both Sides of the Money Market, Canada (1951–1975)

[14] Collis, *Three Essays*.

Recall that the $p_0$ term is an inverse measure of liquidity preference, so that when $p_0$ falls, liquidity preference increases. The period therefore seems to open with an episode of nervousness or bearishness in the financial markets, which then dissipates in the mid-1950s. Later on, there are also two other episodes in which bear sentiment seems to increase. The first of these occurs in the late 1950s and early 1960s, and the second in the late 1960s/early 1970s. Coincidentally or not, there was in fact a recession in Canada around 1960/1961 and another slowdown in growth in the early 1970s. Toward the end of our period on the other hand, there seems to be a large increase in $p_0$ which, among other things, would imply an increase in the rate of inflation itself. Overall, therefore, the results do seem to be consistent with the actual economic history of the 1970s, which was a period of stagflation, high inflation combined with high unemployment. Not only was there high inflation in the 1970s, but there was also another recession in Canada around 1974–1975.

As a second example of how to construct time series for the several exogenous variables, consider an equation to explain the evolution of labour productivity. This will be useful because in most of the theoretical models used so far in this book we have employed the simplification of treating the (natural logarithm of) average labour productivity, $a$, as a constant. When it comes to empirical models, however, it is clearly both possible and desirable to endogenize this variable, as already discussed earlier in *Lecture 4* and elsewhere. We might therefore try the following specification which includes an auto-regressive component. Equation (8.20) further suggests that there is what the literature calls an 'efficiency wage' argument. This is the idea that productivity will depend positively on the real wage rate. Better paid workers will be happier and more productive.

$$a = a_0 + a_1 w + a_2 a_{-1} + error \qquad (8.20)$$

Next, take first differences of equation (8.20) and run the regression using the same Canadian data for 1951–1975 as in the inflation equation.

$$\Delta a = a_{00} + a_1 \Delta w + a_2 \Delta a_{-1} \qquad (8.21)$$

The results are;

$$\Delta a = 0.003923 + 0.655339 \Delta w + 0.016968 \Delta a_{-1} \qquad (8.22)$$
$$(0.006) \qquad (0.143) \qquad (0.159)$$

Again, because of the small sample size, *etc.*, these results should be treated with caution. But, in this case the test statistics do show that the regression explains around 45% of the changes in productivity. (It performs somewhat better in this respect than did the inflation equation.) One of the coefficients (that for $\Delta w$) is statistically significant at conventional confidence levels, but the others are not. In any event, the next step is solve for the series $a_0$ which can be said to represent the autonomous component of productivity growth, or innovation, derived using all the information currently available. The series may then be represented in a graph as in *Figure 8.8*. The solution for $a_0$ is;

$$a_0 = a - 0.65539w - 0.016968a_{-1} \qquad (8.23)$$

The results might be thought of as measuring something similar to the phenomenon of 'Schumpeterian' innovation (after Joseph Schumpeter, and as discussed in *Lecture 2*). Changes in the $a_0$ term can be taken to represent purely exogenous changes in productivity rather than changes in the overall level of productivity as such. *Figure 8.8* shows a record of mostly positive innovations in productivity on balance over this period, albeit with frequent setbacks or checks to the process as, for example, toward the end of the series. This apparently sharp autonomous decline in productivity in the early-to-mid-1970s also seems consistent with the onset of 'stagflationary' conditions at that time, just as were the inflation trends in the previous graph.

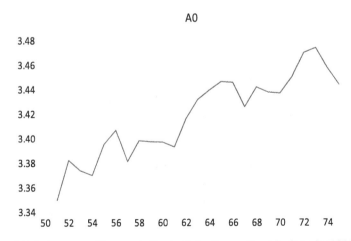

*Figure 8.8*: Autonomous Changes in Productivity (Innovations) in Canada (1951–1975)

# 8.13   Conclusion

This final *Lecture* has provided a detailed set of instructions on the use of the commercially available software package *EViews 11*, for exercises in both computer simulation and time series econometrics, using the example of a specific macroeconomic model, the AMM. The reader should now be in a position to use the same type of procedure for models with any number of equations, and for various different specifications.

If one of the main messages of this book has been that to move forward economics has to take a step back and revert to methods of monetary macroeconomics in the style of Keynes, the later Hicks, and the Post-Keynesians, this chapter has highlighted the contribution that the research methods and techniques of the twenty-first century can make.

In the last century, in the mid-1980s, my colleagues Omar Hamouda, Bernard Wolf, and I organized a conference in Toronto at which one of the speakers (one of whose co-authors was a Nobel Prize winner) put forward the attractive notion of a modern day Keynes;[15]

> ... surrounded by a high-tech 'circus'[16] with ... personal computers ... [and with] ... current problems being attacked by ... intuition ... aided by current technology.

The fact of the matter is, however, that in the 1980s the relevant technology was not yet available. As mentioned, I had already made an attempt in this direction myself, in my doctoral thesis,[17] and the computers of those days could hardly be called 'high-tech'. Now in the twenty-first century the situation is quite different. As is demonstrated, I think, by the material in this final *Lecture,* there need now be no hesitation in suggesting that non-stochastic numerical methods, in discrete time, can provide a theoretical method that can handle fundamental uncertainty, and thereby provide a comprehensive process analysis dealing with historical time. It has also been shown that there can be a robust empirical

---

[15] Ronald Bodkin, Lawrence Klein and Kanta Marwah, 'Keynes and the origin of macro-econometric modelling', in Omar Hamouda and John Smithin, eds., *Keynes and Public Policy after Fifty Years*, vol. 2, *Theories and Method* (Aldershot: Edward Elgar, 1988).

[16] The 'circus' was the name given to the small group of Keynes's closest followers in Cambridge in the 1930s.

[17] Smithin, *Financing of Unemployment Insurance.*

method, soundly based on the principles of abduction or retroduction rather than induction, which is also able to retain and make use of at least some of the results and techniques of time series econometrics that continue to play such a large role in the training of contemporary graduate students.

Printed in the United States
by Baker & Taylor Publisher Service